RENEWALS 458-4574

DATE DUE

Tourists, Migrants & Refugees

TOURISTS, MIGRANTS & REFUGEES

Population Movements in Third World Development

Milica Z. Bookman

LYNNE
RIENNER
PUBLISHERS

BOULDER
LONDON

Published in the United States of America in 2006 by
Lynne Rienner Publishers, Inc.
1800 30th Street, Boulder, Colorado 80301
www.rienner.com

and in the United Kingdom by
Lynne Rienner Publishers, Inc.
3 Henrietta Street, Covent Garden, London WC2E 8LU

Library of Congress Cataloging-in-Publication Data
Bookman, Milica Zarkovic.
  Tourists, migrants, and refugees : population movements in Third World
development / Milica Z. Bookman.
     p. cm.
  Includes bibliographical references and index.
  ISBN-13: 978-1-58826-481-7 (hardcover : alk. paper)
  ISBN-10: 1-58826-481-5 (hardcover : alk. paper)
  1. Tourism—Economic aspects—Developing countries. 2. Tourism—Social
aspects—Developing countries. 3. Visitors, Foreign—Developing countries.
4. Developing countries—Population. 5. Developing countries—Emigration
and immigration. I. Title.
G155.D44B66 2006
304.809172'4—dc22
                                        2006004685

British Cataloguing in Publication Data
A Cataloguing in Publication record for this book
is available from the British Library.

Printed and bound in the United States of America

The paper used in this publication meets the requirements
∞ of the American National Standard for Permanence of
Paper for Printed Library Materials Z39.48-1992.

5 4 3 2 1

To the memory of
Ruth Lowe Bookman and
John Jacob Bookman

Contents

Tables and Figures

Tables

Figures

Acknowledgments

I am grateful to many people for helping me during the creation of this book. For providing an encouraging work environment and supporting three research trips, I want to thank John McCall, George Prendergast, and Brice Wachterhauser. For consistently bringing humor and enthusiasm to the office and infecting all his colleagues, my thanks go to Tom Burke. Marla Gaglione and Bill Conway helped with the background logistics patiently, thoroughly, and efficiently. I am grateful to Larry Swatuk and Nicoli Nattras for answering my questions and to Ljubisa Adamovic for comments on earlier drafts. Ann Szewczyk's rapid response to my data requests is greatly appreciated. David Lyskowski helped with data entry, showing how effective technology can be. My African Economies (2003) students were extremely helpful in the early phases of my research. Special thanks go to Jerry Katen, Jackie Hein, Amra Mehmedic, Anthony Kamara, Juan Aleman, and Zac Coyle. And to Dori Pappas, my wholehearted gratitude—you have been my right (and left) hand in everything I have accomplished over the past fifteen years.

Marilyn Grobschmidt at Lynne Rienner Publishers has been wonderful to work with. Also, two anonymous readers provided invaluable comments that greatly improved the manuscript and for which I am very grateful.

Finally, Richard, Karla, and Aleksandra—you are what it's all about.

—*Milica Z. Bookman*

1

Introduction

Caprivi Strip. For tourists worldwide, the mere name brings to mind exotic wildlife, still waters, idyllic sunsets. By contrast, to social scientists it connotes economic, demographic, political, and social realities that clash with the bucolic landscape. Although the Caprivi Strip has experienced economic development, political turmoil, and social change, it is the multidirectional population movements, intense and concentrated, that have made the region what it is. Indeed, in this corner of southern Africa, where Namibia juts into Botswana along the Zambezi River, just a glance away from Zimbabwe and Zambia, four types of population movements have occurred. The most obvious is the flow of tourists, the raison d'être for the fundamental transformation of the region. Workers from the Botswana and Namibian hinterlands migrated to the region in search of employment in the labor-absorbing tourist sector. Less noticeable are the German nationals who came to build and manage a hotel at the tip of the Strip. Finally, behind the scenes, the indigenous San peoples were displaced from their land because their pastoral ways were incompatible with the burgeoning tourist industry. It is clear, then, that tourists are not the only ones traveling in the Caprivi Strip. A package of supporting population movements is also taking place in order to service, enable, and accommodate the tourists' demands.

All four types of population movements just described are part of a growing worldwide trend loosely associated with globalization. They are part of the increased flow of goods, services, people, information, and commodities across international and domestic boundaries. Population mobility is especially poignant in the new millennium as, more than at any time in history, people are on the move, leading scholars to refer to the post-1990s as the "age of migration."[1] Differences in human capital needs are causing workers to relocate in order to maximize their employment options, wage differentials are attracting workers from low-income to high-income regions, movements of enterprises in search of profit maximization induce workers to follow, high disposable incomes and cheap transportation are enabling leisure travel, widespread famines and environmental disasters are causing unprecedented numbers of refugees to relocate, and wars and secessions are inducing voluntary and involuntary migrations as people of different ethnic groups adjust to new leaders and new borders.[2]

Empirical evidence from across the globe shows that indeed people everywhere are on the move. According to the World Bank, each year some two to three million people emigrate from their countries of origin.[3] At the beginning of the twenty-first century, some 130 million people lived outside their home country, and that number has been rising by about 2 percent a year. Most migrants, however, never cross an international boundary.[4] In China, for example, some 200 million people have moved more than 1,000 miles from home, yet they do not show up in international migration statistics. At the turn of the new millennium, more than fourteen million people worldwide were refugees and asylum seekers.[5] That number pales by comparison to the twenty-five million people who were internally displaced at the end of 2004.[6] According to the US Refugee Service, "large scale movements of refugees and other forced migrants have become a defining characteristic of the contemporary world. *At few times in recent history have such large numbers of people in so many parts of the globe been obliged to leave their own countries and communities to seek safety elsewhere* [italics mine]."[7]

Far exceeding any one of these population movements, however, is the cross-border flow of tourists. Tourists made 700 million international trips in 2000, up from twenty-five million in 1950.[8] According to the World Tourism Organization, international travel is expected to reach 935 million people by 2010, nearly double the 500 million people who traveled abroad in 1993.[9]

Such an increase in traveling cannot but have economic significance. Indeed, across the globe, tourism has become a force to contend with. According to the United Nations Conference on Trade and Development (UNCTAD), tourism has become the world's largest industry.[10] Donald Lundberg, Mink Stavenga, and M. Krishnamoorthy claimed that "tourism has become the world's largest business enterprise, overtaking the defense, manufacturing, oil and agriculture industries."[11] According to the World Travel and Tourism Council (WTTC), the travel and tourism industry accounts for $4.4 trillion of economic activity worldwide.[12] During the 1990s, world tourism grew at twice the rate of world gross national product (GNP).[13] In 2005, it accounted for over 10 percent of world gross domestic product (GDP).[14] It has become the fastest growing foreign income sector worldwide. The World Tourism Organization (WTO) reported that tourism accounted for 8 percent of world export earnings and 37 percent of service exports.[15] The director general of the General Agreement on Tariffs and Trade (GATT) predicted that trade in services (of which tourism is an important component) was likely to surpass trade in goods by 2003.[16] Finally, the WTTC estimated that employment in tourism would account for almost 12 percent of total world employment in 2005.[17] By 2010, it is expected to employ 328 million people.[18]

Although most tourist activity tends to be concentrated in Western countries such as France, Spain, and the United States, this indisputable link between the flow of tourists and its economic impact has not bypassed governments in other countries.[19] In order to increase tourist demand, the Czech Republic is looking for a new one-word name, one that foreigners can more easily pronounce.[20] It is the developing countries, however, that are most impressed with the potential of tourism. They have come to view it as a panacea because it increases the flow of foreign currency, contributing directly to the current account of the balance of payments and generating successive rounds of economic activity. Given tourism's low barriers to entry and its resulting rapid incorporation into the global economy, leaders from less developed countries (LDCs[21]) are quick to offer their natural resources. In the process, they hope to increase government revenue, pay down their foreign debt, and alleviate poverty. In the words of Cynthia Enloe, countries are increasingly putting all their development eggs in the tourist basket.[22] For example, Gabon's president intends to convert 11 percent of the country's territory into national parks for the benefit of tourists, and war-torn Rwanda is building five-star hotels in the expectation that tourism will overcome tea and coffee as the principal income earner.[23] As a result of such endeavors, the WTO has reported that tourism has become a principal export (in the top five) for 83 percent of developing countries and is the principal export for one-third of them.[24]

Tourism does not take place in a vacuum, however, leaving no trace. Instead, with its concomitant linkages, multipliers, and externalities, tourism alters the preexisting patterns of supply and demand as well as production and consumption. It changes the composition of national income as well as the industrial distribution of the labor force. In other words, it leaves a huge footprint on less developed economies.

Tourism, an industry based on population movements *par excellence,* results in yet other kinds of population movements as people adjust to tourism-induced changes in the labor market (as illustrated by the earlier Caprivi Strip example). Thus, one type of movement *induces* others and at the same time is *enabled* by those others in a self-reinforcing causal circular flow.

Because the scope and potential of tourism is so great, the flow of tourist-induced population movements must be at the forefront of development studies. Moreover, given the sheer magnitude of tourists, migrants, and refugees, as well as the number of countries that are either their homes or hosts, global population movements warrant the attention of scholars, policymakers, human rights organizations, and the media. Without adequate attention to all population movements affecting the LDCs—workers, refugees, tourists—political leaders, international organizations, and policymakers will not be prepared for the complex twists and turns that participation in the global economy can bring on. By understanding all the population movements, we can understand how to harness tourism's potential for the benefit of LDC inhabitants.

This Book Within the Context of Social Science Research

Social science research responds to current events. Indeed, the increase in worldwide population movements—both voluntary and involuntary—in the post–cold war period has spurred scholarly research on their destination, their origins, their personal profiles, and the reasons for them.

Some of these studies focus on the voluntary flow of labor. The literature on economic growth and population movements owes a debt to Simon Kuznets, who was the first to identify labor migration as the labor adjustments of growing economies. As his theory is discussed in Chapter 2, suffice it to say here that it is based on a functioning labor market in which supply and demand play crucial roles. Other studies focus on involuntary migration—an area that experienced increased interest in the 1990s—as a result of more public awareness of ethnic cleansing across the globe.[25] Of all population movements, it is tourists who receive the least academic attention. It is odd that the growing number of tourists visiting LDCs, coupled with the evident potential for economic growth to be had with tourism, has not sparked an explosion of academic study of how to harness the benefits to be reaped by this trend. Indeed, author and professor Louis Turner claimed that tourism is the most "under-studied industry impinging on the Third World."[26] To be sure, economists have studied the effects of tourism on economic development, focusing on the direct and indirect economic consequences of tourism.[27] Anthropologists, following the pioneering work of Valene Smith, have been focusing on the cultural effects of tourist penetration.[28] Sociologists such as Emanuel de Kadt, Dean MacCannell, J. Diamond, and later Jozsef Borocz have sparked interest in their field.[29] Political science writings, dating back to the 1970s, took off after Linda Richter's 1983 contribution.[30] Gender concerns have been studied by Enloe, and environmental issues were brought to light in the 1980s by Helen Briassoulis and John Dixon, among others.[31] Scholars of ethnicity (such as Robert Wood) are taking tourism into account in the construction of ethnic identity.[32]

To date, there have been few attempts to merge all these different types of population movements, to observe them in their totality and globality, and to develop a comprehensive international perspective. Such a view is more than the sum of its parts, namely tourist flows, labor flows, and displacement flows. Indeed, all these people on the move do not form one homogeneous group. They originate in a variety of countries, and their destinations are different. Their opportunities are different, as are their incomes and their pushes and pulls. Some are temporary, others are permanent; some are voluntary, others are forced. These differences, although large, do not negate a meaningful aggregation of population movements. On the contrary, by requiring us to stand back and look at population movements in their entirety, we get a broad perspective, one that focuses on the forest rather than individual trees. Observing these flows all together, one sees patterns and relationships that are not visible when focusing on a single movement. It is this generalized aggregate view that is best suited for the study of the relationship between population movements and economic growth, the underlying theme of this book.

It is precisely in this way that this book strives to push the boundaries of academic discourse. It strives to fill the void in the literature pertaining to the synthesis of different population movements by adopting a broad definition of population movements and lumping together voluntary and involuntary movements as well as temporary and permanent. Attributing such an umbrella property to the phrase *population movements* enables a broader perspective than is usually taken. Indeed,

Lucy Lippard noted that "few have looked at those 'other' tourists—the movement of refugees, immigrants, and other displaced people" even if, as Dean MacCannell stated, there are different ways of "being out-of-place."[33] One of those who takes a broader perspective is A. Appadurai, who in his study of globalization introduced the concept of ethnoscapes, namely the flow of people—workers, immigrants, and tourists—across the world.[34] Another broad perspective was offered in the edited volume by C. Michael Hall and Allan Williams, in which the contributors focused on different aspects of the link between tourism and migration.[35] Following a review of the literature, the editors stated that "the tourism migration nexus represents a fertile and still largely virgin territory, offering rich rewards for tourism and migration researchers."[36] It is in that spirit that this book was written.

In addition to employing a broad definition of population movements, this study also attempts to bridge the gap between development studies and tourism studies by focusing on the flow of tourists as an integral part of economic development, an approach thus far outside of the scope of development studies. Indeed, extensive as the tourism literature is, it has not broken into mainstream development studies and therefore has remained quite isolated. One look at popular development textbooks of the twenty-first century indicates that, despite the rising importance of tourism to developing countries, it is largely an ignored phenomenon. Tourism is a service, and as M. Thea Sinclair and Mike Stabler have pointed out, the development literature has overlooked the growth of services in general, focusing instead on industrialization in the 1950s and 1960s and later on agriculture as the source of employment for reducing poverty: "It was not until the late 1980s that the need to examine the service sector was generally recognized, although tourism was rarely acknowledged in either developing or developed countries."[37]

In merging the development and tourism literatures, this study addresses the fundamental difference in the way the two fields approach population movements. In other words, mainstream development literature, based largely on Kuznets's work, deals with migration as the dependent variable (occurring as a result of economic growth). Tourism literature, on the other hand, focuses on population movements as the independent variable. By merging the two fields, this book underscores the fact that population movements must be studied as both independent and dependent variables.

Moreover, missing from tourism studies is a comprehensive assessment of tourism's effect on other population movements. To the extent that studies have focused on population movements, with very few exceptions it has been on the tourist, not the movement induced by the tourist. Alternatively, to the extent that economists have studied the role of the tourist industry in development, they have neglected the labor demands brought about by the growth in the industry. This shortcoming is rectified here.

Finally, this book has an international perspective insofar as it places population movements within the global economy instead of viewing them as isolated phenomena to be tolerated or encouraged by host states. Thus, even though the story told in this book is about population movements and economic growth, the superstory is about globalization and development in the twenty-first century. Although Frances Brown may have criticized tourism studies for being too compartmentalized by discipline and neglecting to take the global perspective, this book confirms that the global perspective, in the form of globalization, has permeated tourism studies of late.[38]

About This Book

The earlier description of the Caprivi Strip illustrates two concepts that underlie the theoretical framework of this book and provide the structure for its chapters. The first has to do with the circular flow of population movements associated with tourism, namely, the fact that one type of population movement (tourists) stimulates other movements (workers and involuntarily displaced peoples) in a causal, self-perpetuating way. The second concept has to do with the relationship between these population flows and economic growth. As in the Caprivi Strip, when tourists spend foreign currency for accommodations, restaurant meals, and local guides, they become engines of growth by stimulating multiple rounds of economic activity. It is argued in this book that a strong relationship exists between the multidirectional population movements (of which tourist flows are an important component) and economic growth in the LDCs. Simply put, these multidirectional population flows are at the root of development, they facilitate development, and they are byproducts of development. As such, population flows are both the cause and the effect of economic growth in less developed countries. It is their role as economic enablers and lubricators that is studied here.

Together, the circular flow of populations and its complex effect on economic development raise numerous questions whose answers must be reflected in national policies pertaining to foreign investment, immigration and emigration, development priorities, and so on. Although the link between population flows and economic growth is strong, there are other offsetting forces operating in developing countries that mitigate the potential impact of tourism. Authorities in LDCs must assess the net effect of these forces as well as the costs and benefits of promoting tourism as part of their development strategy. In this book, it is argued that tourism cannot a priori be viewed as a panacea, nor, as some have claimed, is it always detrimental to economic development. Rather, the determination of its net effect is location specific. In all cases, however, population flows are interdependent, and that interdependence has to be taken into account. As is argued throughout the text, when there are population flows, human costs are incurred, and those need to be considered when planning for tourism.

The circular flow of populations and its relationship to economic growth run through the book chapters in the following way. Chapter 1 introduces the concept of tourism as a population movement and explains the nature of tourist-friendly LDCs. The conceptual definitions, parameters of the study, and introductory country statistics set the stage for the subsequent chapters.

Chapter 2 begins with a study of the spatial distribution of economic activity that induces population movements. It is here that population movements are classified by two independent variables—duration and choice—yielding four different types of movements: tourists and travelers, voluntary labor movements, involuntary labor movements, and displacement of ethnic populations. A theoretical framework that shows how each of these movements is related to economic growth is then presented, along with some policy implications that are then explored in subsequent chapters. This chapter provides a macroperspective on population flows whereas the next three chapters continue the discussion at the microlevel.

Chapter 3 focuses on tourists, those men and women who, through their consumption of a wide variety of goods and services, have the power to transform sleepy regions such as the Caprivi Strip used to be. An understanding of who these people are is crucial to understanding how tourism can be an engine of growth. This chapter includes an analysis of what determines demand for travel to LDCs—important information for promoters of tourism. The supply side of the tourism market is then observed, with specific emphasis on the role of LDC governments, foreign operators, and local communities.

The focus of Chapter 4 is on the labor force and how it is affected by the booming tourist sector. Both voluntary and involuntary movements of workers are studied. In the case of the former, this chapter argues that derived demand draws skilled labor from the West and unskilled labor from the domestic economy. Such migrations are associated with the spatial redistribution of economic activity in tourist destinations. With respect to involuntary movement of workers, this chapter observes movements of workers who have become structurally unemployed by tourism. In the end, this chapter asks what are the costs and benefits of migration and how are they related to economic growth.

In developing countries, economic growth often entails involuntary movement of people. Such displacements, either by a dam, a factory, or, as in the case of the San in the Caprivi Strip, tourism, are studied in Chapter 5. The mechanics of dislocation are discussed as well as the rationale offered by the perpetrating authorities to justify them. In many multiethnic LDCs, such dislocations often occur because tourism's growth potential induces economic competition to take place along ethnic lines. This leads to a discussion of the negative implications of displacement for the very tourist industry that LDC authorities want to promote.

Finally, the concluding chapter returns to the macrolevel of analysis by placing the circular flow of populations into the context of the globalizing modern world economy. It explores the way in which globalization enables tourists, migrants, and displaced peoples to spread cultural, economic, and political ideas. But what happens if authorities in LDCs or more developed countries (MDCs) choose to limit population movements? This chapter also discusses explicit policies aimed at erecting barriers (such as restricting tourist visits and immigration laws) and the effect of these impediments on the circular flow of populations.

A few words about method are in order. First, the study of global population flows is undertaken from the political economy perspective. This approach, underscoring the role played by political institutions in economic activity, has always been popular among scholars in development studies.[39] It is also used in tourism studies, after its pioneering application by S. G. Britton in 1982 and Richter in 1983.[40] Peter U.C. Dieke, in his study of tourism in Africa, argued in favor of the political economy approach because tourism decisions and choices are made with political power considerations in mind and are linked to policy.[41] Moreover, it is necessary to study tourism in a political economy framework because institutions—local, foreign, public, or private—are crucial in the provision of tourist services. The importance of the political economy approach is not limited to the study of economic development or tourism, however, but also lends itself to the study of population movements in general, be they voluntary or involuntary, short term or long term.

Second, since this study did not entail microlevel fieldwork in a single or several LDC destinations, it does not contain the high degree of detail and subtlety associated with such research. Although I have included anecdotal evidence from interviews I conducted in South Africa, Botswana, Zambia, and Panama, this study relies mostly on primary statistical sources and secondary comparative statistics and analyses that provide a global perspective and enable large-scale assessments and comparisons.[42] Indeed, it reflects an underlying interest in exploring comparative complexities of less developed tourist-friendly economies rather than seeking the laws that govern a single case. It must be noted, though, that working with primary statistics is a double-edged sword. Although some sources, such as the World Tourism Organization, UNCTAD, and the World Bank, have extensive tourism data, they are not always compatible and cross-sectional analyses are not always possible. Countries of the world simply do not report some statistics, nor are they always disaggregated or complete. This lack of comparable data has been a problem throughout this book—less so with GNP and growth statistics than with labor force and migration data. Moreover, some data differences transcend efforts at uniformity. For example, temporary mobility statistics are difficult to collect (in part because such mobility is difficult to define), so they do not show up in national statistics compilations.[43] Also, tourism and some employment-related migration take place in the informal sector, which is rarely recorded. In addition, sometimes identities of tourist and worker overlap—a reality not reflected in statistics.

Tourist-Friendly LDCs

As noted above, the population movement that presently trumps all others with respect to sheer magnitude is tourism. Consequently, in this study, LDCs are selected and classified on the basis of the economic role played by the tourist sector. That role can be measured in a variety of ways. Historically, the focus has been on arrival figures, namely how many people came and how long they stayed. More recently, the emphasis has tended to be on indicators of tourism's effect on local economic growth. Accordingly, the WTO classified developing countries as LDCs with prominent tourism sector, less prominent tourism sector, and without significant tourism activities.[44] Some scholars, including Dieke, have opted for a more complicated classification, claiming that the significance of tourism is best measured by a combination of GNP, merchandise exports, and trade in services.[45] In this study, the role of tourism is assessed by the relative size of the travel and tourism industry (as a percent of total GDP).

Given the obvious variety among developing countries, it is useful to group them into categories. Table 1.1 contains a grouping of countries into high, medium, and low categories (A, B, and C respectively), depending on the percentage of GDP derived from the tourist industry.

Table 1.1   Travel and Tourism as a Percentage of GDP, 2004

% GDP	Group A Countries
70–100	British Virgin Islands, Antigua and Barbuda, Maldives, Anguilla (71.9)[a]
50–69.9	Macao, Seychelles, Bahamas, Aruba, Vanuatu, Barbados (52.2)
30–49.9	St. Lucia, Cayman Islands, Jamaica, St. Vincent and Grenadines, Virgin Islands, Mauritius, St. Kitts and Nevis (30.1)
25-29.9	Grenada, Kiribati, Fiji, Guadeloupe, Dominican Republic, Dominica (25.1)

	Group B Countries
20–24.9	Belize, Gambia, Bahrain, Angola (20.3)
15–19.9	Tunisia, Jordan, Cape Verde Islands, Morocco, Egypt (15.3)
10–14.9	Malaysia, Qatar, Tonga, Cuba, Papua New Guinea, Panama, Gabon, Costa Rica, Lebanon, Thailand, Comoros, Kenya, China, Guyana, Trinidad and Tobago, Sri Lanka, Oman, Ethiopia, Cambodia, Indonesia, Solomon Islands, Brunei, Turkey, United Arab Emirates (10.0)

	Group C Countries
8–9.9	Libya, Ghana, Singapore, Botswana, Sudan, Namibia, Venezuela, Democratic Republic of Congo, Mexico, Laos, Uganda, Martinique, Ecuador, Nepal, Tanzania, Bolivia, Kuwait, Saudi Arabia, Peru, Honduras, Vietnam, Uruguay (8.1)
5–7.9	Iran, São Tomé and Principe, Korea, Senegal, South Africa, Yemen, Philippines, Nicaragua, Brazil, Colombia, Argentina, El Salvador, Curaçao, Algeria, Swaziland, Lesotho, Rwanda, Malawi, Syria, Zambia, Mali, Chile, Guatemala, Madagascar, Benin, Burkina Faso, Paraguay, Nigeria, Chad, Pakistan, Reunion, Cameroon (5.0)
<4.9	India, Suriname, Burundi, Haiti, Togo, Central African Republic, Niger, Zimbabwe, Côte d'Ivoire, Guinea, Bangladesh, Myanmar, Congo (Zaire), Sierra Leone (1.9)

Source: World Travel and Tourism Council, *Travel and Tourism—Forging Ahead,* the 2004 Travel and Tourism Economic Research Country League Tables (Madrid: 2004), Table 46.

Notes: Group A countries derive 25–100 percent of their GDP from travel and tourism; Group B countries 10–24.9 percent; Group C countries 0–9.9 percent.

a. The numbers in parentheses indicate the lowest value in the group.

The countries within each category are listed in descending order, and the lowest value in the group is noted in parentheses. Countries not included in the three categories are those for which data were unavailable from reliable and comparable sources. Even for some of the countries included in the table, the reported statistics are unreliable and should be viewed with skepticism (as, for example, the data for Nepal). This classification of countries into three groups is valid for a single point in time, giving a mere snapshot of the tourism industry, without reflecting the fact that it is dynamic, transforming, and expanding almost everywhere. The lines of demarcation between groups of countries are approximations that are not set in stone. Consequently, countries that are at the borders of those demarcation lines are less reliably ensconced in a group than those further from the borders.

Countries in which the travel and tourism industry accounts for more than 25 percent of GDP are listed in Table 1.1 as members of Group A. Even though the range of values is wide (from 95.2 percent of GDP in the British Virgin Islands to 25.1 percent in Dominica), these countries share numerous similarities. Each is an island state. They tend to be small, their populations low, and their economies open. These countries have few resources other than tourism. For example, even in Jamaica, where the role of tourism is smaller than in many of the other countries, tourism has surpassed bauxite in foreign earnings.[46] In the Dominican Republic, tourism had replaced sugar as the primary foreign exchange earner by the mid-1990s.[47] The role of size is huge for these countries, as their options are smaller than in bigger states and the impact of tourism, both good and bad, is greater.

Group B consists of countries in which the travel and tourism industry accounts for between 10 and 24.9 percent of GDP. Although the number of countries is similar to that in Group A, the range of their values is more compact. Few are islands and few are small. In small islands, tourism is of crucial importance, vying for prominence with offshore finance and, in the case of Trinidad and Tobago, energy. Although the remaining countries in Group B vary in size and population, they all have diversified economies. Their tourist sectors are well established, but they do not dominate the economies. Indeed, Morocco, Egypt, Malaysia, and Panama all have other dominant industries.

Group C includes the majority of LDCs, those in which tourist expenditure receipts account for less than 9.9 percent of GDP. It includes countries with well-developed tourist sectors that coexist with other well-developed industries and so by comparison are relatively smaller (including Botswana, Guatemala, South Africa, and Chile, among others). Despite the existence of other industries, tourism is often the principal foreign exchange earner.

Group C also includes countries in which tourist sectors are very underdeveloped, as in Bangladesh, Pakistan, and Sierra Leone. It is useful to differentiate between these two sets of countries by forming a subgroup, low C countries, that includes those whose tourist receipts account for less than 4.9 percent of GDP. These countries coincide with the description offered by the WTO of the poorest countries in the world: they are countries "lacking consistent tourism-related policies," such as Central African Republic, Djibouti, Equatorial Guinea, Mozambique, and Sudan.[48] Countries suffering from instability and therefore having no significant tourism activities include Afghanistan, Burma, Congo (Zaire), Eritrea, Guinea, Guinea-Bissau, Haiti, Liberia, Sierra Leone, Somalia, and Zimbabwe.

The classification presented in Table 1.1 refers to the total travel and tourism industry and thus will be especially relevant in subsequent chapters when growth and employment are discussed. Here it is also useful to disaggregate the tourism industry information to understand the relative role of international receipts. Most studies of tourism in LDCs focus on international rather than domestic tourism. Not only are they two distinct markets, but they also differ in their significance for development, since only the former brings in foreign currency.[49] Even though domestic tourism accounts for some 80 percent of tourist activity, governments would rather promote foreign arrivals because they generate foreign currency.[50] Table 1.2 shows countries grouped according to the proportion of their GDP derived from international tourist receipts. As this measure is less inclusive than the one provided by WTO satellite statistics presented in Table 1.1, the ranking of countries is also different. Those countries that rank in the same category in both tables are ones in which international receipts are a large component of the travel and tourism industry (as, for example, the Maldives, Bahamas, Vanuatu, and so on). In these countries, very little income and product is generated by domestic tourism or by travel-related economic activities that are not subsumed in expenditure by foreign travelers.

LDCs in Asia, Africa, and Latin America are not equally distributed across the three categories described in Table 1.1. As evident from Table 1.3, Group A countries are mostly located in the Caribbean. Group B countries are spread out over the continents, with the largest concentration in Africa and Asia. Only five are islands. Four have coastlines on

Table 1.2   International Tourist Expenditure as a Percentage of GDP, 2002

% GDP	Countries
	Group A
70–100	Turks and Caicos, Cayman Islands, Anguilla (70.9)[a]
50–69.9	Guam, Maldives (57.3)
30–49.9	Aruba, Antigua and Barbuda, St. Lucia, Bahamas (36.7)
25–29.9	Barbados, Monserrat, St. Vincent and Grenadines (25.6)
20–24.9	St. Kitts and Nevis, Vanuatu, Dominica (21.0)
	Group B
15–19.9	Seychelles, São Tomé and Principe, Grenada, Jamaica, Belize (16.9)
10–14.9	Dominican Republic, Mauritius, Fiji, Namibia, Gambia, Mexico (10.4)
	Group C
8–9.9	Eritrea, Guyana, Bahrain, Cambodia, Costa Rica, Tunisia, Jordan (8.0)
5–7.9	Tanzania, Ghana, Malaysia, Morocco, Comoros, Panama, Syria, Laos, Thailand, Turkey, Nicaragua, Singapore (5.1)
<4.9	Lebanon, Honduras, Tonga, Kiribati, Mongolia, Cape Verde, Egypt, Indonesia, Botswana, Zambia, Marshall Islands, Papua New Guinea, Mali, Kenya, Senegal, Uruguay, New Caledonia, Mauritania, Trinidad and Tobago, Madagascar, Ecuador, Benin, Guatemala, Uganda, Nepal, Solomon Islands, Saudi Arabia, Suriname, United Arab Emirates, Philippines, Lesotho, Swaziland, South Africa, Bolivia, Bhutan, El Salvador, Malawi, China, Peru, Colombia, Korea, Burkina Faso, Haiti, Taiwan, Zimbabwe, Sri Lanka, Niger, Chile, Ethiopia, Sierra Leone, Paraguay, Argentina, Côte d'Ivoire, Togo, Iran, Brazil, India, Congo (0.06)

Source: Calculated from various country tables in World Tourism Organization, *Compendium of Tourism Statistics* (Madrid: 2003); World Bank, *World Development Indicators* (CD-ROM, 2003), various tables.

Notes: Group A countries derive 25–100 percent of their GDP from travel and tourism; Group B countries derive 10–24.9 percent; Group C countries 0–4.9 percent.

a. The numbers in parentheses indicate the lowest value in the group.

the Caribbean, thus tapping the same tourist market as countries in Group A (Belize, Panama, Costa Rica, and to a lesser degree Guyana). Although the ten African countries in category B (two of which are islands) represent a large portion of the Group B countries, Group C contains the overwhelming majority of African states.

Given this concentration of African states in Group C, Africa has a special place in the study of LDC tourism with respect to its possible po-

Table 1.3   Group A, B, and C Countries by Geographical Regions

Country Groups	Number of Countries by Geographical Region
A	Africa (2), Asia (2), Caribbean (16), Central America (0), Middle East (0), Oceania (3), South America (0)
B	Africa (10), Asia (8), Caribbean (2), Central America (3), Middle East (7), Oceania (2), South America (1)
C	Africa (34), Asia (11), Caribbean (3), Central America (5), Middle East (4), Oceania (0), South America (11)

Source: Table 1.1.

tential for stimulating development. Unfortunately, with the exception of northern Africa, Africa is distant and costly to get to for Western tourists. Attractions are minimal, compared to historical and architectural draws in other places (Senegal stands out as an exception, touting its slave trading posts). Egypt was a lucrative destination until Islamic militants disrupted tourism. West Africa has malaria and other diseases. Of the sub-Saharan countries, only South Africa is listed in the top forty tourist destinations worldwide. Nevertheless, the continent holds much potential for tourist expansion. Iain Christie and Doreen Crompton of the World Bank noted that "some thirty countries in Sub-Saharan Africa have incipient or flourishing tourism industries, defined by minimum contribution of 2 percent to GDP and of 5 percent to exports."[51]

An overview of countries in Group C leads us to wonder why some have not lived up to the tourist potential that they clearly have (for example, Algeria has beaches; Pakistan has historical sites; Cameroon has rain forests). Although microeconomic issues, including demand and supply, are of course relevant (and will be addressed in Chapter 3), a government's overall propensity toward tourism is a key determinant. Such a propensity is reflected in government policy in general and with respect to tourism (and other population movements) in particular. Countries in Group A are undoubtedly dependent on tourism, and it is likely that government policies reflect that dependency. In other words, countries in Group A desire tourism and have de facto integrated it, and efforts to diffuse growth into other sectors (to the extent that they even exist) have to date either been lukewarm or have not been successful, as indicated by their membership in Group A. Countries in Group C have not developed their tourism sectors and, especially in the low Cs, it is unlikely to be a priority. They are restrained by political turmoil and civil wars (as in Angola, Sierra Leone, Côte d'Ivoire, and Sudan), by religious extremism (witness the Islamic rebel activity in Algeria and Egypt and the antiwestern policies of Iran), or simply by draconian proclamations, as in Malaysia, where the death penalty for trespasses is clearly spelled out at the airports for tourists to ponder. It is the Group B countries in which tourism is growing in importance yet does not dominate the economy. To underscore this difference, Group A countries are said to be tourist dependent, Group B countries can be called tourist friendly, and Group C countries are tourist restrained. These terms encompass the mix of actual (or realized) tourism in the economy as well as the policy that must support it (or not, as the case may be). The use of the word *friendly* can be misleading and warrants further explanation. Attributing the term *tourist friendly* to a country does not imply that its government and population are thrilled at receiving foreigners. As illustrated by Jamaica, it is possible to rely on tourism while resenting both the tourists and the dependency they foster. Still, as long as state policy does not officially curtail or forbid tourist enterprise, it can be designated as tourist friendly. Also, it is unreasonable to argue that Pakistan is more accepting and friendly toward tourists than India, as is suggested by the classification presented in Table 1.1. But that table presents a single indicator of the importance of tourism, namely the travel and tourism industry as a percent of GDP. The fact that Pakistan ranks slightly higher than India should be viewed in light of the approximate nature of the demarcations between categories.

The most interesting group of countries is B, namely the tourist-friendly countries that have not yet realized their tourist potential and therefore have the capacity to expand the sector. Throughout the book, evidence will be provided to illustrate the motivation of these countries to harness the tourist potential even if they forgo a tourist-led development strategy. This does not imply, however, that countries in Groups A and C do not encourage tourism. Most do, in ways that are very similar to those of Group B countries. Their potential for tourist growth and its diffusion throughout the economy is different, however (as will be discussed in Chapter 2).

Ultimately, the designation "tourism friendly" is used to denote a country's position on tourist flows, which by extension has implications for other population flows as well. Indeed, a country that welcomes foreign tourists will also welcome workers to produce the requisite goods and services and might also engage in displacement of populations to enable the development of the industry.

Notes

1. Stephen Castles and Mark J. Miller, *The Age of Migration* (New York: Guildford Press, 1993); Timothy J. Hatton and Jeffrey G. Williamson, *The Age of Mass Migration* (New York: Oxford University Press, 1998).

2. Allan M. Williams and C. Michael Hall point out four reasons why this is so: demographic changes (longer lives allow people more years for possible movements), changing income streams (enabling the consumption of leisure travel), transportation and communication changes (lower transportation costs coupled with email and the Internet), and political changes (liberalization of travel requirements). Allan M. Williams and C. Michael Hall, "Tourism, Migration, Circulation and Mobility: The Contingencies of Time and Place," in *Tourism and Migration, New Relationships Between Production and Consumption,* ed. C. Michael Hall and Allan M. Williams (Dordrecht, The Netherlands: Kluwer Academic Publishers, 2002), pp. 12–17.

3. World Bank, *Entering the 21st Century: World Development Report 1999/2000* (Oxford: Oxford University Press, 2000), pp. 37–38.

4. Permanent population movements within a country constitute the largest number of migrants. The next largest share of migrants moves across national boundaries within less developed countries (LDCs). The remaining migrants move from the LDCs to the more developed countries (MDCs). Although proportionally small, these migrants are large in absolute terms and are growing.

5. U.S. Committee for Refugees, *World Refugee Survey 2000* (Washington, DC: 2000), Table 2.

6. *BBC News,* http/news.bbc.co.uk/go/pr/fr/-/2/hi/Europe/3985159.stm (accessed November 5, 2004).

7. *The State of the World's Refugees,* cited in Donna E. Arzt, *Refugees into Citizens* (New York: Council on Foreign Relations, 1997), p. 101.

8. Philippe Legrain, *Open World: The Truth About Globalization* (London: Abacus, 2002), p. 108.

9. Cited in Donald Lundberg, Mink Stavenga, and M. Krishnamoorthy, *Tourism Economics* (New York: Wiley, 1995), p. 3.

10. Cited in Deborah McLaren, *Rethinking Tourism and Ecotravel,* 2nd ed. (Bloomfield, CT: Kumarian Press, 2003), p. xv.

11. Lundberg, Stavenga, and Krishnamoorthy, *Tourism Economics,* p. ix.

12. Cited in World Bank Group, World Bank Revisits Role of Tourism in Development, 17, no. 12 (1998).

13. Based on a study by the Wharton Economic Forecasting Association, cited in Lundberg, Stavenga, and Krishnamoorthy, *Tourism Economics,* p. 3.

14. *eTurbo News,* www.eturbonews.com, accessed March 27, 2005; World Travel and Tourism Council, March 28, 2005, www.travelwirenews.com/news/28mar2005.htm, accessed March 28, 2005.

15. David Diaz Benavides and Ellen Perez-Ducy, eds., *Tourism in the Least Developed Countries* (Madrid: World Tourism Organization, 2001), p. 231.

16. Cited in Donald Reid, *Tourism, Globalization and Development* (London: Pluto Press, 2003), p. 44.

17. Cited in ibid.

18. World Bank Group, *World Bank Revisits Role of Tourism.*

19. More than two-thirds of all tourism spending occurs in Organization for Economic Cooperation and Development (OECD) countries, although this is slowly changing as more and more third world destinations develop their tourist industries and become accessible. *Business Life*, July/August 2005, p. 18.

20. The tourist authorities have favored Czechia. *Economist*, May 22, 2004, p. 48.

21. There are many different ways of referring to developing countries. Martin Mowforth and Ian Munt used the terms *West* and *the Rest,* implying a division between first world capitalist economies and everyone else (Martin Mowforth and Ian Munt, *Tourism and Sustainability*, 2nd ed. [London: Routledge, 2003], p. 5). The term *third world* provided a way of lumping together the less developed countries of Asia, Africa, and South America. It was short, to the point, and therefore more convenient than the unwieldy *less developed countries.* As David Harrison suggested, the term *third world* is no longer appropriate: with the end of the cold war, there is no longer a second world, so by implication not a third world either (David Harrison, "International Tourism and the Less Developed Countries: The Background," in *Tourism and the Less Developed Countries*, ed. David Harrison [London: Belhaven Press, 1992], p. 1). In this study, the term *less developed countries* is favored, although others are sometimes also used.

22. Cynthia Enloe, *Bananas, Beaches and Bases: Making Feminist Sense of International Politics* (London: Pandora, 1990), p. 32.

23. *Financial Times*, July 9–10, 2005.

24. Diaz Benavides and Perez-Ducy, "Background Note by the OMT/WTO Secretariat," p. 2.

25. Andrew-Bell Fialkoff, *Ethnic Cleansing* (New York: St. Martin's Griffin, 1999); Roberta Cohen and Francis M. Deng, eds., *The Forsaken People, Case Studies of the Internally Displaced* (Washington, DC: Brookings Institution, 1998).

26. Louis Turner, "The International Division of Leisure: Tourism in the Third World," *World Development* 4, no. 3 (1976). Quoted in John Lea, *Tourism and Development in the Third World* (London: Routledge, 2001), p. 1.

27. Lundberg, Stavenga, and Krishnamoorthy, *Tourism Economics*; M. Thea Sinclair and Mike Stabler, *The Economics of Tourism* (London: Routledge, 1997).

28. Valene Smith, ed., *Hosts and Guests, The Anthropology of Tourism*, 2nd ed. (Philadelphia: University of Pennsylvania Press, 1989).

29. Emanuel de Kadt, *Tourism, Passport to Development?* (New York: Oxford University Press, 1979); Dean MacCannell, *The Tourist: A New Theory of the Leisure Class*, 3rd ed. (Berkeley: University of California Press, 1999); J. Diamond, "Tourism's Role in Economic Development: The Case Reexamined,"

Economic Development and Cultural Change, 25, no. 3 (April 1977); Jozsef Borocz, *Leisure Migration, A Sociological Study on Tourism* (Tarrytown, NY: Elsevier, 1996).

30. Linda K. Richter, "Tourism Politics and Political Science: A Case of Not So Benign Neglect," *Annals of Tourism Research* 10 (1983).

31. Helen Briassoulis, ed., *Tourism and the Environment,* 2nd ed. (Boston: Kluwer Academic Publishers, 2000); John Dixon et al., *Tourism and the Environment in the Caribbean,* Environment Department Papers no. 80 (Washington, DC: World Bank, 2001). Incidentally, the reader should note that although presented here by discipline, this scholarly attention has been largely interdisciplinary, as the subject demands. Mowforth and Munt said that "as a personal activity, tourism is practiced by a diverse range of the population; as an industry, it is multi-sectoral; and as a means of economic and cultural exchange, it has many facets and forms. Any comprehensive analysis of the field must therefore be multidisciplinary." Mowforth and Munt, *Tourism and Sustainability,* p. 2.

32. Robert Wood, "Touristic Ethnicity: a Brief Itinerary," www.camden.rutgers.edu/~wood/Papers/touristic-ethnicity.pdf (accessed January 14, 2006).

33. Lucy Lippard, "Foreword," in MacCannell, *The Tourist,* p. xi; MacCannell, *The Tourist.*

34. A. Appadurai, "Disjuncture and Difference in the Global Cultural Economy," *Global Culture: Nationalism, Globalization and Modernity,* ed. M. Featherstone (London: Sage, 1990), pp. 295–310.

35. Williams and Hall, "Tourism, Migration, Circulation and Mobility," p. 3.

36. Ibid.

37. Sinclair and Stabler, *The Economics of Tourism,* p. 143.

38. Frances Brown, *Tourism Reassessed: Blight or Blessing?* (Oxford: Butterworth-Heinemann, 1998).

39. See Michael Todaro and Stephen Smith, *Economic Development,* 9th ed. (Boston: Addison Wesley, 2005).

40. S. G. Britton, "The Political Economy of Tourism in the Third World," *Annals of Tourism Research* 6, no. 3 (1982), pp. 318–329; Linda Richter, *Land Reform and Tourism Development in the Philippines* (Cambridge, MA: Schenkman, 1982).

41. Peter U.C. Dieke, "The Nature and Scope of the Political Economy of Tourism Development in Africa," in *The Political Economy of Tourism Development in Africa,* ed. Peter U.C. Dieke (New York: Cognizant Communication Corporation, 2000), p. 15.

42. Research was undertaken in South Africa (2002), Botswana and Zambia (2003), and Panama (2005).

43. Even the United States, so sophisticated in data collection, does not have a comprehensive data source on commuting by workers.

44. Diaz Benavides and Perez-Ducy, *Tourism in the Least Developed Countries,* p. 44.

45. Dieke, "The Nature and Scope of the Political Economy of Tourism," p. 15.

46. Enloe, *Bananas, Beaches and Bases,* p. 32.

47. Ibid.

48. Diaz Benavides and Perez-Ducy, *Tourism in the Least Developed Countries,* p. 44.

49. This distinction is blurred somewhat by the tourists who are expatriates, going to their home countries to visit friends and family, as it is unclear if they should be considered domestic or international tourists. For the purposes of this study, if they bring in foreign currency, they are the latter.

50. Dieke, "The Nature and Scope," p. 16.

51. World Bank, "Tourism in Africa," Findings Report no. 22617, *Environmental, Rural and Social Development Newsletter* (July 2001), p. 1.

2

Growth and Population Movements in Tourist-Friendly Economies

At the beginning of the new millennium, many LDCs were experiencing unprecedented economic growth. India's economy expanded by 8.2 percent in 2003,[1] and China is said to have supplanted the United States as the capitalist engine of the world.[2] An African country, Botswana, had the highest rates of economic growth in the world in 2002.[3] Although there are undoubtedly still problems of poverty, unequal distribution, acquired immunodeficiency syndrome (AIDS), production bottlenecks, and institutional constraints, these glowing rates of growth portend well for the ability of these countries to address those problems. How, in fact, does that growth manifest itself?

When a society experiences economic development (also known as modern economic growth), fundamental alterations occur in the structure of its economy.[4] There is a change in what is produced, how it is produced, where it is produced, and who produces it. During economic development, an increase in income per capita is achieved by the widespread application of innovative technology to the production process (which serves to make inputs more productive and/or to change the way in which they are used in the production function). The definition of economic development also includes an aftermath: namely, it results in a structural transformation of the economy according to which the sectoral distribution of national income changes, as does the industrial classification of the labor force.[5] With respect to the former, the contribution of the agricultural sector to national income declines while the contribution of manufacturing grows by a lot, then stabilizes and even contracts. The importance of the services sector continues to rise in the course of economic development (in the

United States, it accounted for nearly 70 percent of national output by the end of the twentieth century).[6] The labor force and the labor markets also undergo changes during the structural transformation process. As these are discussed in detail below, suffice it to say here that as the sectoral contribution to national income changes in the course of economic growth, so too does the nature of the work that workers perform. The importance of agriculture as the principal employer diminishes while that of the manufacturing sector first increases and then falls off. Services continue to absorb labor.

LDCs have, more or less, followed the pattern described above. Most are becoming more industrial and less agricultural, and the two developing giants, India and China, are a case in point.

Given the focus of this book, one might ask if economic growth is different in tourist-friendly LDCs. In other words, does the prominence of the travel and tourism industry alter the nature of the structural transformation? Donald Reid said that in discussing the structural transformation and tourism, it is necessary to distinguish between less developed countries and the more developed, as the manifestations of the structural transformation will be different. M. Thea Sinclair and Mike Stabler also said that viewing the structural transformation in the usual sense is misguided in the case of countries where tourism is important.[7] Tourism is classified as an invisible export industry, an intangible service that one cannot touch, like insurance and banking; it does not produce capital-intensive megaprojects that are usually associated with growth and modernization. It also does not entail the proliferation of big factories that was the core of the traditional growth experienced by Western industrialized countries a century or two ago, when manufacturing fueled the economy. To the contrary, in the third world, luxurious enclaves coexist with profuse poverty, side by side, with differing degrees of integration. The lack of visible signs of modernization is even more acute in those tourist-friendly countries where tourism accounts for a significant portion of the country's economy.

Before the potential of tourism was noted, many third world governments introduced aggressive policies to stimulate the structural transformation of the economy (including industrialization policies as well as tax, trade, pricing, and marketing policies—all aimed at stimulating manufacturing). In the early aftermath of their independence, many developing countries turned to the Soviet Union, the country that experienced the quickest structural transformation, for guidance with planning methods.[8] Others adopted authoritarian systems with huge public sectors; still others embraced an unbridled and unregulated capitalism. Some developing countries achieved growth while bypassing the industrial stage altogether. The oil-rich countries did it, as did those with abundant gold and diamonds. Service economies that relied on banking and shipping also did it, as the experience of Singapore attests. The demonstration effect of those examples was huge, and third world leaders turned to introspection to assess their capacity for such growth. They found that tourism offered a similar promise, namely the possibility of riches while bypassing the long industrialization process.

In this chapter, two independent variables—duration and choice—are introduced that enable a classification of population movements in tourist-friendly LDCs. The effect of those very different population movements on economic growth is then discussed.

Population Movements as Labor Adjustments to Economic Growth

Economic growth requires resources to fuel it, irrespective of the sector in which it is concentrated. Capital and labor are needed to produce output, and without them, growth cannot occur. Therefore, in order to understand growth, we need to understand resources. That includes the movement of resources.

Why do resources move from one place to another? With special reference to labor, what determines the migratory flows of workers and how are they related to economic conditions? These questions have been answered by scholars representing different schools of thought. According to world systems theory, the division of labor across the globe sets the stage for movements from the periphery to the core. Following Immanuel Wallersteins's pioneering work,[9] Lúcie Cheng and Edna Bonacich claimed that migration occurs in the course of capitalist development, as the core requires more workers for its development and the periphery cannot sustain its workers owing to underdevelopment.[10] Theories that draw on the concept of the dual labor markets stress that immigrant labor tends to be concentrated in the secondary market, where income is low, job security is nonexistent, workers are unproductive, and so on. Rational choice theories state that people attempt to maximize their benefits relative to their costs, so they will migrate if that is called for by their personal cost-benefit analysis. J. R. Harris and Michael Todaro expanded this idea by combining push-and-pull factors to indicate that migration will continue from a sending area to a target area as long as expected earnings in the latter exceed expected earnings in the former.[11] Earnings tend to be high in a growing region, in which there is economic activity that raises the demand for labor and keeps the wages relatively higher.

Migration as an economic phenomenon has been studied most comprehensively by Simon Kuznets.[12] He stated that as an economy grows and becomes more industry and service oriented, its requirements for workers undergo a transformation. In other words, as the sectoral contribution to national income changes in the course of economic growth, so too does the nature of the work that workers perform. The importance of agriculture as the principal employer of labor diminishes, whereas that of the manufacturing sector first increases and then falls off. Services continue to absorb labor.[13] Thus economic change, coupled with new developments in technology and transportation, alters the demand and supply of labor such that the location of productive activity changes (computers are not produced on a farm; shipping does not take place on a mountain). The demand for agricultural workers, being a derived demand, keeps pace with the demand for the product those workers produce. As the demand for agricultural goods fails to keep up with overall increases in consumption, so too the demand for agricultural workers tends to fall off. The demand for industrial and service sector workers increases along with consumer demand for products from those sectors. In addition, labor-saving technological change takes place in agriculture and manufacturing, whereas service sector production tends to be labor intensive, thus absorbing large quantities of white-collar labor. As a result, the labor demands of the economy are no longer necessarily met by the *preexisting* labor force working in *preexisting* locations. It is often necessary for labor to re-locate, commute, or otherwise geographically respond to market stimuli in new geographical locations. Such migration occurs between rural and urban areas, across regional boundaries, and over international borders. Empirical evidence supports this view of migration as an adjustment to economic change. In the post–World War II period, Germany's economy needed labor for its reconstruction efforts, hence the labor recruitment efforts in Italy to fill labor shortages.[14] In a similar fashion, since the mid-1970s, more than 90 percent of South Asian migrants have gone to the oil-exporting countries of western Asia that are receptive to foreign labor for their growing industries.[15]

Ever since Kuznets published his pioneering study of how the manpower demands of a growing economy are met through geographical mobility, scholars have focused on both the volume of labor movements as well as the characteristics of the migrant worker. In the Kuznets tradition, John Lansing and Eva Mueller presented their detailed assessment of the nature of mobility in the US economy, thereby setting the stage for the theoretical discussion that ensued over the next few decades.[16] They said, "The geographical mobility of labor is one of the basic processes of adjustment in the economy. . . . As new developments occur in technology, demand and transportation, changes take place in the location of productive activity. Failure of human resources to adjust to these changes leads to inefficiency, poverty and dependency."[17] Theirs and other early studies of the link between economic development and labor requirements formed the underpinnings of a wide range of academic disciplines. Now, it has become the basis for demographic theories concerned with population movements, sociological theories pertaining to migration, economic theories explaining economic growth and development, and regional studies theories focusing on location of industrial clusters and transportation networks.

Toward a Comprehensive
View of Population Movements

The preceding discussion focused on population movements as labor adjustments to economic growth. That, however, leaves other kinds of movements unaccounted for. Indeed, as was clear from the description of the Caprivi Strip in Chapter 1, labor migrations are but one of the movements taking place in tourist-friendly LDCs. Here we turn to a more comprehensive view of population movements, including those in countries where *economic growth comes from tourism*, thus building the theoretical framework of this study.

As noted in Chapter 1, the link between tourism and migration has not been sufficiently studied. Rare examples include R. J. Wolfe, who in 1967 equated tourism with migration.[18] M. Bell and G. Ward compared temporary mobility with permanent migration.[19] Others focused on overlapping forms of mobility; R. V. Bianchi, for example, studied the migrant tourist worker.[20] Bell and Ward placed mobility on a continuum of space and time, where space is defined as local, regional, and national and time is measured in hours, days, weeks, months, and years.[21] Tourism falls somewhere in the middle, farther from home than shopping or excursions, less permanent than seasonal labor. Tim Coles, David Duval, and C. Michael Hall analyzed conceptual linkages between tourism and temporary mobility. Although they studied tourism as a form of temporary mobility "analogous in scope and meaning to

other forms of movement (e.g. travel to second homes, return migration, emigration)," they also studied forms of tourism that have arisen
as a result of enhanced global mobility.[22]

Allen Williams's and C. Michael Hall's contribution to the study of
tourism and migration stands out for its significance and breadth. Their
study focused on five forms of what they called tourism-informed migration: labor migration, entrepreneurial migration, return (labor) migration, consumption-led economically active migration, and retirement migration.[23] They claimed that this classification was neither
exhaustive nor were the categories discrete; instead they existed along
a continuum. Individuals may have multiple motives and therefore
slide between one category and another at different points in time. The
most important aspect of their typology was that it sought to differentiate between production- and consumption-led migration, and therein
lies their huge contribution to academic research (they differentiated
between these two insofar as the former deals with migrants who aim
to work in the tourism industry and the latter refers to migrants who
aim to partake in the tourist industry as guests).[24]

Williams's and Hall's five-part typology was not adopted in this
book, as the focus on LDC tourism renders some of their categories irrelevant. Indeed, three of their categories, namely return migration,
consumption-led economically active migration, and retirement migration, occur mostly in the more developed countries from which their research was drawn, countries that have higher incomes and where tourist
activities, both as hosts and guests, have long prospered. In most less
developed countries, where tourism is just beginning to take off and
where retirement is an option for very few people, the migrations of importance are the labor and entrepreneurial migrations. Moreover, this
book's emphasis on developing countries necessitates the inclusion of
involuntary population movements, which continue unabated in numerous countries under study. Williams and Hall did not deal with involuntary migration, as their focus was on Western states where contemporary manifestations are smaller in incidence and magnitude (in
contrast with the past in which Western countries have had their share
of involuntary dislocations—witness dislocations of native populations
in Canada, the United States, and Australia).

This book also departs from the work of Williams and Hall in another way. Williams and Hall introduced a four-phase model of tourism
migration that described tourist movements to destinations that then, in
phase two, stimulated temporary worker movements and in phase three
induced permanent migration. Phase four was complex insofar as it in-

cluded visiting friends and relatives (VFR) tourists, return migrants, and temporary labor migrants, among other types.[25] Their model illustrated that "not only does tourism lead to migration but migration may generate tourism flows," as, for example, VFR tourism.[26] Williams and Hall focused on the stimulus of friendship, ethnic, and kinship ties to generate new tourism, whereas this book focuses on the role of tourism in economic development and, in turn, its effect on tourism.

To that end, the world is divided into the MDCs and the LDCs (Figure 2.1). The population movements that originate in the former and go to the latter include tourists, other travelers, and skilled workers. The former two do not stay long—tourists might stay for a week of sun and sand, travelers on business might stay overnight in town to close a deal. Foreign nationals from the West also go to developing countries for work, often in the tourist or extractive or other high growth industries. They stay for a specific duration, until their job is done.

With respect to international population movements that originate in the LDCs, emigrants are the largest category, certainly larger than tourists. Although some international tourism undoubtedly exists and some temporary exchange occurs involving, for example, students and specialists, these are insignificant by comparison. As discussed in Chapter 3, since tourism is largely determined by income, poor developing

Figure 2.1   Circular Flow of Populations

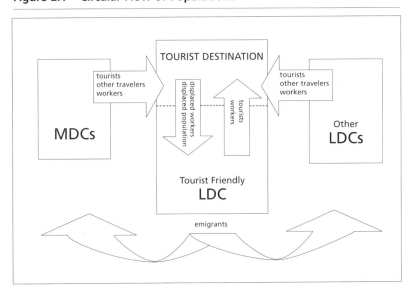

countries are less likely to generate it unless they are huge, like India and China.

Most population movements take place *within* developing countries, entailing no border crossing. They consist of economic migrants voluntarily moving in search of work as well as people involuntary displaced from their homes or jobs. Also, this category includes domestic tourists. Domestic tourism is not considered growth promoting because it brings in no foreign currency.[27] Still, its sheer volume in countries such as South Africa, China, the Philippines, and India has attracted attention. Worldwide, 80 percent of all tourists are domestic. In India the foreign tourist inflow is less than 3 million per year, whereas the domestic tourist traffic is about 234 million visits per year.[28] How can we study the diverse population movements depicted in Figure 2.1? Indeed, how can we lump together tourists traveling long distances to see exotic lands, managers posted in a resort town to run a hotel, an underemployed farmer moving across state to get a job in the restaurant business, and an indigenous tribe member forced to evacuate prime beach property and relocate into a camp for displaced peoples? At the core, each of these movements is economic insofar as each entails actions based on considerations of scarce resources. Also at the core, they all involve human actions and so, by definition, entail imperfections and irregularities. To be useful, however, scholarly analysis of population movements must transcend those two commonalities. To that end, two variables are introduced here: duration of stay and freedom of choice. By looking at the *duration of stay*, we can place population movements along a spectrum ranging from temporary (minimum one day) to permanent (a lifetime). Of course, tourists are on one end; permanent immigrants are on the other. With respect to *freedom of choice*, the spectrum of population movements includes leisure tourist travel at one end and ethnic cleansing at gunpoint at the other.

The Temporal Dimension

Population movements vary in duration from one day to forever. Tourists leave their cruise ships to visit Aruba for a few hours or cross the border into Dubai for a day of shopping. At the other extreme, people make permanent trips with one-way tickets, planning never to return home. In between these two extremes are the multitude of other possible durations of people in motion between their origin and destination.

These people also differ by intent, as some migrations are a priori permanent, rather than becoming so a posteriori. Under those circumstances, how long must migrants be in a new location before their movements can be classified as permanent? In other words, at what point does a temporary visit become permanent? There is no clear demarcation point, and permanence cannot be measured scientifically. Its existence is identified qualitatively, rather than in empirically quantifiable ways. In the common definitions of migration as incorporating some degree of impermanence, Williams and Hall stated that "the idea of permanence is problematic, for there is no theoretically grounded definition of 'permanence.'"[29] Researchers rely on arbitrary time limits such as twelve months. As there is no single definition, varying terms have emerged to deal with temporary migrants: seasonal workers, nomads, long-distance commuters, peripatetic lifestylers, temporary migrants, among others.[30] Irrespective of the terminology, the migrant's duration of stay might be measured by how he or she has integrated into the host society, both socially and politically. In this way, a quantifiable indicator of permanence is the taking of the host country's citizenship. Such a step implies that the migrant has made a commitment, has invested in learning the host country's language and laws, has enrolled children in local schools, earns an income, and pays taxes.

The Choice Dimension

A fundamental difference among people is the extent to which their decision to travel is born from free choice. Failure to recognize the importance of choice in migration decisions has retarded much research and postponed our understanding of the nature of population movements. Graeme Hugo pointed out this deficiency, stating that initial research on population movements in LDCs was based "either explicitly or implicitly on the premise that population movement is a fundamentally voluntary process. This is due to an inappropriate transfer of concepts and models developed in contemporary Euro-American society."[31]

All population movements are either voluntary or involuntary. Voluntary migration results from a personal cost/benefit analysis that indicates that relocation will maximize utility. The choice to migrate is assumed to be rational; the process of assessing costs and benefits is assumed to be an informed one. Voluntary migration for the tourist involves an assessment of the price of the trip relative to the value derived from it. Most voluntary migration is motivated by expected economic benefits, namely a better job (including higher wages, improved working conditions, greater status, more possibility for advancement, increased job satisfaction, and so forth). Sometimes the voluntary migrant bases his or her decision on nonpecuniary considerations such as family bonds, political inclinations, and so forth. Whatever the motivation, the migrant exercises free choice in the migration decision and bears the responsibility for that decision.

During forced (or involuntary) population movements, the decision to travel is imposed on the individual or group. Involuntary migration includes both the forcible physical removal of individuals from their homes and the exertion of pressures that make survival in the present location untenable. Without the use of force, the creation of conditions that essentially amount to the absence of volition in migration has been called environmental refugeeism.[32] Another form of involuntary migration, human trafficking, has been receiving attention as the number of children and women who are forcibly sold across borders grows at alarming rates. Either way, people are evicted or transferred. They have no choice in the migration decision.

There are numerous reasons why involuntary migration occurs. These can be classified into two broad categories: natural and man-made disasters.[33] The latter includes displacement for economic purposes and political reasons. When disasters such as floods, droughts, landslides, and earthquakes occur, people are involuntarily moved from their homes. Even though such calamities obliterate homes and destroy livelihoods and thus create displacement as certainly as armed troops, the ensuing encampment of people is rarely long term. Once the affected area is reconstructed, migrants return home. It is the economic and political reasons for involuntary migration that are more likely to produce permanent dislocation.

Among the economic reasons, the most common is dislocation for the purposes of labor exploitation. When Europeans moved to the New World, they needed cheap workers to exploit the land and they turned to the blacks of Africa for their labor needs. From the mid-fifteenth century to the late nineteenth, some twelve million Africans made the voyage to the Western Hemisphere.[34] Before and after, millions more had trekked by foot to the Middle East, where Arab traders sold them on the market. Everywhere they went, slaves dug in mines, cleared land, planted, and harvested. Inside homes, they cooked, cleaned, washed, and tended to children. The transportation of chained Africans to the New World has modern parallels. Indeed, the movement of Jewish and Slavic laborers during Nazi rule in Germany and the forcible treks of Karen men in Myanmar for jungle clearance projects are all examples of involuntary labor migration. In the twenty-first century, human trafficking for the purposes of labor exploitation is on the rise.

It includes debt bondage, peonage, and involuntary servitude, all of which entail coercing a person to perform labor (including commercial sexual activity). As Kevin Bales pointed out, such modern slavery exists in LDCs (such as Mauritania, Pakistan, India, and Thailand, among others) as well as in MDCs, where a market for smuggled women and men is thriving. Linda Richter noted that many forced workers across the world are children.[35]

Land exploitation is also an economic reason for population dislocation. Historically, native populations were displaced so their land could be taken over (Zulu lands in South Africa, Aboriginal lands in Australia). Contemporary examples of population displacement for the sake of land exploitation, occurring now for the sake of tourism, are discussed in Chapter 5.

Political reasons for involuntary migration include international and domestic circumstances. Among the former are wars involving armed intervention and/or political warfare (such as propaganda or a victorious new political system).[36] With respect to domestic pressures on populations to involuntarily relocate, the most important is turbulence of various forms: a violent government change, such as one associated with a revolution or a coup d'état that carries with it either policies adverse to a given people or simply violence. In this environment, persecution on the basis of religion, race, or ethnicity, whether by sporadic harassment or planned genocide, is apt to arise and result in displacement (for example, the Armenian exodus from Turkey, the Indian flood from Guatemala, the Muslim exodus from Myanmar). When ethnicity is at the root of involuntary displacement of populations, then *ethnic cleansing* is the term of choice.[37] It is noted that minorities are not the only ones suffering, however, from what might be a brutal, dictatorial government that harasses members of society: the political opposition may also be a target, resulting in political migration (for example, the exodus of political opponents of Pinochet from Chile or of the Ayatolla Khomeini from Iran).[38]

Clearly then, both voluntary and involuntary population movements characterize contemporary society. Although population movements have occurred since the beginning of time, however, most of them were not voluntary. Indeed, it was not until the 1840s that annual voluntary European migration to the Americas exceeded the involuntary African migration.[39] In fact, fewer than 10 percent of the estimated nine to fifteen million transatlantic migrants before 1800 were free.[40] And even then, the movements were not about tourism but rather in response to economic, political, or religious pushes and pulls. Tourist travel is voluntary by definition, and although it has existed since ancient times, especially for medicinal purposes, it did not take off until the second half of the twentieth century.[41]

A Comprehensive Typology of Population Movements

Using two independent variables, duration of stay and choice in decisionmaking, four categories of population movements can be identified (presented in Table 2.1). All are related to economic growth, albeit in different ways. Short-term voluntary movements consist mostly of tourists, who are largely viewed as engines of growth in their travel destination. Long-term voluntary movements are labor adjustments to growth. Also adjustments to growth are short-term involuntary movements, namely those that occur because a skill becomes obsolete or a business closes down. These are involuntary, but they are forms of structural unemployment. They differ from the fourth category of long-term involuntary migrants. Clearly, different types of migrations coexist. They are not necessarily mutually exclusive, and so, as Nazli Choucri pointed out, "complicate any simple accounting of migration at any point in time."[42]

Temporary and Voluntary: Population Movements as Engines of Growth

The temporary and voluntary category consists of tourists as well as other travelers who may travel to a destination for shopping, medical care, visits to friends and family, or miscellaneous business (the latter group is not included in the labor categories discussed below because

Table 2.1   Population Movements Classified by Duration and Choice

Duration	Voluntary	Involuntary
Temporary	Tourists and other travelers (engine of growth)	Labor (structural and cyclical unemployment)
Permanent	Labor (workforce adjustments to growth)	General population (interethnic economic competition and ethnic cleansing)

their labor is not necessarily associated with the tourist industry). All of these travelers, irrespective of the reason for their travel, arrive at a destination and use accommodations, restaurants, transportation, and entertainment.

As a result of their consumption of local services and products, tourists and travelers have a stimulating effect on the local economy. They bring foreign capital both directly by spending and indirectly by inducing investment. In the process, the domestic service sector is developed, and its linkage and multiplier effects spread throughout the economy. Thus, the principal economic impact of tourism is on foreign exchange, GDP, and employment. This is discussed below.

Foreign capital. Since the early 1900s, economists have focused on the important role of capital accumulation for economic growth. The neoclassical model put forth by Robert Solow claimed that growth depended on the supply of capital and labor.[43] R. Harrod and E. Domar argued that the savings rate is crucial for growth, since it is positively related to capital accumulation.[44] In developing countries, a deficiency of private savings is compensated for with public savings and debt. If private and public domestic savings are still inadequate for the desired levels of capital accumulation, then international sources of capital fill the gap. Indeed, multilateral and bilateral flows of capital have compensated for domestic deficiencies and promoted economic growth in Asia, South America, and Africa. Singapore's phenomenal growth is often attributed to the successful encouragement of such capital inflows in the form of direct foreign investment.[45]

In tourist-friendly LDCs, foreign visitors bring foreign capital. That happens in two ways (both studied in Chapter 3).[46] First, tourist consumption of related goods and services (such as accommodation, transport, entertainment, food and beverage, recreation, and so on) entails the transfer of money, often in foreign currency, into local hands. According to the World Bank, visitors' expenditure outside their hotels can range from half of to nearly double the in-hotel expenditures.[47] Second, the more important form of capital infusion is the foreign investment, private and direct, that follows tourists. Profit-seeking foreign and multinational firms provide the supply that the tourist industry seeks. They become part of the tourist industry, an enormous umbrella business that includes a multitude of small and not so small subcomponents within the areas of travel, accommodation, food and beverage, ground transportation, attractions, recreation, retail, and so forth. They also participate in funding the secondary demands of tourism, including industries that produce automobiles (for rental cars), cameras and film, sunscreens, tennis rackets, and so on.

When these tourist services and goods are sold to residents of other countries, then the industry is classified as an export and has balance-of-payments implications (obviously domestic tourism, even though income generating, does not have this property). As a result of this international component of tourism, two aspects of trade theory can be used to analyze developments in the tourism industry. First, in the past century, the more and the less developed countries had different patterns of economic activity and trade (simply, LDCs export primary products and import manufactured goods). Tourism gives them the opportunity to export something for which demand is growing and that has a high income elasticity of demand. Second, we can infer that third world countries will export goods and services produced using the abundant factor of production. In tourist-friendly countries, that includes wildlife, beach, and indigenous populations, in other words, the exotic factor, also known as natural capital. Although it may not be surprising that tourism is an important component of Caribbean exports, it is less obvious that tourism continues to be the biggest service export of the United States.[48]

Economists have long argued that international trade and participation in the international financial markets are positively related to economic growth.[49] In order to ensure sustained economic growth, a country must have access to markets both for the sale of its output and the purchase of its inputs. Those countries with sufficient domestic demand for output and a domestic supply of inputs need not actively search for international markets. In reality, it is rare that countries do not reach out into the global economy for the most low-cost alternatives and the most lucrative sales. In the 1970s, the phenomenal growth experienced by the Asian countries known as the Four Tigers—Taiwan, Hong Kong, South Korea, and Singapore—re-ignited the hope that export-oriented policies would be the panacea for small countries.[50] Such promotion of exports of manufactured goods (rather than primary products) during the 1970s and 1980s increased foreign exchange earnings, improved the trade balance, and stimulated growth in these four countries. Many third world countries are hoping trade in tourist services will do the same for their economies.

Linkage and multiplier effects. The infusion of foreign capital and the development of services in tourist-friendly states not only contribute directly to raising the gross domestic product but also have forward and backward linkages that enable a multiplier effect throughout the economy. In other words, tourist-induced economic growth will have linkages that result in industrialization, employment beyond the tourist industry, increases in incomes, and increases in aggregate demand. These in turn will increase production and supply and set the country on a growth trajectory. Several multipliers are particularly relevant, including sales, output, income, and employment multipliers. The latter two, the most common gauge of tourism's role in economic activity, measure the ratio of the initial increase in tourism expenditure to its final impact on incomes or employment. The higher the multiplier coefficient, the greater the amount of additional income or employment created by an increase in tourism expenditure. Typically, multipliers in developing countries range between 2 and 3 (namely, for each dollar spent by tourists, two to three dollars of output are created in the economy).[51]

Thus, tourists and travelers induce the infusion of foreign capital, the incorporation of LDCs into the global economy through service exports, and the multiplier effects of linkages throughout the economy that are, in theory at least, conducive to economic growth. The extent to which these voluntary and temporary population movements *actually* stimulate economic growth depends on a variety of factors (addressed in Chapters 3 and 4). Despite what are often huge leakages, the WTO has argued that in fact tourism has *greater* potential for economic growth than other sectors for the following reasons.[52] First, tourism is consumed at the point of production, so there are other additional services and products that might be consumed when the consumer travels to the destination.[53] Second, export industries depend on financial, productive, and human capital. Although tourism also depends on those, in addition it draws heavily on natural capital such as scenery, beaches, wildlife, traditional peoples, and so on. In this way, tourism is different from other goods because, as Brian Copeland noted, "the bundle of goods and services purchased by a tourist is consumed jointly with unpriced natural amenities such as climate and scenery."[54] Most LDCs have abundant and untapped natural capital, enabling the supply of tourist facilities and services to be highly responsive to demand. Third, tourism is extremely labor intensive. The ramifications of this are explored in Chapter 4, so suffice it to say here that by using many workers, income is distributed across a broader range of people who in turn spend it in the local economy. Fourth, tourism is not really a sector unto itself, as tourist activities overlap and blend with other economic activities. As a result of this breadth and diversity, tourism offers more scope for wide participation and the development of the informal sector (cruise ship tourism is an exception).

Given then that voluntary and temporary flows of population can potentially be an engine of growth, we must ask if that potential is constant across countries pursuing tourism as a development strategy. In other words, do tourists traveling to countries in Groups A, B, and C (as discussed in Chapter 1) have the same stimulating effect on local economies? Given structural and resource limitations of multiplier and linkage effects, it is unlikely that the effect would be the same. To the contrary, the more important the role of tourism in the economy, the greater the number of tourist visits but the less tourism is an engine of growth. Indeed, even though tourism is an engine of growth at all stages (or at least it can be in theory), it is not equally effective at all stages (this is explored in Chapter 3 by using an analysis of the tourist market as well as empirical evidence of growth in countries A, B, and C). This has at least two policy implications. First, there is a small window of opportunity in which tourist population movements can stimulate economic growth, and third world tourism policy must reflect that. Second, it is not uncommon for tourist demand to be overpowered by tourist supply. In other words, the supply of capacity by LDC governments, foreign travel agencies, airlines, world banking institutions, and so on has been overwhelming relative to the demand. Those governments that have responded to a temporary and fickle demand with permanent structures must make adjustments in their future policy to reflect that imbalance.

Permanent/Voluntary and Temporary/Involuntary: Labor Force Adjustments to Growth

At the onset, some terminology requires explanation. The labor market is assumed to have players who voluntarily take jobs, who take jobs for pay, and who can leave those jobs. They are assumed to make choices, conduct personal cost/benefit analyses, and pursue their own self-interests.[55] Wherever people have no effective choice to respond to labor market conditions, where they have no choice to travel and take new jobs, where they cannot freely sell their labor, there is no functioning labor market. Therefore, assuming the absence of structural constraints to selling one's labor, a functioning labor market consists of employers who respond to changing economic circumstances by hiring, transferring, or discharging workers; closing or opening facilities; or moving their operations to new locations. Workers respond to changing economic or personal conditions by changing employers, occupations, or geographical locations. Clearly, supply and demand of labor are crucial concepts in understanding where people try to find work and where the jobs are located.

Labor mobility in its broadest form includes the following. When product demand, labor productivity, level of investment in human capital, family circumstances, or general economic conditions change, some workers find it advantageous to change employers, occupations, geographic locations, or some combination of these three. Alternatively, it is the employers who might initiate changes in the labor market. Indeed, they might respond to changing economic circumstances in the ways described above, namely by hiring, transferring, or laying off workers; closing or expanding facilities; or moving operations to new locations. Together, the actions by workers and firms generate movement of labor from job to job and place to place.

What makes people migrate? Albert Hirschman proposed a microlevel framework for analyzing individual choice in order to explain behavior. He said that when an organization fails to meet its expectations, individuals can express their disappointment in the form of exit (namely, stop buying the products) or voice (namely, protest in hopes of changing the objectionable practices).[56] Ishtiaq Ahmed applied this framework to migration: an individual will migrate if the location of residence fails to live up to its economic, social, and/or political expectations; in other words, the individual will exit.[57]

When the home region does not meet the economic expectations of a potential migrant (especially with respect to employment and income), such failure is a push that induces emigration. At the same time, economic expectations pertaining to opportunities in the host country exert a pull on the migrant. Potential migrants calculate, implicitly or explicitly, their chances of finding employment that is preferable to their current one (in terms of salary, benefits, future prospects, working conditions, and so on). Although numerous economists, including J. Hicks, W. A. Lewis, G. Ranis, J.C.H. Fei, J. R. Harris, and Michael Todaro, have focused on these economic considerations in migration, others have stressed that migration decisions cannot be viewed strictly in economic terms.[58] Instead, the decision to migrate is made on the basis of economic and noneconomic considerations. Although determining the single most important of these is realistic only on a case-by-case basis, some broad outlines of economic and noneconomic considerations that determine the propensity to migrate include personal characteristics, government policy, institutions, and infrastructure. These four variables determine labor mobility insofar as they describe what facilitates mobility, what contributes to the push and pull of workers, and what smooths out their relocation process (studied in Chapter 4). At the same time, they also encompass the obstacles to mobility. As such, each of them determines the capacity as well as the incentive to migrate.

The preceding discussion clearly refers to voluntary migration, situations in which workers make their own decisions about relocating. Yet, this category (namely, permanent/voluntary and temporary/involuntary) includes temporary involuntary movements also. These then are the movements of workers who are displaced by the business cycle or by structural changes in the economy and can no longer find employment in a given location. They do not want to move, but the search for employment forces them to do so. It is justifiable to include them in this section because they, like voluntary workers wishing to relocate permanently, are seeking better work. They are classified as temporary because they think they may go back (even if most do not). Incidentally, this category also includes involuntarily displaced migrants who have crossed international borders.

Whether voluntary or involuntary, are manpower adjustments to economic growth the same across all countries? The answer is no: the more tourist oriented the country, the greater the manpower adjustment of its population and therefore the greater the inflows of foreign and domestic workers. To the extent that this does not occur, it is owing to the imposition of artificial barriers that impede the circular flow of populations (as discussed in Chapters 4 and 6).

Permanent/Involuntary: Interethnic Competition and Economic Growth

When people are forcibly displaced for reasons other than natural disasters, they rarely have an option to return. Their movement then is both involuntary and permanent.

In most cases of man-made displacement, the displaced people are of different ethnicities[59] (or religions, races, or linguistic groups) than those who displace them.[60] This reality underscores the important role of ethnicity in involuntary migration, as examples from Rwanda, Bosnia, and Turkey clearly indicate. Moreover, ethnicity underlies government policy toward involuntarily displaced populations (for example, India welcomes refugees from Tibet but not from Bangladesh).[61] In tourist-friendly LDCs, dominant ethnic groups use force to displace marginalized weaker groups. With few exceptions, such as Fiji, the dominant groups wield economic and political power within their societies, whereas the weaker groups, usually indigenous populations, are smaller in number and are economically and politically weaker. They are displaced for economic reasons, in an effort to establish control over choice resources (as the San in the Caprivi Strip were displaced because their pastoral activities were incompatible with the development of a tourist infrastructure). This is, then, what I have called elsewhere interethnic economic competition.[62]

The more lucrative the tourist industry, the more acute this interethnic competition for its benefits. Indeed, when the potential for growth is as great as it is in the tourist industry, there is competition for control of tourist-related resources. When authorities pursue policies of displacement for the sake of tourism development, they are crossing moral boundaries set by the international community. But more important for this study, involuntary population movements are counterproductive because they translate into the obliteration of the very exotic peoples who attract tourists to LDCs. They are shortsighted, based on short-term benefits without consideration of long-term consequences, and must be reassessed on economic grounds.

Notes

1. *New York Times*, October 1, 2004.

2. Ted Fishman, "The Chinese Century," *New York Times Magazine*, July 4, 2004.

3. This statistic is based on growth of aggregate GDP during the 1980–1992 period. World Bank, *World Development Report 1994* (Washington, DC: 1994), Table 2.

4. It is necessary to underscore the difference between economic growth and economic development (or long-term modern economic growth, as some economists, including Simon Kuznets, have referred to it). Economic growth is simply defined as an increase in income per capita. It comes about from an increased use of resources, principally land, labor, and capital.

5. Additional ramifications often follow. In the MDCs these ramifications include rising employment, increased labor productivity, higher real wages, and reduced inequality. This is not necessarily the experience of the LDCs.

6. This transformation occurs because rising incomes associated with economic growth entail a change in the nature of demand, shifting as it does into those sectors with higher income elasticities, such as manufactured goods and services. Moreover, some sectors have experienced more technological innovation than others, enabling higher rates of growth. Some US data aptly illustrate the structural transformation that occurred during the nineteenth and twentieth centuries: At the turn of the 1800s, agriculture accounted for some 90 percent of the national income; years later, that number was about 5 percent. Manufactur-

ing, on the other hand, accounted for 5 percent and 20 percent respectively. Finally, services grew from some 2 percent to 75 percent of national income over 200 years (Bradley Schiller, *The Macro Economy Today*, 8th ed. [Boston: Irwin McGraw-Hill, 2000], pp. 29–30).

7. Donald Reid, *Tourism, Globalization, and Development* (London: Pluto Press, 2003); M. Thea Sinclair and Mike Stabler, *The Economics of Tourism* (London: Routledge, 1997), p. 143.

8. The structural transformation in the West took centuries to complete. It was a process that evolved in a complex symbiotic relationship with both technological change and democratization. Less developed countries today are acutely aware of their underdevelopment as communications make snapshots of Western life readily available. They feel they are falling behind, and with globalization heightening the speed of change, they are increasingly impatient to get on with development. Unwilling to wait centuries for the structural transformation to alter the economy as it did in the West, LDCs want to catapult from traditional agricultural poverty into modernity.

9. Immanuel Wallerstein, *The Modern World-System: Capitalist Agriculture and the Origins of the European World Economy in the Sixteenth Century* (New York: Academic Press, 1974).

10. Lucie Cheng and Edna Bonacich, eds., *Labor Immigration Under Capitalism: Asian Workers in the United States Before World War II* (Berkeley: University of California Press, 1984).

11. John Harris and Michael Todaro, "Migration, Unemployment and Development: A Two-Sector Model," *American Economic Review* 60, no. 1 (1970).

12. Simon Kuznets, *Population Redistribution and Economic Growth, United States: 1870–1950* (Philadelphia: American Philosophical Society, 1960).

13. In addition, during economic development, the occupational structure of the labor force changes: the proportion of blue-collar workers decreases as the proportion of white-collar workers increases. An analysis of the US industrial classification of the labor force indicates that over the past 100 years, the proportion of agricultural workers dropped significantly, whereas the proportion of industrial workers and workers employed in services rose. Moreover, in 1950 blue-collar workers accounted for almost two-thirds of the labor force; by 1990, they had decreased to less than half (down from 62.5 percent to 43 percent). Over the same time period, the white-collar workforce grew from 37.5 percent to 57.1 percent (Anna Kutka, "Demographic Trends in the Labor Force," in *The Changing U.S. Labor Market,* ed. Eli Ginsberg [Boulder, CO: Westview Press, 1994], p. 17).

14. The German-Italian labor recruitment agreement signed in 1955 was a program of guest worker recruitment to fill labor shortages. Later, similar agreements were signed with Spain, Greece, Turkey, and Portugal. Germany's importation of foreign labor occurred through a regulated program; France's program, however, relied on the market to determine levels of inflows. Both countries were aggressive importers of workers.

15. Tomas Hammar and Dristof Tamas, "Why Do People Go or Stay?" in *International Migration, Immobility and Development*, ed. Tomas Hammar, Grete Brochmann, Dristof Tamas, and Thomas Faist (New York: Berg, 1997), p. 6.

16. John Lansing and Eva Mueller, *The Geographic Mobility of Labor* (Ann Arbor, MI: Institute for Social Research, 1967).

17. Ibid., p. iii.

18. R. J. Wolfe, "Recreational Travel, the New Migration," *Geographical Bulletin* 9 (1967), pp. 73–79.

19. M. Bell and G. Ward, "Comparing Temporary Mobility with Permanent Migration," *Tourism Geographies: International Journal of Place, Space and the Environment* 2, no. 3 (2000), pp. 87–107.

20. R. V. Bianchi, "Migrant Tourist-Workers: Exploring the Contact Zones of Post-Industrial Tourism," *Current Issues in Tourism* 3, no. 2 (2000).

21. Bell and Ward, "Comparing Temporary Mobility," p. 93.

22. Tim Coles, David Timothy Duval, and C. Michael Hall, "Tourism, Mobility, and Global Communities: New Approaches to Theorising Tourism and Tourist Spaces," in *Global Tourism*, 3rd ed., ed. William Theobald (Amsterdam: Elsevier, 2005), p. 464.

23. Allan M. Williams and C. Michael Hall, "Tourism, Migration, Circulation and Mobility: The Contingencies of Time and Place," in *Tourism and Migration, New Relationships Between Production and Consumption,* ed. C. Michael Hall and Allan M. Williams (Dordrecht, The Netherlands: Kluwer Academic Publishers, 2002), p. 25.

24. Ibid.

25. These population movements do not end in phase four, nor are all phases necessary. Ibid., pp. 8–12.

26. Ibid., p. 11.

27. Some studies contradict this. The WTO cited recent research in the Philippines that showed domestic tourists are in fact more "valuable" than international tourists because they spend about 6 percent more per day than international tourists. David Diaz Benavides and Ellen Perez-Ducy, eds., "Background Note by the OMT/WTO Secretariat," *Tourism in the Least Developed Countries* (Madrid: World Tourism Organization, 2001), p. 231.

28. World Tourism Organization, *Enhancing the Economic Benefits of Tourism for Local Communities and Poverty Alleviation* (Madrid: 2002), p. 28.

29. Williams and Hall, "Tourism, Migration, Circulation and Mobility," p. 4.

30. The authors who coined these terms were discussed in ibid., p. 5.

31. Graeme Hugo, "Postwar Refugee Migration in Southeast Asia: Patterns, Problems and Policies," in *Refugees: A Third World Dilemma*, ed. John R. Rogge (Totowa, NJ: Rowman and Littlefield, 1987), p. 237.

32. Nazli Choucri, "Cross-border Movements of Population in a 'Fair Globalization,'" *Development* 48, no. 1 (2005), p. 46.

33. This classification roughly coincides with Rogge's distinction between politically induced refugees and ecological refugees. John R. Rogge,

Too Many, Too Long: Sudan's Twenty-Year Refugee Dilemma (Totowa, NJ: Rowman and Allanheld, 1985), pp. 2, 4.

34. *Economist*, Millennium Special Edition, December 31, 1999, p. 69.

35. Kevin Bales, *Disposable People: New Slavery in the Global Economy* (Berkeley: University of California Press, 2004); Linda Richter, "Not a Minor Problem: Developing International Travel Policy for the Welfare of Children," *Tourism Analysis* 10, no. 1 (2005).

36. War situations provoked Chinese population movements in Indochina following the victory of North Vietnam; Jewish emigration from Germany, Poland, and Croatia during World War II; and residence exchanges among Greeks and Turks following the Greco-Turkish war of 1922. New political systems were responsible for the pressure on Germans to leave the Soviet Union and Eastern Europe following World War II and on Asians to leave Uganda in the 1970s. Wars of liberation or decolonization provoked a mass exodus of Portuguese from Mozambique and whites from Malawi and Rhodesia. There are many others examples.

37. Andrew Bell-Fialkoff, who wrote the most comprehensive book to date on the practice, defined it as "a planned, deliberate removal from a certain territory of an undesirable population distinguished by one or more characteristics such as ethnicity, religion, race, class or sexual preference. These characteristics must serve as the basis for removal for it to qualify as cleansing." He went on to describe a spectrum of population removal, with genocide on one end, emigration under pressure on the other, and in the middle deportation/expulsion, transfer, and exchange. Andrew Bell-Fialkoff, *Ethnic Cleansing* (New York: St. Martin's Griffin, 1999), p. 3.

38. Not all governments that cause population movements do so out of design or malice. Some are simply incompetent and are unable to lead their populations or offer them adequate standards of living. For example, government incompetence led to hunger in Somalia and Ethiopia, political instability in Lebanon in the 1970s led to chaos, and both created destabilizing population movements.

39. D. Eltis, "Free and Coerced Transatlantic Migrations: Some Comparisons," *American Historical Review* 88 (1983), p. 255, quoted in Timothy J. Hatton and Jeffrey G. Williamson, *The Age of Mass Migration* (New York: Oxford University Press, 1998), p. 7.

40. Herman M. Schwartz, *States Versus Markets* (New York: St. Martin's Press, 1994), p. 117.

41. Although tourism has existed throughout history, Cohen stated that the earliest mention of the term *tourism* dates back to the late 1800s in Europe. E. Cohen, "The Sociology of Tourism: Approaches, Issues and Findings," *Annual Review of Sociology* 10 (1984), pp. 373–392.

42. Choucri, "Cross-border Movements," p. 47.

43. Robert Solow, "A Contribution to the Theory of Economic Growth," *Quarterly Journal of Economics* 70, no. 1 (1956); Robert Barro, "Economic Growth in a Cross-Section of Countries," *Quarterly Journal of Economics* 106, no. 2 (May 1991).

44. R. Harrod, "An Essay in Dynamic Theory," *Economic Journal* 49 (1939); E. Domar, "Capital Expansion, Rate of Growth and Employment," *Econometrica* 14 (1946).

45. The anticommunist countries of East Asia were also the recipients of US economic and military aid that unequivocally fueled their growth. Dictatorial regimes there provided the "best business climate" for Japanese and US capital. See Kwang Yeong Shin, 'The Political Economy of Economic Growth in East Asia," in *The Four Asian Tigers,* ed. Eun Mee Kim (San Diego, CA: Academic Press, 1998), p. 18.

46. Usually when we speak of population movements and capital in the same breath, we are referring to human capital and brain drain. Tourists do not bring human capital, but they do induce the flow of physical capital.

47. World Bank, "Tourism in Africa," Findings Report no. 22617, *Environmental, Rural and Social Development Newsletter,* July 2001.

48. Donald Lundberg, Mink Stavenga, and M. Krishnamoorthy, *Tourism Economics* (New York: Wiley, 1995), p. 8.

49. Some short-run exceptions to this lead countries to erect trade barriers, restrict the flow of foreign investment, curtail the activities of multinational organizations, restrict immigration and emigration, limit exposure to foreign cultures, restrict tourism, and so on. See, for example, Hla Myint's pioneering work, *The Economics of the Developing Countries*, 4th ed. (London: Hutchinson, 1973).

50. For some recent assessments of the success of the Four Tigers, along with the effects of the financial crisis of 1977, see Victor Mallet, *The Trouble with Tigers: The Rise and Fall of South-East Asia* (New York: HarperCollins, 1999); Robert Garran, *Tigers Tamed: The End of the Asian Miracle* (Honolulu: University of Hawaii Press, 1998); Ross McLeod and Ross Garnaut, eds., *East Asia in Crisis: From Being a Miracle to Needing One?* (London: Routledge, 1998).

51. Anil Markandya, Tim Taylor, and Suzette Pedroso, "Tourism and Sustainable Development: Lessons from Recent World Bank Experience," www.pigliaru.it/chia/markandya.pdf (Web site accessed January 20, 2005).

52. Diaz Benavides and Perez-Ducy, "Background Note by the OMT/WTO Secretariat."

53. Moreover, tourism is purchased without inspection. Sinclair and Stabler, *The Economics of Tourism*, p. 1.

54. Brian Copeland, "Tourism, Welfare and De-Industrialization in a Small Open Economy," *Economica* 58 (November 1991), p. 516.

55. This definition of the labor market excludes systems in which slavery is the dominant form of labor relationships, according to which workers are not free to sell their labor to an employer of their choice (as was the case historically on US plantations and presently in parts of Africa). It also excludes present-day feudalism, in which workers are bound to employers as a result of a series of constraints and thus cannot respond to labor market incentives (as in regions of rural India where indebted farmers and their future offspring are bound to a landlord).

56. Albert O. Hirshman, *Exit, Voice and Loyalty: Responses to Decline in Firms, Organizations, and States* (Cambridge: Harvard University Press, 1970), chap. 7.

57. Ishtiaq Ahmed, "Exit, Voice and Citizenship," in *International Migration, Immobility and Development,* ed. Tomas Hammar, Grete Brochmann, Dristof Tamas, and Thomas Faist (New York: Berg, 1997).

58. J. Hicks, *The Theory of Wages* (London: Macmillan, 1932); W. A. Lewis, "Economic Development with Unlimited Supplies of Labour," *The Manchester School of Economic and Social Studies* 22 (1954); G. Ranis and J.C.H. Fei, "A Theory of Economic Development," *American Economic Review* 51 (1961); J. R. Harris and Michael P. Todaro, "Migration, Unemployment and Development: A Two-Sector Analysis," *American Economic Review* 60 (1970); Michael Todaro, *International Migration in Developing Countries: A Review of Theory* (Geneva: International Labour Organization, 1976).

59. According to Anthony Smith, an ethnic group is composed of a people that share a cultural bond and that perceive themselves to share a common origin. Anthony Smith, "Chosen Peoples: Why Ethnic Groups Survive," *Ethnic and Racial Studies* 15, no. 3 (July 1992), p. 450.

60. The question of how to classify and define peoples remains unresolved and continues to dominate debates on ethnicity and nationalism. Possible categories abound, such as ethnicity, race, language, and so forth, and despite their overlap and imprecision, they serve to group populations across the globe. For the sake of simplicity and convenience, in this study of encampments, ethnicity is referred to as the distinguishing characteristic even though it is not universally applicable. Indeed, sometimes race is the crucial distinguishing characteristic (as in South Africa), or it is language (as in Canada) or religion (as in Bosnia). *Ethnicity* is therefore used in the text as an umbrella term that includes race, religion, language, nation, as the case may be. In that sense, this study heeds the 1997 proposal of the American Association of Anthropologists, suggesting that the US government use ethnic categories in federal data to reflect the diversity of the population and to phase out the use of race, which is a concept that has no scientific justification in human biology. Editorial, *Nature Genetics* 24 (February 2000), p. 97.

61. US Committee for Refugees (USRC), *World Refugee Survey* (Washington, DC: 1997), p. 129.

62. Milica Z. Bookman, *The Demographic Struggle for Power* (London: Frank Cass, 1997), chap. 2.

3

Tourists and Other Travelers

Tourism is the starting point for the study of the circular flow of populations. The underlying logic for this choice is that tourist demand sets in motion other voluntary and involuntary population movements.

To understand this demand, we must ask who the tourists are, where they come from, and what they hope to experience in less developed countries. Why do they forgo traditional attractions such as the Eiffel Tower, the Empire State Building, or the Canadian Rockies and instead traverse long distances at great expense in order to visit what until recently would have been overlooked destinations? In these locations, overt signs of underdevelopment are usually undeniable within moments of arrival, overwhelming tourists' senses. Did these tourists to developing countries pay money in order to participate in what J. Hutnyk called "a voyeuristic consumption of poverty"?[1] Is the discomfort of obvious poverty offset by physical beauty and indigenous color and the novelty of it all? That question brings to mind nineteenth-century European dictionaries that defined tourists as people who travel, among other things, "for the joy of boasting about it afterwards."[2] To the extent that such boasting serves to induce and perpetuate the fastest-growing industry in developing countries, some explanations are in order to set the groundwork for fundamental reevaluations of traditional concepts of economic development. Therefore, the first step in understanding LDC tourism and its role as an engine of growth is to assess the profile of its principal protagonists: the men and women who travel. Understanding who they are, where they come from, and what determines their demand is crucial for nurturing the industry and guiding its future expansion.

45

Tourist demand does not exist in isolation, however, and cannot independently realize the industry potential. Indeed, as with any market, the supply of tourism must complement demand, since in the absence of either there is no transaction or exchange. Microeconomic theory provides essential tools for studying the tourist market in developing countries. This chapter begins with a discussion of the demand for LDC tourism before delving into its supply by central governments, foreign operators, and local communities.

Demand for LDC Tourism

Tourists and Other Travelers

A recent survey of eighty academic studies found forty-three different definitions for the terms *traveler, tourist,* and *visitor.*[3] The WTO defines tourists as people who travel outside their usual environment for a period of less than one year. As the purpose of the travel is not relevant, this definition includes travel for leisure, business, pilgrimage, medical treatment, visiting friends and relatives, education, and so on.[4] James Mak suggested calling tourists only those who travel for pleasure and pay their own way, as they are fundamentally different from business travelers, who travel for someone else's benefit.[5] Mak's distinction by purpose is similar to that of William Theobald, who defined travelers as individuals making a trip between two geographical locations and then went on to break them down into visitors and other travelers.[6] The former includes tourists (overnight visitors) and same-day visitors, whereas the latter includes everyone else (commuters, migrants, nomads, diplomats, armed forces, refugees, and so on). For the purposes of this study, tourists are those who voluntarily travel for pleasure, and other travelers include everyone else who also voluntarily takes trips (thus excluding armed forces and refugees).[7] This distinction is adopted here, despite the contention by Donald Lundberg, Mink Stavenga, and M. Krishnamoorthy that tourists and travelers are virtually the same in the US government's lexicon.[8] However, when we discuss choice and duration of travel (Chapter 2), then tourists and other travelers (including those traveling on business unrelated to the tourist industry) are lumped together, as they are all individuals who *voluntarily* make *short-term* trips.[9]

In an effort to further clarify terms, it is useful to define tourists by both their *capacity* to travel as well as their *incentive*. With respect to the former, it is noted that not everyone is or can be a tourist. In order for tourism to appear in an individual's consumption equation, that person must have both leisure time and discretionary income. These preconditions explain why tourism appeared in Western societies long after the Industrial Revolution had enabled the achievement of significant increases in living standards. The technological change associated with the Industrial Revolution propelled economic growth by making factors of production more productive. This aspect of the structural transformation of economies was discussed in Chapter 2, so suffice it to say here that productivity increases result in higher discretionary income and that over time, after basic needs have been met, individuals begin to consume luxury goods of their choosing. One of these is travel.

In addition to money, travelers must have enough free time to travel. In contemporary societies, leisure time is no longer the luxury it was when Theodore Veblen proposed his theory of the leisure class. A century or so later, Dean MacCannell again examined the link between leisure and luxury.[10] As a mass phenomenon, leisure time and leisure activities appeared in the United States when the workweek decreased from sixty hours to forty-eight, then to forty. Valene Smith cited other factors, including labor unions that increased paid vacations, the trend to observe national holidays on Mondays or Fridays, early retirement and increased longevity, pension schemes and investment income, and good health, which makes for youthful senior citizens. All of these contribute to the overall ability of workers to have leisure time.[11] Donald Reid explained how in the West, the division between work and leisure became very clear with the Industrial Revolution. Most traditional societies do not have that segmentation of time, and many languages do not have a word for leisure in their vocabulary. Certainly in those societies, leisure is not a commercial enterprise.

In addition to leisure, other factors are also relevant in determining the capacity to consume tourism. The availability of credit markets enables individuals to travel now and pay later. Also, since the advent of mileage programs of airlines, distant, expensive locations have become accessible.

The availability of excess income and leisure time defines the capacity to travel, but what about the incentive? Not everyone who has excess disposable income spends it on tourism. Numerous factors define incentives. Among these is the idea suggested as early as 1969 by David Inkeles: that a modern person is more prone to travel because he or she has broader horizons. This argument is even more relevant in the 2000s, when communications and media enable people to know what is happening across the world, and the Internet enables both armchair travel and inexpensive spread of information pertaining to destinations and prices. Moreover, increasingly people want instant happiness. According to Valene Smith, "the extra money once saved for home, car or a rainy day becomes the means to travel."[12] Other determinants such as taste and cultural predispositions, discussed later, serve to underscore that not all people have the same incentives at any given level of income.

Thus, an individual must have the capacity as well as the incentive to be a tourist. These are both more likely to occur in Western countries, where incomes, leisure, and culture predispose individuals toward exploratory travel.

Homing in on the Third World Tourist

When Thomas Cook first organized tours abroad, the destinations were always European sites (with a few warm weather exceptions such as Egypt). At the time, Britain and other European powers were riding the waves of empire, and no one would have traveled to the third world for pleasure. The weather was deemed unpleasant, the diseases rampant, one could not buy foods and drinks considered essential, and anyway, what was there to see in the colonies?

It seems unbelievable that some 100 years later tourism has become diversified and global. In addition to ancient sites and museum attractions, now nature draws the ecotourists. Religious travel brings the devout to Mecca, Medjugorije, and Varanasi; the so-called dark travel includes visits to Poland's concentration camps and Vietnam's Ho Chi Minh Trail. Theme parks, a US staple, are popping up across Asia. People travel to taste food and wine or simply to visit friends and family.[13] They go to India for open-heart surgery, to Brazil for vision correction, and to Costa Rica for dental work in what has become known as medical tourism. Sex tourism is booming—Thailand now offers child sex, displacing southern Africa's reign as the capital of the sex industry where once-forbidden interracial sex was the lure.[14] Elephants and lions in their natural habitat draw people on safari, and the more endangered the animal, the greater the appeal.[15] "Wild animal" parks have become popular among domestic tourists in China, who pay to watch animals attack each other while the audience eggs them on, throwing chickens into their cages.[16] Similarly, political relics have an exotic cache, as Michel Houellebecq noted in reference to Cuba: "It's one of the last communist countries, and probably not for much longer, so it has a sort of 'endangered regime' appeal, a sort of political exoticism."[17] Ukraine is touting its orange revolution of 2005 by offering political tours[18]; Korea and Cyprus offer tours into demilitarized zones[19]; Ireland is the place to go to give birth because of its generous citizenship rules.[20] The dropping of sanctions against Libya has set its tourist industry in full gear, drawing the traveler in search of the exotic.

Few attractions are more exotic than foreign people—the more foreign, the better. If their bodies are pierced and they wear strange masks and dance scantily clothed, then they are attractive. Different. Unique. Indigenous. Exotic. It used to be that tourists sought out the four Ss: sun, sea, sand, and sex. Although those pursuits are undoubtedly still popular, they have been supplemented with the three Ts: traveling, trekking, trucking (and, for some tourists, with two more Ss: security and sustainability).[21] While trekking, globe-trotting individuals seek to break out of the tourist bubble and *experience* foreign culture. Indigenous/cultural tourism is addressed in depth in Chapter 5, so suffice it to say here that many tourists seek greater immersion into cultures that are different from theirs. They have "done" Paris and London. Given how homogenized the world is becoming, people have to travel farther and farther off the beaten track in order to see something different. That brings them to the developing countries. (The preceding discussion clearly applies to the Western tourist. Although there are a growing number of tourists from parts of Asia and the oil-rich states, they tend to be drawn to Western sites or to domestic sites, where they do not spend foreign currency.)

Determinants of Demand

Although price determines the *quantity* of third world travel demanded by a tourist, demand is determined by factors such as taste, income, substitutes (their availability and price), and expectations (about income, prices, tastes, conditions, terrorism, and so on). No single determinant alone defines tourist demand. Aggregate demand for third world tourism—namely, the sum of individual demands—is discussed below.

Price. Price determines the quantity of travel demanded by an individual. According to the law of demand, the higher the price of the trip (including travel, accommodation, food, entertainment, and so on), the fewer trips will be purchased. The best prices are available on the most traveled routes, and for that reason the most popular destinations for international travel from the United States tend to be Cancun, Jamaica, and so on. As with all luxury products, however, some travelers are willing to pay more for the privilege of being alone on a remote island or in a highly exclusive resort.

Just how sensitive are tourists to changes in price of foreign travel? How much does price have to increase in order for them to forgo their trips? The answer lies in the price elasticity of demand: the higher the elasticity, the more sensitive tourists are to price changes. Elasticity is dependent on a variety of factors. Among these is the nature of the good in question: is it a luxury or necessity? Clearly travel is not a necessity, although, in high income economies, it undoubtedly appears more frequently in the consumption function. Also relevant is the relative importance of the product in the individual's budget: the higher the importance, the higher the price elasticity (Thea Sinclair and Mike Stabler have shown how the relative and absolute importance of tourism in people's expenditure budgets has risen dramatically[22]). The price elasticity also depends on the time available for travelers to adjust to price changes. Hendrick Houthakker and Lester Taylor did a study of the US consumer and found that price elasticity for foreign travel was highly inelastic in the short run (.14) and became elastic in the long run (1.77).[23]

Related to the concept of travel price is value—what one gets for one's money. The World Bank said that "as tourists at all price levels become more sophisticated in the global market, value, in addition to price, becomes a critical element in the decision to visit one destination rather than another."[24] In other words, holding price constant, tourists question what they get in one destination that they do not get in another.

There is evidence that tourists are willing to swallow a price increase if they feel it is for a good cause. Several "willingness to pay" studies of African tourism have shown that tourists are willing to pay an extra fee when the purpose is explained to them. For example, tourists will pay "entrance fees and environmental taxes to conserve a specific asset provided that the funds are earmarked rather than allocated to general budgetary revenues."[25]

Taste. From the study of travel patterns and modes of traveling by geographers and psychologists, and from economic analyses of tourist motivations, it is clear that taste in travel is complex.[26]

Some people simply do not like to travel. They do not like living out of a suitcase, they prefer their regular routine, they have little interest in other cultures, or they have fear of flying. For such people, taste determines their lack of participation in the tourist industry. As for the others, taste determines their inclination to travel as well as where they go, how they get there, and what they do once they are there. Some want to learn about colonial history, so they travel to lands ruled by their ancestors; others simply want to get a suntan. Some go to exotic places in order to, as M. Sarup said, discover their identities.[27] Others perceive travel, especially third world travel, as a status symbol, one to be boasted about. Nelson Graburn noted that "tourists almost ritualistically send postcards from faraway places to those whom they wish to impress."[28] Some, who want to get away from it all and have adventures in less touristy locations, are willing to pay more for the privilege of uniqueness; others are inclined toward mass tourism that provides herd comforts. Other tourists get utility from maximizing the number of countries visited, which by definition increases the demand for the third world where most countries are located. Valene Smith noted that "humans everywhere seek status symbols to reaffirm their identity, and some western tourists count countries as evidence of their widened experience."[29] The existence and popularity of the Century Travelers Club is a case in point (membership is limited to those who have visited a minimum of 100 countries).

A discussion of taste must also include an aggregate across the population, as it is a factor in a country's consumption function, not just that of the individual. In other words, some peoples/nationalities are more inclined to travel than others, especially to foreign destinations. Although this societal propensity to travel is in part determined by geography and location, it is also partly cultural. For example, Lundberg. Stavenga, and Krishnamoorthy found that New Zealanders and Australians travel abroad more than their income per capita would suggest, and on a per capita basis, the Scandinavians travel more than North Americans.[30] *Business Life* reported that within Europe, it is Greek, Spanish, French, and Italian citizens who are most likely to vacation at home whereas Belgians, Germans, and Austrians are least likely to do so.[31] Americans and Japanese seem least bothered by long distances and vacation the farthest from home, despite the fact that they take the shortest vacations. Also, MacCannell pointed out that "leisure is constructed from cultural experiences," meaning that people in different cultures will use their leisure time differently.[32]

Income. The greater the personal disposable income of the tourist, the more is available for consumption of nonessentials, including travel. Being a normal good, travel is positively related to income.

Sinclair and Stabler stated that "the relative and absolute importance of tourism in people's expenditure budgets has risen dramatically."[33] Numerous studies of tourism have quantified this by calculating income elasticity.[34] It has been found that the demand for foreign travel is elastic (3.08), so that when income rises, demand for foreign travel rises faster. There is variety within the category of tourism, for example between short-distance and long-distance trips, but nevertheless travel demand remains elastic.[35]

The positive relationship between income and tourism extends also to the tourist's country of origin. The amount of travel and per capita income are positively correlated with gross national product, although not perfectly because the propensity to travel depends on other factors (such as tastes).[36] This is because the higher the income of the originating country, the greater the capacity to demand third world travel. As noted earlier, travel requires income in excess of subsistence. Such excess income—and the leisure time it can buy—is more prevalent in countries with high per capita incomes.

Thus, the more developed world dominates the pattern of international tourism. In the 1990s more than 90 percent of world tourism flows originated in the more developed countries.[37] In 2004, the top ten countries ranked by personal travel and tourism were, in descending order, the United States, Japan, Germany, the UK, France, Italy, Spain, China, Canada, and Australia.[38]

Despite a predominance of Western tourists, travelers to developing countries may be rich citizens of other developing countries or even of the host country itself. Irrespective of national origin, tourist demand tends to come from the middle to upper middle classes. Even when they are roughing it, these travelers are "nomads from affluence," a term E. Cohen gave to the voluntary poverty of youthful middle-class tourism.[39] Although there are ample opportunities for travel among the working class, such travel tends not to be to exotic destinations that are often too far and too expensive compared to local packages. It is this precondition of wealth that led Melanie Smith to refer to LDC destination tourists as "post-tourists," children of Western capitalist consumerist societies, not representative of the global tourism industry.[40]

Demand for LDC travel may have reached a ceiling in Western countries because available free time and income allocated to tourism may have leveled off. Income growth in other countries, however, will make up for this deficiency. For this reason, those in the tourist industry place high hopes on indicators of worldwide economic growth. They hope that data such as the growth of the world economy at 8 percent in 2003 will herald a new golden age in tourism.[41] All eyes are turned to China in expectation of a miracle. In 2003, the Chinese overtook the Japanese as Asia's biggest travelers because of the growth of their middle class and the growth of China's excess income.[42]

Substitutes. The 1987 coups in Fiji showed how easy it was to substitute travel destinations. As most tourists to Fiji came from Australia (in fact, 43 percent), the ensuing bad publicity induced them to go to domestic resorts that were roughly at the same latitude.[43] In a similar fashion, Kenya's decades-old position as the center of African tourism was shaken by South Africa's reentry onto the global radar after apartheid. Thus, over a short period, Kenya was dethroned by another African country touting its game, local color, and mountains and beaches. The terrorist attack on the US embassy in Nairobi further shifted the tourist nucleus southward, to regions of Africa with fewer Muslim populations.

This pattern of substitution has been experienced across the globe, highlighting clearly the fact that many destinations are interchangeable and that alternatives for LDC travel destinations are plentiful. For many tourists, one sunny beach is perceived to be like another, one exotic person like another. Product differentiation succeeds in fostering brand or place loyalty only among a certain type of tourist.[44] The extent to which a destination achieves monopoly status depends on real and perceived factors. Among the former are tangible sights or natural resources that cannot be duplicated: there is, for instance, only one Eiffel Tower. Few developing countries have yet to promote any such unique feature.

Expectations. Tourist demand for LDC travel is determined by expectations both at the point of origin and at the destination. With respect to the former, questions of future employment and personal income are crucial in making present-day consumption decisions. These are tied to expectations about the state of the macroeconomy and its ability to grow. In addition, tourist demand also depends on expectations about future prices of travel. For example, expectations of a fare sale in the future will result in less travel today. Tourists also expect their tastes to change over time and might be inclined to take a more adventuristic vacation at a younger age and put off more sedentary vacations for the future.

Expectations pertaining to the destination also determine the demand for third world travel. Events in these locations, whether manmade or not, are taken into account by potential travelers (the former include festivals and holiday celebrations; the latter include natural disasters). Travelers to the Caribbean closely monitor hurricane reports, and after 2004, travelers to the Indian Ocean worry about tsunamis. Expectations about events such as coups, political upheavals, and terrorism play a large role in tourist demand.[45] Indeed, when Idi Amin came to power, tourism to Uganda dropped off precipitously in expectation of what he might do.[46] According to a World Bank study of African tourism, fluctuations in tourist demand were mainly due to country conditions such as terrorist attacks, civil unrest, natural disasters, crime, and public health problems (rather than price).[47] In the tourist regions of the Caribbean, fiscal deficits grew owing to a slowdown of tourists after September 11, 2001.

Number of tourists and market demand. Microeconomic theory points to the importance of the number of buyers in determining the market demand for a product. Clearly, in the case of tourism, the number of tourist visits to a destination is crucial in determining total demand. An increase in market demand can come about from various sources. It can include more tourists visiting a destination, or it can include the same tourists making repeat visits or extending their stay. Indeed, if a tourist stays longer and consequently spends more money at the destination, the bottom line is the same as if there were multiple visitors. This last point was highlighted by the World Tourism Organization's study on how to enhance the economic benefits of tourism in developing countries. It was proposed that the length of stay increase—in other words, to increase demand in terms not only of numbers of visitors but also of quantity demanded by each visitor.[48] Those tourists who seek out a unique experience are unlikely to be repeat visitors, so the composition of tourists will change as they pass on to other tourist destinations or other consumer goods. Nevertheless, there will be other travelers coming of age and into income brackets to be able to participate in the product cycle.

Does Supply Create Its Own Demand?

A recent edition of *Town and Country Travel* magazine contained an article entitled, "Build It (and They Will Come)."[49] It is based on the premise that an innovative hotelier can and will succeed in creating demand for his product in the West Indies. In other words, Say's Law is alive and well in the tourist industry, and supply creates its own demand, at least as long as it builds on a preexisting demand. In creating that demand, suppliers in the tourist industry advertise, give prizes, upgrade, offer tie-ins, and use other creative marketing techniques. In addition, they tap travelers on nontourist trips. Dean MacCannell noted how Uganda tried to attract businesspeople who would then do some sightseeing and would perhaps go back home and talk about it.[50] US troops on leave from Vietnam served a similar purpose in Southeast Asia. The idea is to get people hooked. *Get people hooked!*

Which individuals, groups, or institutions are aiming to hook people on LDC tourism? Three come to mind: LDC governments, private foreign operators, and international organizations. These three entities together are responsible for creating the supply of tourism in developing countries. They are all involved in tourist sector capacity building. The interplay of these three entities was evident in the immediate aftermath of the Asian tsunami disaster of 2004, when they pooled their resources to get the tourist industry back on track as quickly as possible. Although Sinclair and Stabler claimed that to date there is no coherent theory of tourism supply,[51] this chapter contains some observations on how each of the three entities contributes to supply.

Conspicuously absent in this discussion are local communities in developing countries, those who are most directly affected by the construction of a resort, the noise of an airport, and the village electrification program. It is local communities that come into contact with the tourist, not the government or the international lending institution. Still, they are ignored in this chapter; their role is analyzed in Chapter 5, which is entirely devoted to the effect of tourism on local populations.

Supply of Tourism I: Third World Governments

In Thomas Mann's novel *Death in Venice,* the local government takes extraordinary measures to misinform and conceal the reality that Venice is in the grips of pestilent cholera, all in order to protect the lucrative tourist industry. Stepping from fiction to nonfiction, a century later, government involvement in the tourist industry is no less direct and often just as desperate. It is so because tourism is important.

It is important in the United States, a Western developed country, where almost one million businesses are related to tourism.[52] Even in the countryside, tourism is now a bigger earner than farming.[53] This relative importance of tourism is even more pronounced in many developing countries, where other sectors of the economy are by comparison less prominent. Although recognized for over thirty years, tourism was not viewed as a serious industry by mainstream economists nor as clearly associated with modernization and growth as a large capital goods factory. Work in tourism was seen as nonwork. All that changed when it became a leading sector, and many countries singled it out as the productive sector with the most potential (witness the Moroccan government's proclamation that tourism was one of the major growth sectors whose potential had yet to be tapped, even if it generated more than 15 percent of the country's foreign exchange earnings[54]).

Thus, as Melanie Smith contended, "tourism . . . *has become a force to be reckoned with*, irrevocably transforming destinations, traditions and lifestyles [italics mine]."[55] LDC tourism-friendly governments have recognized this force and are responding to this unexpected interest in their natural resources and indigenous peoples by promoting, taxing, and regulating tourism. They promote it because tourism is viewed as a panacea for their development problems; they tax it in hopes of generating government revenue; and they regulate it because, as Smith said, there are irrevocable changes that tourism brings on, not all of which are positive. These public sector activities are discussed below.

Despite its numerous shortcomings, the public sector has taken the leading role in the LDC tourism industry. With the exception of a handful of multinationals (largely based in India, Thailand, and South Africa), local private capital lacked sufficient strength to sponsor the required investment, and foreign capital had associated problems. This reality was recognized by the WTO: "It is widely recognized that the market alone cannot be relied upon to deliver sustainable development."[56] Moreover, the role of the public sector in policy formulation and planning for tourism, highlighted by C. L. Jenkins and B. N. Henry, among others,[57] was formalized in 1996, when the Lomé IV Convention strongly emphasized the need to formulate policies in the tourism sector rather than letting it develop haphazardly.[58] In the absence of a plan, countries suffer negative environmental, social, and economic consequences.[59] Thus, tourism is one of the few sectors left in which governments still do extensive planning. In theory at least, they consider limited resources, scarcity, opportunity costs, and cost/benefit analyses. They consider the short run and plan for the long run, with special attention to ensure sustainable long-term growth. In their plans, some governments make decisions about the expansion of infrastructure, the reduction of leakages, the maximization of linkages, and the encouragement of pro-poor economic growth. When government is involved in planning the tourism industry, it can, if it is so inclined, identify and monitor tourism activities, measure and evaluate the impact of tourist activity on the infrastructure and resources, integrate tourism into regional and national macroeconomic plans, and consult with the host community if it deems it appropriate. It can also better coordinate tourism policies with other government agencies and international agencies. That, of course, is the best possible scenario.

This is not to say that LDC governments do not promote the private sector. On the contrary, tourist-friendly countries have increasingly found that, as in other sectors of the economy, private business tends to be dynamic and adaptable; it tends to respond quickly to technological change and financial incentives, at the level of transnational corporations as well as the level of microbusinesses. Governments in southern African countries (with the exception of Angola) have been formulating policy about tourism with a role for the private sector since they recognized that it plays a key role in financing and implementing future developments.[60] In Morocco, government bias toward private ownership led to the privatization of publicly owned hotels (so that by 1999, twenty-four of thirty-seven had been sold[61]). Sectoral analysis of the private/public mix in tourism highlights the successful cooperation in nature-based tourism (where, as Ralf Buckley pointed out, private companies are in partnership with the government[62]). Therefore, most tourist-friendly countries have tourism policies such as the one announced in India in 2001, namely "government-led, *private-sector driven* and community-welfare oriented [italics mine]."[63]

In their efforts to plan the tourism industry, LDC governments consider how to promote it, tax it, and regulate it. In the process, they are often faced with contradictory goals. Stephen Wanhill identified some decisions that governments must make because policy objectives are often at odds with each other: maximize foreign exchange earnings versus actions to encourage the regional dispersion of visitors; attract high-spending tourists versus policies to continually expand the number of visitors; maximize job creation by generating high volume of tourists versus conservation of the environment; and community tourism development versus mass tourism.[64] It is useful to keep these in mind in the discussion that follows.

Promotion of Tourism

The Swiss government developed computer models of the Alps, with virtual tourists, in order to decide just how much to subsidize farmers to graze their cows in the mountains. Cows eat young trees, and that in turn results in better vistas for tourists.[65] This anecdote conveys just how far governments will go to promote tourism. In promoting it, governments must make choices about the product they are supplying, they have to take steps to ensure personal safety for their visitors, and they have to develop the national infrastructure. Each of these costs money, and government expenditure must be channeled into the appropriate program. According to the World Travel and Tourism Council, in 2004 the top spenders (in descending order, as measured by the percentage of total government expenditures going to tourism) were Cayman Islands (28.9 percent), Antigua and Barbuda, British Virgin Islands, St. Lucia, Seychelles, Aruba, Dominican Republic, Guadeloupe, Virgin Islands, and other Oceania (19.3 percent).[66] These are all island countries, largely dependent on tourism. More indicative of policy was the growth of government expenditure on tourism in 2004. The top ten countries according to government expenditure on tourism worldwide were Croatia (13 percent), Chad, St. Kitts and Nevis, Qatar, Sudan, Latvia, Ethiopia, Suriname, Libya, and Madagascar (7 percent).[67] Also of interest was the ranking of countries according to total domestic capital investment in 2004, including public and private sectors. The countries with the highest percentage investment into the tourist industry (as a percentage of total capital investments) were Aruba (76.2 percent), Macao, Antigua and Barbuda, other Oceania, Bahamas, Barbados, Virgin Islands, Anguilla, British Virgin Islands, and Cayman Islands (52.4 percent).[68] Again, a ranking by the growth in capital investments showed a different group of countries: Macao (16.9 percent), Mexico, China, Malaysia, Argentina, Chinese Taipei, Madagascar, Libya, Brazil, and the United States.[69]

Choice of tourist product. Tourist destinations in developing countries range from shabby and overcrowded towns to high-end luxury resorts in which the price per day is in the thousands of dollars. Which of these do third world governments want to promote? This question is often posed in terms of mass versus luxury tourism. Mass tourism, also known as herd tourism, involves large numbers of people purchasing low-quality accommodations and services; luxury tourism is successful in Namibia, Botswana, and the Seychelles. Is it better to promote small numbers of high spenders or large numbers on tight budgets? The answer reflects the goal underlying the development of the tourist industry, namely maximization of revenue. In other words, rather than maximizing the number of visitors, a policy of tourist promotion aims to maximize the revenues that visitors generate. As revenue depends on price and quantity, suppliers of the tourist industry must make decisions pertaining to estimates of those variables. Ultimately, however, pure maximization of value per tourist is difficult because tourist expenditure is not exactly associated with the number of visitors: according to the WTO, "the average receipt per arrival of an international tourist in Africa in 1999 was $385, compared with $800 in South Asia."[70] They considered, for example, that packaged holidays tended to yield small profit margins (according to a World Bank study, they were 1–2 percent of sales),[71] whereas customized tourism, catering to high-income spenders, tended to have higher margins.

In addition to revenue, governments have to consider tradeoffs in terms of degradation of resources and strain on facilities associated with large numbers. Also, they must weigh direct and short-term gains from mass versus luxury tourism against indirect and long-term losses.

In their cost/benefit analyses, LDC leaders come up with widely differing results and therefore different policies. Nepal, for example, promotes its image as the hippie mecca for Western youth or, in M. Hampton's words, the backpacker tourist.[72] MacCannell said that "some Third World countries willingly accept, even encourage visits . . . from hippies and others who are sometimes seen as 'undesirables.'"[73] By contrast, Botswana has focused on the top end of the market, luring the discriminating tourists who have the capacity and incentive to pay for individualized service. The vast majority of developing countries offer both types of resorts, therefore catering to both types of tourists. This approach carries with it other problems, since mass and luxury resorts are sometimes mutually exclusive. As Brian Copeland pointed out, crowding by tourists is a negative externality that can inhibit the flow of foreign visitors.[74] Ultimately, the lucky countries are the ones that can attract many high-paying customers, in other words, high price and high quantity. In the mid-2000s, Asian countries that cater to Chinese tourists are getting both high numbers of visits and high expenditures. The Chinese, the fastest-growing tourist group, tend to travel abroad in package tours, as individual travel is bureaucratically cumbersome and expensive.[75] Surprisingly, they have proven to be generous spenders, outspending the Japanese in many parts of Asia.

Whether LDC governments decide to promote mass or luxury tourism, they must also seek out a niche that will give them an advantage in the highly competitive tourist markets. Such product differentiation entails offering a unique product (or at least one that people believe is unique). For Catholics, there are no substitutes for pilgrimages to Rome; for Muslims, there are no substitutes for pilgrimages to Mecca. These locations attract a limited number of niche travelers, however. For the most part, no single country has a monopoly on attractions, and many tout an as yet unexplored angle, trying to create a monopoly by drumming up demand. An entire literature has cropped up on the competitive strategies of tourist destinations.[76]

Provision of a safe environment. When travelers went elsewhere after the 1987 coup, 80 percent of the staff in Fiji's hospitality industry lost their jobs, the currency was devalued by 17 percent, reduced tourism receipts boosted inflation, and public servants took a 15 percent cut in pay.[77] Similarly, when Ugandan president Idi Amin came to power, tourist visits dropped from 85,000 in 1971 to 6,000 in 1972.[78] In the aftermath of September 11, 2001, many US tourists stayed close to home. Although some travelers take risks, most do not visit dangerous places or voluntarily expose themselves to danger during their voyages. Because they have a choice in how and where they spend their leisure time, risk-adverse tourists tend to avoid locations, modes of transport, or foods they deem unsafe. Travelers who take trips for business or expatriates who visit friends and family are more likely to visit a broadly defined "dangerous area" while taking the necessary precautions (hiring bodyguards in Colombia, carrying kidnapping insurance in Brazil, avoiding tap water in India, and so on).

Governments that want to promote their tourism industry need to take steps to provide a safe environment for their visitors. In so doing, the first step is defining what constitutes danger. In the post–September 11 world, the primary security issue that comes to the Western mind is terrorism. Be it real or perceived, this threat has covered some tourist destinations with a blanket of suspicion. For Western tourists, the difference between terrorism and internal instability is often too subtle to matter. For this reason, countries with internal instability due to warring political, ethnic, or religious factions have tried to ensure that the conflict is contained outside the tourist areas.

In the aftermath of internal strife and war, countries must be quick to dismantle vestiges of past dangers. Eritrea focused on tourism even while reconstructing its war-torn land.[79] Its government promoted tourism by reassuring potential visitors that the war was indeed over. By contrast, in Mogadishu in 2004, years after the US-led intervention, landmines had yet to be cleared, and a sign was posted in front of the remains of a cathedral, cautioning "beware of landmines."[80]

Most governments also include robbery and swindling in their definition of danger. To the extent that these activities are concentrated in the tourist areas, where foreigners are easy prey, authorities have attempted to control them.[81] In Egypt, security guards accompany guided tours to temples, tombs, and pyramids; armed guards are posted at various locations; and tour vans on lengthy travel are accompanied by armed militia. Where the public sector does not take charge, private firms offer the provision of tourist security. Indeed, in Mogadishu in 2004, the Sharmo Hotel recommended that guests hire at least ten armed guards to accompany them from the airport.[82]

To the extent that danger is culturally determined, LDC governments must go by the tourists' definition if they wish to promote tourism. In Islamic countries where the norms for gender-differentiated behavior are different from those in the West, accommodations must be made. Cynthia Enloe asserted that governments that have decided to promote international tourism have "decided to be internationally compliant enough that even a woman traveling on her own will be made to feel at home there."[83] That has not been done nearly enough. Linda Richter's study of Pakistan indicated that, as in Saudi Arabia and Nigeria, women alone were not comfortable and secure.[84]

Development of supporting infrastructure. Economic infrastructure is defined as the underlying amount of physical and financial capital embodied in roads, railways, waterways, airways, and other forms of transportation and communication plus water supplies, financial institutions, electricity, and public services such as health and education.[85] Infrastructure facilitates and integrates all economic activities. Indeed, the quantity and quality of infrastructure are crucial determinants of the pace and diversity of a country's development of the service industry.[86] Improvements in infrastructure contribute to the tourist industry, and at the same time, they serve the local population and increase its standards of living.[87] When infrastructure is deficient and inadequate, then transportation systems prevent flows of goods that serve the tourist industry; financial institutions cannot provide capital for investment in accommodations, restaurants, car rental agencies, and shops; communications cannot foster the link to home that tourists often demand; and so forth. Such conditions hamper the development of the tourist industry and ultimately derail aspirations for national economic growth. Indeed, according to a World Bank study of tourism in Africa, infrastructure investments have not kept up with expanding tourism,[88] and the overuse and congestion that have been created have prevented tourism from reaching its potential. A government policy that promotes tourism will use its scarce resources to ensure that transport, power, and water are explicitly favored in the tourist regions by exerting its discretion over investment, as in the sectors discussed below. In most cases, the local population also gets to enjoy the benefits.

Telecommunications. To the extent that the end of the twentieth century witnessed a revolution, it was in telecommunications. With the increases in telephone usage per capita, the ease with which international media have permeated the lives of distant communities, and the astonishing growth of the computer and the Internet as personal and business tools, telecommunications have modernized production and enhanced international competitiveness. This applies to the tourist sector as much as to any other. As a result of enhanced communication, potential tourists have the capacity to more readily gain information about their desired destinations. Tour operators and airlines are able to provide pricing information, and tourists are better able to reap the benefits of competition by easily comparison shopping. The Internet has played an especially large role in government promotion of tourism by providing valuable information. Thus, telecommunications have succeeded in spreading information about distant locations faster and more thoroughly than any tool previously used by tourists.

Transport. Since the time of the ancient Romans, transportation systems have been recognized as key components for economic development insofar as they enable the movement of goods, services, and resources and thereby enable commercial relations to thrive. Indeed, Roman emperors were quick to build the Via Aurelia linking the southern capital with the northern regions; the British built roads and ports in the Indian subcontinent; and the Chinese exploited their river systems for transportation purposes.[89] A developed, maintained, and functioning transportation system is likely to stimulate the flow of populations, not just tourists but also the migrants who respond to the labor demands of the tourist industry. In contrast, a deteriorating infrastructure (consisting of traffic congestion, inadequate traffic management, insufficient airport security, lapsed maintenance of roads and ports, and an outdated urban transport strategy) acts to restrain the flow of populations.

Power. Power has yet to reach many people across the world; it is likely that these were not people located in resorts, since modern tourist facilities require power.[90] There are some exceptions, such as remote safari camps, where the lack of power is part of the decor and where the generators are turned on for several hours a day, enough to enable wealthy Western tourists to download their digital photos onto their laptops. As in the case of other infrastructure, LDC authorities are faced with the choice of powering resorts versus bringing electricity into non-tourist destinations. In countries with an active tourist agenda, the opportunity cost of forgoing the tourist region is enormous. As a result, in a tourist-friendly country such as South Africa, only 11 percent of rural households had access to electricity (even though 70 percent of black Africans resided there[91]).

In electrified regions of LDCs, whether they are tourist spots, capital cities, or remote farms, unreliable power supply restricts production, and blackouts and brownouts in power systems disrupt economic and private life.

Water. Investments in water systems are made for a variety of reasons, including providing drinking water, moving waste, irrigating, and producing goods and services. Intermittent water supplies, insufficient coverage, and inadequate purifying methods are all impediments to the development of a Western-oriented tourist industry and to economic development in general. Indeed, when the Nusa Dua Resort in Bali was constructed, all infrastructure had to meet high standards.[92] With assistance from the World Bank, the water supply (as well as waste management and drainage) was planned and developed in the early stages, as the luxurious resort could not have functioned without it.

Waste management. Brochures promoting tourist resorts in LDCs often show beautiful poolside sunbathers sipping piña coladas. Potential travelers are unlikely to ponder how the sunbathers' waste is managed. Yet, waste disposal and sewage treatment are crucial to the functioning of a tourist destination that attracts people, who, by definition, create waste. Donald Reid said that this issue is acute in less developed countries where sophisticated technology is not available or where it is too expensive to install and maintain.[93] Yet its importance is not lost on governments of tourist-friendly states. The strategy of Malaysian development of rural tourism specifically noted the need to address the "serious problem of . . . dumping of waste material."[94] In the Cape Verde islands, insufficient water and energy supply and sanitation hamper tourism development, as waste collection is very poor and recycling plants do not exist.

Tourists and waste disposal are tied together in a mutually self-reinforcing cycle insofar as the presence of tourists increases the need for a waste disposal system while the absence or inadequacy of such a system negatively affects tourists. This last point includes the fact that tourists face a health hazard if waste is improperly managed, as was the case in Belize City. In addition, it means that tourists will avoid those spots where this particular lapse in infrastructure development is evident.

Money and banking. The function of the banking system is to ensure a safe store of assets, provide a market for credit, facilitate the flow of funds into investment, and enable the execution of monetary policy. The first two functions are relevant for this study. With respect to a store of assets, tourists demand the ability to easily export their bank assets to their holiday destinations. LDC authorities must either provide banks where this is possible or allow foreign banks to have branches in the tourist destinations. Automated teller machines (ATMs) must be ample in number and convenient in location. Clearly, the greater their accessibility, the greater the tourists' spending potential, and so the greater the economic footprint they can leave.

The second function of the banking system, namely the provision of the credit market, also affects the tourist industry. To the extent that modern banking systems (with their fully disclosed interest rates and preplanned payments schedules) replace the village moneylender (whose exorbitant fees and interest rates are decided at whim), access to credit for investment in a tourist-related good or service becomes a realistic possibility for local entrepreneurs. Governments provide microlevel credit to enable individuals to invest in bed and breakfasts, motorized guide services, and other tourist-related small businesses. They also encourage partnerships and joint ventures with existing tourism entrepreneurs and companies so as to minimize and spread risks (this is discussed further below).

Taxing Tourism

Sinclair and Stabler claimed that with few exceptions, public sector economists had largely ignored the role played by tourism and the potential of tourism on public sector finance.[95] Yet, through taxation, LDC governments can benefit from the lucrative tourist industry. Indeed, as the WTO has pointed out, taxation of tourism has become a lucrative source of government revenue.[96]

Tax income is generated by tourism because tourist businesses and individuals are subject to direct taxation, like any other economic activity. Direct financial benefit to the government comes from three types of taxes. Business taxes are those imposed on private sector accommodations, beverages, and gas as well as airports and other forms of transportation. Consumer taxes include the sales tax imposed on each transaction involving goods and services. Income taxes are paid by the population employed in the tourist sector. Together, these three direct types of taxes account for most revenue earned by governments.

When there is a tourist industry, LDC governments also benefit indirectly, as the concomitant increased economic activity diffuses throughout the economy and provides new sources for taxation. More-over, increased private economic activity might stimulate the domestic production of goods that otherwise might have to be provided by the public sector, leaving more revenue for other expenditures. Also, tourists pay indirect taxes on goods and services they consume. They also pay customs duties, which in some places are the greatest source of revenue (in the Bahamas, for example, the government collects most of its tourist revenues through import duties). Finally, many countries have introduced taxes aimed specifically at the tourist sector (for example, in Tunisia, a 1 percent tax on hotel revenues is allocated to environmental projects[97]).

Taxes can stimulate tourism if tax incentives are used for investment. Examples include making capital goods used for business free from importation sales tax, allowing the losses incurred during the first year or two of operation to be carried forward into subsequent years, not taxing dividends and capital gains, and so forth.

Taxes can also stifle tourism, however. If they are too high, potential investors and consumers will go elsewhere. Taxes are part of the cost of doing business and part of the price of the travel experience, and as such are negatively related to demand. Authorities grapple with the question of how high is too high by estimating elasticity. With respect to foreign investment, a World Bank study on tourism in Africa claimed that investors were willing to pay taxes since they deemed other factors to be more important (such as "appropriate and stable policy, legislative and regulatory frameworks for tourism"[98]). Still, governments tread carefully where taxes on foreign investments are concerned. Their trepidation extends to foreign tourist consumers also, as a recent dilemma faced by Mexican authorities attests. In 2004, a proposal was made to levy a tariff on cruise passengers (who hardly spend any money on their land visits even though their ships bring pollution and congestion). Such a tariff would have put them at a disadvantage relative to other Caribbean resorts, and so its implementation was delayed.[99] Rival destinations compete against each other, often causing a spiral of downward pressure on tax revenue.

Regulating Tourism

At one extreme, governments prohibit tourism on their territory. Although China and Albania adopted such policies at various times in their history, autarkic measures are rare. Instead, leaders come close to outright prohibition by strongly discouraging tourism, as President Sukarno of Indonesia did during the 1945–1966 period. Indeed, even the most closed countries have succumbed to the lure of easy tourist earnings. Cuba is now accepting foreign tour operators as well as hotels, and conservative Islamic states of the Middle East are condoning tourist bubbles that require their governments to close its eyes. Increasingly, leaders of developing countries seem blinded by the glitter and prefer not to exercise their sovereign right to discourage the foreign tourist industry.

Even though they do not discourage it, many regulate it. Although the motivations for such regulation vary from country to country, three broad categories have emerged that address the following: environmental degradation, foreign ownership, and the demonstration effect.

Governments concerned with environmental degradation associated with increased population traffic might restrict the number of tourists per time period (for example, Bermuda limited cruise ship activity to five or six visits per year to keep the islands from being inundated). Such environmentally motivated regulation is discussed in Chapter 5; suffice it to say here that governments are increasingly instituting rules because even environmentally friendly tourism has been found to have negative effects on local land, populations, and wildlife. (This is because, according to *New Scientist* magazine, many ecotourist projects are unaudited, unaccredited, and "merely hint they are based on environmentally friendly policies and operations. The guidelines that do exist address such obvious issues such as changes in land use . . . [and] cutting down trees."[100])

Alternatively, regulation may be motivated by sovereignty issues aimed at imposing domestic control of national resources through restrictions on foreign investment. Regulation of foreign involvement in the tourism industry came about because of the negative externalities and leakages associated with laissez-faire practices that usually overpowered the positive effects of multipliers and linkages. Leakages that reduce the impact of tourism on economic development come from one or more of the following: repatriation of profits, imported skills, expatriate labor, imported commodities and services, imported technology and capital goods, and increased oil imports. Moreover, tourism brings with it demand for goods that are not produced locally, so they have to be outsourced. According to UNCTAD,

> Leakage is the process whereby part of the foreign exchange earnings generated by tourism, rather than being retained by tourist-receiving countries, is either retained by tourist generating countries or remitted back to them. It takes the form of profit, income and royalty re-

mittances; payments for the import of equipment, materials and capital and consumer goods to cater for the needs of international tourists; the payment of foreign loans; various mechanisms for tax evasion; and overseas promotional expenditures.[101]

Financial leakages and other negative externalities of tourism have their roots in the very nature of tour operations. As most LDC travel is done in packages, and those packages are paid for up front, only a small proportion of the tourist expenditure ever reaches the host country. John Lea found that only 40–50 percent of the tour retail price remained in the host country; if both airlines and hotels were foreign owned, this number dropped to 22–25 percent.[102] Martin Mowforth and Ian Munt estimated that more than 50 percent of payments made by travelers to tour companies for travel in developing countries never reached the host country. They also said, citing *Survival International*, that 60 percent of Thailand's $4 billion per year tourism revenues left the country.[103] According to Reid, over 50 percent of tourist payments never reach the host country.[104] All-inclusive holidays are worse for developing countries than package holidays because every expense is paid for in the home country. Melanie Smith's study of inclusive holidays in the Gambia highlighted the reality of tourists' spending no money outside the hotel compound.[105] Moreover, it is not as though tour operators bring much needed capital into the country. Large tour operators and owners of capital rarely invest their own capital in developing countries but seek funds from private and government sources locally, thus minimizing their own risk.

The variety of regulatory policies in developing countries reflects the fact that there is variety in the magnitude of the negative externalities and leakages. E. A. Pye and T. Lin claimed that the leakage was reduced when tourism became a larger part of the economy. They even cited the example of South Korea, where the foreign exchange leakage in tourism was smaller than in other industries (in electronics it was 50 percent, in machine industry 23 percent; in tourism, however, it was 19.7 percent).[106] Also, remote rural areas are likely to have higher leakages (and lower multipliers) than resort regions. Similarly, countries with fewer other options, such as Nepal and Gambia, have higher leakages than countries with diversified industries. These differences show up in government policy toward foreign investment, involvement, and consumption in the tourist industry.

Governments also regulate to avoid the demonstration effect whereby the behavior of foreign tourists affects the behavior of local populations. One type of demonstration effect is cultural and social in nature. It has to do with the perceived negative effect of exposing the local population to the customs and cultures of tourists, especially Western tourists who are viewed as having loose morals and uninhibited dress and who act in what is considered an ungodly fashion. Some countries want their culture preserved and so limit the number of tourist visas they give. Bhutan, when it opened its borders to tourism, allowed only 1,000 people per year (and stipulated a daily spending requirement).[107] This policy limits social interactions while generating hard currency.

Another type of demonstration effect centers on consumption behavior of foreign tourists. Sometimes Western tourists crave their own foods, cigarettes, and alcohol. To the extent that these are produced locally, scarce resources are diverted away from other goods for domestic consumption. Alternatively, those goods have to be imported, thus creating yet one more leakage in leakage-prone economies. Either way, LDC authorities may limit the availability of those goods so they reach only the foreigners and not the general population. In order to avoid the demonstration effect, they might impose regulations on what locals can buy (for example, in Japan, Cable News Network [CNN] is broadcast only to international hotels). In the absence of a direct discriminatory ban on consumption, price manipulation can achieve the same result.

Supply of Tourism II: Private Foreign Involvement

A typical Western tourist planning a week's vacation in an LDC resort will purchase an airline ticket on a Western airline[108] and book his or her stay in a recognizable brand-name hotel (usually a Western one).[109] The rental car that the tourist hires is likely to bear a Western name such as Hertz or Avis, and to the extent that land tours are prebooked, they will also be booked through a Western company such as American Express or Thomas Cook. If the tourist travels to a wildlife park, it is likely that such a park is also under Western control.[110]

All this implies that the foreign component of LDC tourism is huge. In fact, it is much larger than the domestic share, both private and public. The largest form of foreign participation is through foreign direct investment (FDI), which takes place in two ways. A foreign company may purchase or build a tourist facility from scratch, or it may lend investment capital to a domestic tourism enterprise. Such joint ventures are common. As mentioned in Chapter 2, LDC governments welcome FDI because it satisfies the high capital requirements in the initial investment in infrastructure and facilitates, transfers some of the risks to foreign firms, facilitates the transfer of technology and managerial know-how, is a reliable source of tax revenue, and stimulates development in other parts of the economy through backward linkages. Authorities often adopt policies that entail provision of venture capital to construct resorts and hotels. These are then favored with tax and investment incentives.

Problems in foreign ownership and control of LDC tourism, as discussed earlier, have led to regulation, however. Indeed, there are high leakages due to repatriation of profits and incomes, and foreign business activities may drive out domestic competition and suppress local entrepreneurship. There is only limited participation of the local community, especially given the trend toward all-inclusive holidays. Also, foreign investors often do not help governments in making tourism more sustainable; the investors may produce unsuitable products, stimulate incompatible consumption patterns, or adopt inconsistent technologies. In fact, the foreign involvement may hurt the local population. Brian Copeland found that in the presence of foreign ownership of immobile factors such as land, an increase in tourism can reduce welfare of the population if the increase in the flow of repatriated earnings is large enough.[111]

In addition to private foreign investment, foreign involvement in the LDC tourist industry comes about through the intermediary sector, namely tour operators and travel agents. There are many such operators, and the market is highly competitive. In order to thrive in such an environment, tour operators differentiate their product by coming up with niche tourism: designer, personalized, customized, specialized tours.[112] Foreign tour operators know well the effect of changing consumer tastes and international conditions.[113]

Supply of Tourism III: International Institutions

Somalia has not had a single officially acknowledged tourist since 1992. Nevertheless, it has a minister of tourism who would like foreign funding for rebuilding a national park where there are no animals left (they were eaten by the population during the wars).[114] Somalia, like numerous other developing countries, is looking to international institutions to provide the funding that private investors find is too risky or yields insufficient returns. Two types of international institutions are involved in the supply of LDC tourism: international lending institutions and international nongovernmental organizations (NGOs). The former sees tourism as a panacea for development and facilitates its expansion, whereas the latter seeks to regulate it for the benefit of local populations. The efforts of both are reflected in the final supply of tourism. Both are discussed below.

There is also investment by foreign governments through development assistance programs, but this is not private (international organizations involved in the supply of tourism are discussed in the next section). There are also bilateral arrangements between foreign and national governments, as in the case of Ivorian-German cooperation in the tourism development in Tai National Park.[115] Donor governments and their aid packages are not discussed here.

International Lending Institutions

In his assessment of Namibia's tourist industry, Carson Jenkins pointed out that without the assistance of the European Union, "development planning for tourism would have been beyond the resources and capacity of Namibia."[116] Other developing countries follow a similar path by turning to international lending institutions to access the resources they lack. An official of the World Travel and Tourism Council, the world's largest organization of private sector tourism industry executives, said that "there is an increasing role for international development institutions such as the World Bank, to play in the tourism industry."[117]

These lending institutions include multilateral banks such as the World Bank and the Inter-American Development Bank. Also, United Nations agencies such as the United Nations Development Programme (UNDP) and the Global Environment Facility are involved in tourism projects, although not primarily in a lending capacity. Crucial in the functioning of all these international institutions is the World Tourism Organization, an association of 138 government tourism boards with over 350 affiliate members. The WTO coordinates with multilateral and bilateral aid agencies and development banks in the provision of tourist-related projects. It is the World Bank, however, that potentially has the largest role in the tourism development of tourist-friendly countries. It disbanded its tourism department in the 1980s as a result of an unimpressive performance. Still, the World Bank remained active in promoting tourism as a tool for development. In the five years leading up to 2004, the World Bank undertook approximately 100 projects involving fifty-six countries, representing 3 percent of the Bank's total investment.[118] During that time, the Bank avoided projects in which tourism was central to the project (in terms of both investment and outcome). Instead, the vast majority were programs in which tourism had a minor component or where the tourist outcomes were significant. The Bank's projects are based on the linkages between tourism and sustainable development in the economic, environmental, and social areas.[119] Although this proportion of Bank activity is relatively small, it has been growing to reflect the growing importance of tourism for many of the Bank's client countries.

The World Bank, along with other international multilateral institutions, offers assistance in formulating tourism policies, provides loans and grants, coordinates public and private sectors, and formulates a behavioral and legal framework within which third world governments can operate.[120]

Formulation of tourism policies. International institutions help tourist-friendly governments integrate tourism into broader policy frameworks. They help focus on tourism with development as the final objective. They help formulate and manage indicative development plans. If needed, they train local and central governments to build capacity and manage growth in that sector. They provide guidance with feasibility studies, risk assessment, and, later, monitoring and evaluation. The WTO is most involved in counseling countries in developing strategies for attracting investment.

Provision of loans and grants. Lending institutions provide capital for developing countries to exploit tourist demand. They are the visionaries that foresee potential; they are the risk takers that bank on their investments.

To date, infrastructure is the sector in which most lending has occurred. Developing local infrastructure, as well as health and education services, improves the overall investment environment for tourism and thus attracts investors. It provides those inputs that private tour operators require (such as roads, bridges, and airports) but will not invest in themselves. The World Bank has considerable experience in infrastructure investment, including hospital, roads, water and sewerage systems, communications, and transport systems. Indeed, most of its loans to third world countries have been major infrastructure development projects.[121] Its loan to preserve assets around Peru's Machu Picchu has as an integral element the improvement of infrastructure throughout the valley, including a regional solid waste management system; its loans of some $1.075 billion to Vietnam are aimed mostly for eight transportation projects. Recently, under pressure to pay attention to the local populations, World

Bank lending has started to change emphasis from large infrastructure projects to more community-based projects (discussed in Chapter 5). Other lending institutions, including the Inter-American Development Bank, which has been funding tourism projects for decades, are also scaling down their mega infrastructure investments.

In addition, a crucial component of the inflow of capital is the technical capacity to make the best use of it. With this goal in mind, international lenders are involved in providing technical assistance where needed (WTO takes a leadership role in the organization of such assistance). Other international institutions are involved in the actual training and development of a local human capital base. One example is the United Nations Development Programme/International Labour Organization (UNDP/ILO), which is creating skilled labor in Bangladesh by establishing the National Hotel and Tourism Training Institute that, since its inception in 1974, has trained thousands people.

Coordination with the private sector. The WTO offers support to third world governments by fostering a business environment that gives private investors the possibility for profitable tourism projects, including commercially viable private/public partnerships. International lenders are acutely aware of the private sector role in developing countries and are keen to promote and build partnerships for action in the tourist industry. As part of the structural adjustment programs implemented in many developing countries, the World Bank and the International Monetary Fund (IMF) supported rolling back the role of the state, privatizing the economy, promoting foreign investment, and thus creating a positive environment for the tourist industry.[122] In that environment, partnership blossomed. In Bali, the Nusa Dua Resort was assisted by the World Bank and managed by the Bali Tourism Development Corporation, a public corporation owned by the government that functions as an autonomous body.[123] In collaboration with the Vietnamese National Park Administration, the United Nations implemented a program in 1999 for the development of tourism in the Babe National Park.[124] Also, in collaboration with the Jordanian Ministry of Tourism and Antiquities, the World Bank funded a $44 million project in 1998 for comprehensive tourism development.[125]

International institutions also promote giving assistance to communities to negotiate tourism and other joint ventures with the private sector. They also provide community investment funds to provide resources to participate in those joint ventures, as will be discussed in Chapter 5.

Behavioral and legal framework. International institutions are leaders in the establishment of behavioral norms for the tourist industry, including the protection of human rights, employment regulations, migrant worker protection, and so on. Increasingly, they also promote broad social inclusion in their projects. With respect to ecotourism, they encourage countries to be signatories to the 1972 Ramsar Convention, the 1992 Biodiversity Convention, and the 1979 Convention on Migratory Species. Campaigns for ethics in consumption and corporate social responsibility are increasing. Among these, the WTO's Global Code of Ethics for Tourism has been exemplary. Its Article 5 says that local populations must share in the economic benefits they generate, and Article 9 refers to the rights of self-employed workers.[126] Also, there is a new Tour Operators Initiative for Sustainable Tourism Development that is supported by the United Nations Environment Programme (UNEP), the WTO, and the United Nations Educational, Scientific, and Cultural Organization (UNESCO). The World Bank has partnered with indigenous people to launch a new initiative that aims to support sustainable and culturally appropriate development projects.[127]

International institutions are also involved in the provision of a legal framework for the development of tourism as exemplified by the existence of negotiated agreements such as the General Agreement on Trade in Services and the inclusion of LDC tourism in, for example, the Uruguay Round.

Nongovernmental Organizations

Nongovernmental organizations came into existence in reaction to problems associated with international lending institutions. Indeed, even though international institutions provide an invaluable resource for developing countries in their quest for tourism, those institutions' activities raise numerous concerns. Among these, the question of autonomy and dependency is foremost. When developing countries accept loans from international institutions in order to develop their tourist industries, is their sovereignty compromised? This question has recently been raised by a dispute between UNESCO and Myanmar about who decides what is appropriate use of international funds. Although UNESCO worked with Myanmar in the 1980s in a joint restoration project to repair damage of an earthquake in 1975,[128] in the 1990s they parted ways because of disagreement over how to repair the temples. Government authorities rebuilt old temples with red brick and modern designs across all the country's best-known historical sites, whereas UNESCO advocated a more authentic approach. Should local authorities or international donors decide how to restore national treasures? This question remains unresolved.

Another concern has to do with the motivation of lending institutions. The IMF and the World Bank have been active in supporting a partnership between the rich and poor countries (the former have the tourism know-how, whereas the latter have the attractive destinations) because they see this as a potential industry to be exploited, allowing the countries sufficient income to be able to pay back their debts. In order to pay back their debts, developing countries are pressured by the world organizations to open doors to foreign investments. The long-term consequences are rarely considered, as by then the loans will be paid off. Is it acceptable for lending institutions to put emphasis on their rates of return, even if the negative externalities to the home country are large? That is another question that remains unresolved.

Finally, the implicit and explicit costs that involvement with international organizations entails are often criticized. Crucial among these are the structural adjustment programs and how they negatively affect countries trying to develop a tourism industry.[129] In his study of the IMF, Robert Poirier found that although IMF had been a driving force in the development of tourism, the concomitant adjustment policies put limitations on its potential to be an engine of growth.[130]

For all the above reasons, NGOs came into existence and set out to advocate regulation of tourism aimed at offsetting negative side effects. These organizations are both Western and based in developing countries; they work independently or with governments. Some NGOs are broad and cover the entire gamut of issues related to tourism (such as the Open Africa initiative[131]). Others are small and have a narrow focus. Perhaps the largest area of concern to NGOs is the extent to which local populations do not participate in the gains from tourism. Tourism Concern launched the Fair Trade in Tourism Network in 1999 as a partnership among industry, NGOs, and universities to examine the effect of tourism on LDC communities.[132] It was found that in order to benefit destination communities, it was necessary to adopt ethical trading practices. Corporate Social Responsibility was developed,[133] designed to give developing countries a fair share of the returns from the sale of their products. Fair Trade in Tourism incorporates five areas in which greater equality is necessary: international trade agreements, transnational corporations, independent investors, destination community policies, and destination government policies.

None of these concerns is the monopoly of any given NGO. On the contrary, overlapping of goals and duplication of efforts serve to strengthen the cumulative drive. Fair Trade in Tourism, for example, is not alone in paying attention to the destination community's populations. It is complemented by area-specific NGOs that deal with local problems. Alternatively NGOs deal with a single issue at the global level. British-based Survival is entirely devoted to displaced populations. World Wildlife Fund focuses on ecotourism, and Rethinking Tourism draws attention to green-washing—the practice of depicting products, services, and destinations as ecofriendly when in fact they are not.[134] Sometimes a whole range of NGOs is concentrated in a single country, as in Namibia. As a result of this concentration, local NGOs (such as Women's Action for Development, the Namibia Development Trust, and the Namibia Community-Based Tourist Association) had an effect on government policy and the creation of the Community-Based Tourism Policy of the Ministry of Environment and Tourism.

It remains to be seen whether international NGOs and international lending institutions end up contradicting each other and even working against each other, or whether they will manage to overcome their differences and synthesize their efforts on behalf of those countries they profess to want to help.

Tourism: An Engine of Growth

Of the forty-nine countries within the UN-designated category of least developed countries, only Botswana has graduated out of the group, largely owing to its tourism industry. Four other potential graduates, Cape Verde, Maldives, Samoa, and Vanuatu, are all tourism based.[135] In these countries, tourism seems to be an engine of growth (at least in terms of strict economic variables such as per capita GDP, even if not in terms of variables such as life expectancy).

In an effort to understand how the market for LDC tourism is related to economic growth, two growth statistics are observed: the growth rate of GDP per capita in 2003 and the growth rate of the travel and tourism industry in 2004. The former statistics come from the World Bank, except in a small number of cases for which data were unavailable and Central Intelligence Agency (CIA) sources were used. The latter are from the WTTC satellite statistics. Both growth numbers are presented in Table 3.1, in parentheses following each country listing (countries are placed in

Table 3.1 Growth of GDP and Growth of Travel and Tourism Industry in Developing Countries by Group

% GDP	Group A Countries	Average % Change in GDP, 2003	Average % Change in Travel and Tourism, 2004	Ratio
70–100	Anguilla (2.8[b]; 10.4), Antigua and Barbuda (3.2; 15.6), British Virgin Islands (1[a]; 11.5), Maldives (9.2; 10.3)	4.05	11.95	.34
50–69.9	Aruba (–1.5[a]; 6.3), Bahamas (3[d]; 12.5), Barbados (1.3; 16.3), Macao (15.6[c]; 16.4), Seychelles (–5.1; 9.6), Vanuatu (2; 7.3)	2.55	11.4	.22
30–49.9	Cayman Islands (1.7[a]; 8.1), Jamaica (2.3; 16.7), Mauritius (3.2; 19.6), St. Kitts and Nevis (0; 18.5), St. Lucia (1.8; 17.9), St. Vincent and Grenadines (4.1; 14.8), Virgin Islands (2[a]; 11.6)	2.16	15.31	.14
25–29.9	Dominica (–0.6; 15.4), Dominican Rep. (–0.4; 23.6), Fiji (4.8; 16.3), Grenada (5.8; 16.1), Guadeloupe (na; 0), Kiribati (2.5; 17.9)	2.42	17.86	.14
	Unweighted Average Group A	2.80	14.13	.20
	Group B Countries			
20–24.9	Angola (4.5; 8.8), Bahrain (5.6[d]; 5.9), Belize (9.4; 15.1), Gambia (6.7; 19)	6.55	12.2	.54
15–19.9	Cape Verde Islands (5; 9.4), Egypt (3.2; 16.5), Jordan (3.2; 11.7), Morocco (5.2; 11.8), Tunisia (5.6; 18)	4.44	13.48	.33
10–14.9	Brunei (3.2[a]; 8.1), Cambodia (5.2; 13.3), China (9.3; 12.2), Comoros (2.5; 14.1), Costa Rica (6.5; 11.8), Cuba (na; 15.7), Ethiopia (–3.7; 11.8), Gabon (2.8; 9.7), Guyana (–0.7; 15.6), Indonesia (4.1; 9.3), Kenya (1.8; 12.1), Lebanon (2.7; 16), Malaysia (5.3; 14.7), Oman (1.2[d]; 4.8), Panama (4.1; 12.2), Papua New Guinea (2.7; 11), Qatar (8.7[d]; 8.9), Solomon Islands (5.1; 17.9), Sri Lanka (5.9; 13.6), Thailand (6.9; 7.5), Tonga (2.5; 10.7), Trinidad and Tobago (13.2; 10.4), Turkey (5.8; 13), United Arab Emirates (5.7[d]; 13.3)	4.38	11.83	.37
	Unweighted Average Group B	5.11	12.50	.41

Table 3.1   Continued

% GDP	Group C Countries	Average % Change in GDP, 2003	Average % Change in Travel and Tourism, 2004	Ratio
8–9.9	Bolivia (2.5; 15.1), Botswana (5.4; 15.1), Democratic Republic of Congo (5.6; 8.8), Ecuador (2.7; 7.5), Ghana (5.2; 15.9), Honduras (3; 8.3), Kuwait (9.9; 8.3), Laos (5; 17), Libya (4.9[d]; 13.8), Martinique (na; 15.5), Mexico (1.3; 9.3), Namibia (3.7; 10.2), Nepal (3.1; 15.4), Peru (3.8 10.1), Saudi Arabia (7.2; 10.2), Singapore (1.1; 11.9), Sudan (6; 11.8), Tanzania (7.1; 18.5), Uganda (4.7; 12), Uruguay (2.5; 2.4), Venezuela (–9.4; 6.8), Vietnam (7.2; 10.5)	3.93	11.38	.35
5–7.9	Algeria (6.8; 7.8), Argentina (8.8; 7.5), Benin (4.8; 8.2), Brazil (–0.2; 6.6), Burkina Faso (6.5; 10.5), Cameroon (4.7; 8.4), Chad (11.3; 39.8), Chile (3.3; 7.1), Colombia (4; 7.8), Curaçao (na; 22.1), El Salvador (1.8; 8.9), Guatemala (2.1; 11.6), Iran (6.6; 2.5), Korea (3.1; 5), Lesotho (3.3; 10.8), Madagascar (9.8; 12.6), Malawi (4.4; 13.8), Mali (6; 8), Nicaragua (2.3; 18.4), Nigeria (10.7; 10.1), Pakistan (5.2; 8.8), Paraguay (2.6; 3), Philippines (4.5; 8.6), Reunion (2.5[d]; 13.9), Rwanda (3.2; 16.3), São Tomé & Principe (4.5; 10), Senegal (6.5; 13.4), South Africa (1.9; 5.2), Swaziland (2.2; 8.7), Syria (2.5; 6.1), Yemen (3.8; 7.9), Zambia (5.1; 12.8)	4.66	10.33	.45
<4.9	Bangladesh (5.3; 5.8), Burundi (–1.2; 7), Central African Republic (–7.3; 8.5), Congo (Zaire) (2.7; 7.8), Côte d'Ivoire (–3.8; 6.9), Guinea (1.2; 7.1), Haiti (0.4; –4), India (8.6; 9.1), Myanmar (–1.3[d]; 2.5), Niger (5.3; 8.1), Sierra Leone (6.6; 10.6), Suriname (5.2; 17.4), Togo (2.7; 11.4), Zimbabwe (-8.2[d]; –7.5)	1.16	6.48	.18
	Unweighted Average Group C	3.25	9.40	.35

Sources: World Travel and Tourism Council, *Travel and Tourism—Forging Ahead,* the 2004 Travel and Tourism Economic Research Country League Tables (Madrid: 2004, Tables 46, 41; World Bank Development Indicators, http://devdata.worldbank.org/data-query (accessed June 28, 2005).

Growth data indicated by a superscript note callout come from the Central Intelligence Agency Factbook, www.cia.gov/cia/publications/factbook/geos (accessed June 29, 2005).

Notes: Group A countries derive 25–100 percent of their GDP from travel and tourism; Group B countries 10–24.9 percent; Group C countries 0–9.9 percent. The first numbers in parentheses are GDP growth rates per capita for 2003 (unless otherwise noted); the second numbers are the growth rate of the travel and tourism industry for 2004. a. Refers to 2002; b. refers to 2001; c. refers to 2003; d. refers to 2004. na = not available.

the appropriate category, depending on the role of tourism in their economy, as in Table 1.1). Table 3.1 also contains average growth rates of GDP per capita and of travel and tourism for Country Groups A, B, and C (as well as their subgroups). Finally, the ratio of the average growth rates (GDP growth rate divided by travel and tourism growth rate) is included to indicate the extent to which overall growth and growth in tourism move in tandem. Throughout, unweighted averages are used, although this sometimes skews some values. For example, the phenomenal growth of the travel and tourism industry in Chad in 2004 (39.8 percent) biases upward the average in Group C countries, even though that growth is due to activity associated with international relief organizations' dealing with the refugees from Sudan rather than the development of traditional tourism destinations.

According to Table 3.1, Group B countries have the highest average growth of GDP per capita (5.11 percent), followed by Group C (3.25 percent), and last, Group A (2.8 percent), indicating that the most tourist dominated countries are experiencing the lowest growth rates. If we focus on the growth of travel and tourism, however, then Group A countries take the lead (14.13 percent), followed by Group B (12.5 percent), and finally Group C (9.4 percent). This descending order makes sense, given how tourist oriented Group A economies are.

With respect to the travel and tourism industry, only two countries experienced negative growth: Haiti and Zimbabwe. Both are members of the lowest subcategory of Group C (in other words, the countries that derive less than 4.9 percent of their GDP from tourism). They are also countries in which political unrest has greatly damaged tourist potential. With minor exceptions, countries typically experienced travel and tourism growth together with GDP growth. The exceptions refer to the existence of negative growth of GDP coupled with growth in travel and tourism. In Group A, this pattern occurred in only four countries (Seychelles, Aruba, Dominican Republic, and Dominica). In Group B, two countries experienced this combination (Guyana, Ethiopia), and in Group C, it showed up in six countries, four of which are in the bottom subgroup (Burundi, Central African Republic, Côte d'Ivoire, Myanmar).

With respect to the relative size of the growth in GDP and of travel and tourism, in all countries the latter is greater than the former. The closer the growth rates, the lower the ratio of the two will be. This ratio is highest in Group B countries (0.41), and within that group, it is highest in those countries that are most tourist oriented (0.54). The lowest ratio exists in two subgroups of Group A countries as well as the least tourist oriented subgroup of Group C countries (0.14 and 0.18, respectively). This indicates that in both tourist-dominated and tourist-restrained countries, growth of the overall economy and growth of the tourist industry are not aligned.

The empirical evidence presented in Table 3.1 relates to the discussion in Chapter 2 where it was stated that the more important the role of tourism in the economy, the less tourism is an engine of growth. Indeed, although tourism is an engine of growth at all stages (or at least it can be in theory), it is not equally effective at all stages. It is in Group B countries that the expansion of tourism is most likely to generate the greatest linkage and multiplier effects. It is these countries that are poised to benefit from the expansion of tourism. By contrast, in Group A, any further expansion of tourism will not result in large-scale infrastructure projects or major expansion of car rental or restaurant services. Construction will be localized, and it is likely to increase competition for existing tourist goods and services rather than expand them. In other words, the expansion of tourism in tourist-dependent countries will serve to heighten competition in an already competitive market. The experience of Group A countries should serve as a lesson to others, and this brings us to a policy implication introduced in Chapter 2, namely, that there is a small window of opportunity in which tourist population movements can stimulate economic growth, and tourism policy in developing countries must reflect that.

Despite the small window of opportunity, LDC governments across Groups A and B continue to invest in tourism. Together with international institutions and foreign investors, they consider the opportunity costs of focusing their development policy on some alternative economic activity. They weigh direct and short-term gains from new income and employment against indirect and long-term losses. In the end, they have invested heavily in LDC tourism, overpowering tourist demand by tourist supply. In other words, the supply of capacity by LDC governments, foreign travel agencies, airlines, world banking institutions, and so on has been overwhelming relative to the demand. The demand for temporary travel gives rise to disproportionately permanent responses with respect to investments and promotion of tourist industry. The supply of tourism, as clear from the above discussion, is broad and deep, whereas the demand of tourism in any single location, even in Group A countries, is shallow and fickle. Tourist demand is a flow, yet the infrastructure, accommodations, and restaurants that are built to accommodate those tourists are permanent. They are a stock. They cannot easily be put to alternative uses: five-star hotels are unlikely to be transformed into low-cost motels or schools. Therefore, those governments that have responded to a temporary and fickle demand with permanent structures must make adjustments in their future policy to reflect that imbalance. Measures to control excess capacity need to be taken sooner rather than later.

Crucial in the discussion of tourism as an engine of growth in all groups of countries is the concept of expectations. Expectations about the future were discussed earlier in reference to tourist demand. Here the concept is applied more broadly to the economy in general. Continuity, reliability, and predictability of the source of growth are all embodied in this term. Will the source of growth continue into the future, is its supply predictable, can we base future expectations on its reliability, and can we predict its continued presence? If answered in the affirmative by a country's economic participants, the result is a stimulation of growth. How do countries differ in their future growth outlook? A country that has the capacity to generate capital for investment is more likely to have continuous growth than one that relies on the vagaries and fickleness of foreign aid or foreign direct investment. A country that has the ability to produce its own human capital or attract it from the global labor markets has greater prospects for future growth. When the source of growth is unreliable and when its future cannot be predicted, social and political disturbances may occur.

Even though tourism in developing countries has been consistently growing, it is anything but reliable and predictable. This is true largely because of both price and income elasticity of demand. All leisure travel is a luxury, and the more expensive it is, the greater its income elasticity of demand. In other words, recessions and layoffs in Western countries have a magnified effect on consumption of LDC tourist services. This volatility of demand is further aggravated by the high price elasticity of demand for any single destination. It was seen earlier how competitive the market is and how abundant the substitutes for any single destination. For this reason, tourist destinations must constantly re-create themselves. They must be one step ahead of the game and focus on future demand before it becomes the present. At the first whiff of change, they must respond. This lesson was learned the hard way by countries with coastal resorts that declined in popularity when cultural tourism, ecotourism, and adventure tourism came into being. Those that were able to combine creative attractions with beaches survived (for example, Sharm el Sheik offers visits to the Pyramids, Belize scuba divers visit the Mayan ruins, Senegal touts its slave route). In addition to price and income, tourists are also sensitive to the political climate, as noted aptly by Linda Richter.[136] With increased terrorism potential worldwide, tourist demand for travel to developing countries will be first to disappear, earlier than to Paris or London. If one constructed a fear elasticity of demand to reflect this sensitivity, then demand for exotic travel would have a higher fear elasticity coefficient than demand for traditional tourism (given, among other factors, the perception of lax security in developing countries).

At the end, one cannot but wonder if perhaps governments do not even consider the issues, raised above, for and against tourism as a development strategy. Perhaps they chose tourism because tourism chose them. As Donald Reid said, "the selection of tourism as an engine of growth by many LDCs may be a result of a lack of alternatives rather than a matter of preference."[137] It is often the cheapest alternative, since resources are already in place and exploiting them usually does not require much domestic capital. A. Mathieson and G. Wall predicted that tourism decreases in importance once industrialization occurs.[138] Where tourism has been lucrative, however, industrialization has not occurred, skewing the structural transformation of the economy. Authorities in these countries have been unwilling to give up the tourism income—a reality reflected in policies not advantageous to manufacturing industries. By default, this leaves authorities with a development strategy based on maximizing linkages and minimizing leakages.

Notes

1. J. Hutnyk, *The Rumor of Calcutta: Tourism, Charity and the Poverty of Representation* (London: Zed Books, 1996), p. 11.

2. Gilbert Sigaux, "The History of Tourism," *Dictionnaire Universel du xxixe Siecle* (Geneva, Switzerland: Edito Service, 1876), cited in Donald Lundberg, Mink Stavenga, and M. Krishnamoorthy, *Tourism Economics* (New York: Wiley, 1995), p. 5.

3. John Lea, *Tourism and Development in the Third World* (London: Routledge, 2001), p. 4.

4. James Mak, *Tourism and the Economy* (Honolulu: University of Hawaii Press, 2004), p. 3.

5. Ibid.

6. William Theobald, "The Meaning, Scope, and Measurement of Travel and Tourism," in *Global Tourism*, 3rd ed., ed. William Theobald (Amsterdam: Elsevier, 2005), pp. 19–20.

7. The term *tourist* is then further subdivided. For example, Smith identified five types of tourists: ethnic, cultural, historical, environmental, and recreational. Valene Smith, *Hosts and Guests*, 2nd ed. (Philadelphia: University of Pennsylvania Press, 1989), pp. 4–6.

8. Donald Lundberg, Mink Stavenga, and M. Krishnamoorthy, *Tourism Economics* (New York: Wiley, 1995), p. 5.

9. Although tourists and other travelers are lumped together, they are not equally important in the economies of developing countries. Indeed, very few of the top ten countries by tourism growth are also among the top ten by growth of business travel (the former are Venezuela, Singapore, Dominican Republic, Chinese Taipei, Chad, Sudan, Solomon Islands, Angola, Malaysia, and Tunisia. The latter are Libya, Sudan, St. Kitts and Nevis, Cambodia, Chad, China, Malaysia, Vietnam, India, and Latvia). World Travel and Tourism Council, *Travel and Tourism—Forging Ahead,* the 2004 Travel and Tourism Economic Research Country League Tables (Madrid: 2004), Tables 3, 8.

10. Dean MacCannell, *The Tourist: A New Theory of the Leisure Class,* 3rd ed. (Berkeley: University of California Press, 1999).

11. Smith, *Hosts and Guests*, p. 1. By contrast, Juliet Schor claimed that Americans actually worked more hours at the end of the twentieth century than they did some hundred years before (Juliet Schor, *The Overworked American* [New York: Basic Books, 1992]).

12. Smith, *Hosts and Guests*, p. 2.

13. Steven Boyne, Fiona Carswell, and Derek Hall, "Reconceptualising VFR Tourism," in *Tourism and Migration,* ed. C. Michael Hall and Allan M. Williams (Dordrecht, The Netherlands: Kluwer Academic Publishers, 2002), p. 241; Priscilla Boniface, *Tasting Tourism: Travelling for Food and Drink* (Aldershot, Hampshire, UK: Ashgate, 2003); Dallen Timothy, "Tourism and the Growth of Urban Ethnic Islands," in *Tourism and Migration,* ed. C. Michael Hall and Allan M. Williams (Dordrecht, The Netherlands: Kluwer Academic Publishers, 2002).

14. David Crouch and Luke Desforges, "The Sensuous in the Tourist Encounter: Introduction to the Power of the Body in Tourist Studies," *Tourist Studies* 3, no. 1 (April 2003).

15. Heidi H. Sung, "Classification of Adventure Travelers," *Journal of Travel Research* 42, no. 4 (April 2004).

16. *Miami Herald*, February 25, 2005.

17. Michel Houellebecq, *Platform* (New York: Knopf, 2003), p. 21.

18. *Miami Herald*, May 10, 2005.

19. Dallen Timothy, Bruce Prideaux, and Samuel SeongSeop Kim, "Tourism at Borders of Conflict and (De)militarized Zones," in *New Horizons in Tourism,* ed. Tej Vir Singh (Cambridge, MA: CABI Publishing, 2004).

20. *Economist*, June 5, 2004, p. 49. In 2003, one in four of the births in Dublin had a non-Irish mother; non–European Union nationals accounted for 82 percent of all foreign births.

21. Martin Mowforth and Ian Munt, *Tourism and Sustainability,* 2nd ed. (London: Routledge, 2003), p. 26.

22. M. Thea Sinclair and Mike Stabler, *The Economics of Tourism* (London: Routledge, 1997), p. 15. Also see Larry Dwyer, Peter Forsyth, and Prasada Rao, "Destination Price Competitiveness: Exchange Rate Changes Versus Domestic Inflation," *Journal of Travel Research* 40, no. 3 (2002).

23. Hendrick Houthakker and Lester Taylor, *Consumer Demand in the United States: Analysis and Projections* (Cambridge: Harvard University Press, 1970).

24. World Bank, "Tourism in Africa," Findings Report no. 22617, *Environmental, Rural and Social Development Newsletter* (July 2001), p. 1.

25. Ibid.

26. See, for example, Peter Johnson and Barry Thomas, *Choice and Demand in Tourism* (London: Mansell, 1992).

27. M. Sarup, *Identity, Culture and the Post-Modern World* (Edinburgh: Edinburgh University Press, 1996), p. 127.

28. Nelson H.H. Graburn, "Tourism: The Sacred Journey," cited in Smith, *Hosts and Guests,* p. 33.

29. Smith, *Hosts and Guests*, p. 201.

30. Lundberg, Stavenga, and Krishnamoorthy, *Tourism Economics*, pp. 9–11.

31. *Business Life*, July/August 2005, p. 18.

32. MacConnell, *The Tourist*, p. 34. Incidentally, culture also plays a role in determining whose tastes count in the travel decisionmaking process. It has been found that in Western countries, working wives tend to be the decisionmakers in the choice of family vacation destinations (Valene Smith, "Women, the Taste-makers in Tourism," *Annals of Tourism Research* 6 [1979], pp. 49–60).

33. Sinclair and Stabler, *The Economics of Tourism*, p. 15.

34. See, among others, Rodney Falvey and Normal Gemmer, "Are Services Income Elastic: Some New Evidence," *The Review of Income and Wealth* 42 (September 1996).

35. Geoffrey Crouch, "Demand Elasticities for Short-Haul Versus Long-Haul Tourism," *Journal of Travel Research* 33, no. 2 (1994).

36. Lundberg, Stavenga, and Krishnamoorthy, *Tourism Economics*, p. 9.

37. World Tourism Organization, "Contribution of the World Tourism Organization to the SG Report on Tourism and Sustainable Development for the CSD 7 Meeting," "Addendum A: Tourism and Economic Development," April 1999, p. 14.

38. World Travel and Tourism Council, *Travel and Tourism,* Table 1.

39. E. Cohen, "Nomads from Affluence: Notes on the Phenomenon of Drifter-Tourism," *International Journal of Comparative Sociology* 14, no. 1–2 (1973).

40. Melanie Smith, *Issues in Cultural Tourism Studies* (London: Routledge, 2003), p. 5.

41. *Economist*, September 18, 2004, p. 49.

42. *Miami Herald*, October 24, 2004.

43. Lea, *Tourism and Development*, p. 33.

44. Duarte B. Morais, Michael J. Dorsch, and Sheila J. Backman, "Can Tourism Providers Buy Their Customers' Loyalty?" *Journal of Travel Research* 42, no. 3 (2004).

45. John T. Coshall, "The Threat of Terrorism as an Intervention of International Travel Flows," *Journal of Travel Research* 41, no. 1 (2003); Abraham Pizam and Aliza Fleischer, "Severity Versus Frequency of Acts of Terrorism: Which Has a Larger Impact on Tourism Demand?" *Journal of Travel Research* 40, no. 3 (2002).

46. Lea, *Tourism and Development*, p. 23.

47. World Bank, "Tourism in Africa."

48. World Tourism Organization, *Enhancing the Economic Benefits of Tourism for Local Communities, and Poverty Alleviation* (Madrid: 2002).

49. Pamela Fiori, "Build It (and They Will Come)," *Town and Country Travel*, Summer 2004.

50. MacCannell, *The Tourist*, p. 170.

51. Sinclair and Stabler, *The Economics of Tourism*, p. 9.

52. Lundberg, Stavenga, and Krishnamoorthy, *Tourism Economics*, p. 7.

53. Philippe Legrain, *Open World: The Truth About Globalization* (London: Abacus, 2002), p. 224.

54. Indeed, in 1999 tourism generated more than 15 percent of Morocco's foreign exchange earnings (outpacing remittances of Moroccans living abroad) and generated 7.5 percent of total employment. World Bank, "Sustainable Coastal Tourism Development," Project Appraisal Document, Report no. 20412-MOR (June 16, 2000), pp. 2, 3.

55. Melanie Smith, *Issues in Cultural Tourism*, p. 11.

56. World Tourism Organization, "Contribution of the World Tourism Organization," p. 18.

57. C. L. Jenkins and B. N. Henry, "Government Involvement in Tourism in Developing Countries," *Annals of Tourism Research* 9, no. 3 (1982).

58. Peter U.C. Dieke, ed., *The Political Economy of Tourism Development in Africa* (New York: Cognizant Communications Corporation, 2000), p. 10.

59. Isaac Sindiga and Mary Kanunah, "Unplanned Tourism Development in Sub-Saharan Africa with Special Reference to Kenya," *Journal of Tourism Studies* 10, no. 1 (1999). The authors claimed that decades of unplanned expansion had led to the breakdown of the physical infrastructure, environmental deterioration, wildlife-human conflicts, social problems, uneven distribution of benefits, and an undeveloped domestic tourism sector.

60. Carson L. Jenkins, "Tourism Policy Formulation in the Southern African Region," in *The Political Economy of Tourism Development in Africa*, ed. Peter U.C. Dieke (New York: Cognizant Communication Corp, 2000), p. 62.

61. World Bank, "Sustainable Coastal Tourism Development," p. 4.

62. Most nature-based tourism involves private companies in public protected areas. Ralf Buckley, "Public and Private Partnerships Between Tourism and Protected Areas: The Australian Situation," *Journal of Tourism Studies* 13, no. 1 (2002).

63. World Tourism Organization, *Enhancing the Economic Benefits*, p. 28.

64. Stephen Wanhill, "Role of Government Incentives," in William Theobald, ed., *Global Tourism*, 3rd ed., ed. William Theobald (Amsterdam: Elsevier, 2005), p. 370.

65. *Economist*, September 18, 2004, p. 83.

66. World Travel and Tourism Council, *Travel and Tourism,* Table 12.

67. Ibid., Table 13.

68. Ibid., Table 18.

69. Ibid., Table 19.

70. David Diaz Benavides and Ellen Perez-Ducy, eds., "Background Note by the OMT/WTO Secretariat," *Tourism in the Least Developed Countries* (Madrid: World Tourism Organization, 2001).

71. World Bank, "Tourism in Africa."

72. M. Hampton, "Backpacker Tourism and Economic Development," *Annals of Tourism Research* 25, no. 3 (1998).

73. MacCannell, *The Tourist*, p. 171.

74. Brian Copeland, "Tourism, Welfare and De-Industrialization in a Small Open Economy," *Economica* 58, no. 4 (November 1991), p. 527.

75. In September 2004, the Chinese government added some European countries to the list of fifty-four worldwide considered "approved destinations." The United States is not on that list, nor is any major Latin American country.

76. See, for example, P. Kotler, J. Bowen, and J. Makens, *Marketing for Hospitality and Tourism* (Upper Saddle River, NJ: Prentice Hall, 1996); Jansen Verbeke, *Marketing for Tourism* (London: Pitman, 1988); C. A. Gunn, *Tourism Planning; Basics, Concepts, Cases* (London: Taylor and Francis, 1994).

77. Lea, *Tourism and Development,* p. 33.

78. Ibid., p. 23.

79. Peter Burns, "Planning Tourism in a Reconstructing Economy: The Case of Eritrea," in *The Political Economy of Tourism Development in Africa,* ed. Peter U.C. Dieke (New York: Cognizant Communications Corporation, 2000), p. 98.

80. *Economist*, March 6, 2004, p. 42.

81. Peter E. Tarlow and Gui Santana, "Providing Safety for Tourists: A Study of a Selected Sample of Tourist Destinations in the United States and Brazil," *Journal of Travel Research* 40, no. 4 (2002).

82. *Economist*, March 6, 2004, p. 42.

83. Cynthia Enloe, *Bananas, Beaches and Bases: Making Feminist Sense of International Politics* (London: Pandora, 1990), p. 31.

84. See the discussion on Pakistan in Linda Richter, *The Politics of Tourism in Asia* (Honolulu: University of Hawaii Press, 1989).

85. Infrastructure has been discussed by development economists such as Paul Rosenstein-Rodan, Ragnar Nurkse, and Albert Hirshman. They used the term *social overhead capital* when referring to infrastructure. Both concepts included activities that share technical features (such as economies of scale) and economic features (such as spillovers from users to nonusers). See World Bank, *World Bank Development Report* (New York: Oxford University Press, 1994), p. 2. Also, there are other definitions of infrastructure. A. D. Chilisa, in his study of government policies in Botswana, divided infrastructure development into soft infrastructure and hard infrastructure. The former includes the

development of the environment for consuming between public and private sectors, whereas the latter refers to what is traditionally included in the tourism supply, such as roads and telecommunications. A. D. Chilisa, "Tourism Development in Botswana" in Peter U.C. Dieke, ed., *The Political Economy of Tourism Development in Africa* (New York: Cognizant Communications Corporation, 2000), p. 156.

86. Michael Todaro and Stephen Smith, *Economic Development*, 9th ed. (Boston: Addison-Wesley, 2005), p. 741.

87. There are exceptions; one example is that of government investment into accommodations for tourists (such as hotels, motels, bed-and-breakfasts, and so on). When scarce resources are used for tourist accommodations, that policy choice flies in the face of the housing shortage for the population.

88. World Bank, "Tourism in Africa."

89. See S. J. Page's study, which highlights the role of transport in tourism and the effect of its improvement on tourism development (*Transport for Tourism* [London: Routledge, 1994]).

90. In 1994, two billion people lacked access to electricity. World Bank, *World Development Report*, p. 1.

91. Only 7 percent had access to flush toilets and 5 percent to garbage collection. Hein Marais, *South Africa Limits to Change* (London: Zed Books, 1998), p. 107.

92. World Tourism Organization, *Enhancing the Economic Benefits*, p. 41.

93. Donald Reid, *Tourism, Globalization and Development* (London: Pluto Press, 2003), p. 42.

94. World Tourism Organization, *Enhancing the Economic Benefits*, p. 39.

95. Sinclair and Stabler, *The Economics of Tourism*, p. 11.

96. World Tourism Organization, *Tourism Taxation* (Madrid: 1998).

97. World Tourism Organization, "Contribution of the World Tourism Organization," p. 6.

98. World Bank, "Tourism in Africa."

99. *Economist*, October 9, 2004, p. 34.

100. "Massive Growth of Ecotourism Worries Biologists," www.NewScientist.com (accessed March 4, 2004).

101. Cited in Peter U.C. Dieke, "The Nature and Scope of the Political Economy of Tourism Development in Africa," in *The Political Economy of Tourism Development*, ed. Peter U.C. Dieke (New York: Cognizant Communications Corporation, 2000), p. 17.

102. Lea, *Tourism and Development*, p. 13.

103. Mowforth and Munt, *Tourism and Sustainability*, 2003, p. 51.

104. Reid, *Tourism, Globalization and Development*, p. 11.

105. Smith, *Issues in Cultural Tourism*, p. 54.

106. E. A. Pye and T. Lin, *Tourism in Asia: The Economic Impacts* (Ottawa: International Development Research Center, 1983), cited in Smith, *Hosts and Guests*, p. 6.

107. Smith, *Hosts and Guests,* p. 15.

108. Developing countries have tried to create regional airlines on several occasions (such as in the Caribbean and East Africa), but these have never been successful.

109. Instances of hotel multinationals based in the LDCs, such as the Indian Oberoi Group, are rare. Only one of the top fifty hotel chains has its headquarters in Africa (South Africa's Sun International).

110. John S. Akama, "Neocolonialism, Dependency and External Control of Africa's Tourism Industry," in *Tourism and Postcolonialism,* ed. C. Michael Hall and Hazel Tucker (London: Routledge, 2004), pp 145–146.

111. Copeland, "Tourism, Welfare and De-Industrialization," p. 516.

112. This desire for differentiation exists despite, or perhaps as a result of, the fact that the standardization of the tour package makes each destination substitutable for another. Especially when one is looking for sand and sun, it means that any individual country has very little control over its own tourist industry. John Lea pointed out how brochures for exotic destinations use the same words to describe locations, thus underscoring that they really could be anywhere. Lea, *Tourism and Development,* p. 110.

113. Economists have applied product cycle theory to tourism and come up with the tourism resort cycle model to describe foreign tour operators' adaptations to changes. Sinclair and Stabler, *The Economics of Tourism,* p. 132; Mowforth and Munt, *Tourism and Sustainability,* 2003, p. 85.

114. *Economist,* March 6, 2004, p. 42.

115. World Tourism Organization, *Enhancing the Economic Benefits,* p. 48.

116. Carson Jenkins, "The Development of Tourism in Namibia," in *The Political Economy of Tourism Development in Africa,* ed. Peter U.C. Dieke (New York: Cognizant Communications Corporation, 2000), p. 128.

117. World Bank Group, "World Bank Revisits the Role of Tourism in Development," *World Bank News* 17, no. 12 (1998).

118. World Tourism Organization, Tourism Policy Forum, "Tourism's Potential as a Sustainable Development Strategy" (October 19–20, 2004), George Washington University, Washington, DC, p. 2.

119. The projects where tourism was crucial tended to be funded by the World Bank's affiliate, the International Finance Corporation (IFC). Anil Markandya, Tim Taylor, and Suzette Pedroso, "Tourism and Sustainable Development: Lessons from Recent World Bank Experience," www.pigliaru.it/chia/markandya.pdf, pp. 10–12.

120. See, for example, World Bank, *Sustainable Coastal Tourism Development,* p. 6.

121. Markandya et al., "Tourism and Sustainable Development."

122. Robert A. Poirier, "Tourism in the African Economic Milieu: A Future of Mixed Blessings," in *The Political Economy of Tourism Development in Africa,* ed. Peter U.C. Dieke (New York: Cognizant Communications Corporation, 2000), p. 33.

123. World Tourism Organization, *Enhancing the Economic Benefits*, p. 41. Additional hotels were developed near the resort, making use of the economies of scale.

124. Ibid., p. 43.

125. *Jordan Times*, July 5, 2000, www.jordanembassyus.org/07052000004 .htm (accessed January 20, 2005).

126. Diaz Benavides and Perez-Ducy, "Background Note by the OMT/ WTO Secretariat."

127. World Bank Group, "The World Bank Grants Facility for Indigenous Peoples," October 2003, www.sacredland.org/news_items/WORLD_BANK _GRANTS.html (accessed January 20, 2005).

128. *Economist,* February 28, 2004, p. 42.

129. See Reid, *Tourism, Globalization and Development,* pp. 87, 98–99.

130. Poirier, "Tourism in the African Economic Milieu," p. 29.

131. Noel de Villiers reported that the Open Africa initiative was an African think tank with a clear goal: "to optimize Africa's tourism potential in a manner that will nourish and restore its resource base." Noel N. de Villiers, "Open Africa: An African NGO Tourism Initiative," in *The Political Economy of Tourism Development in Africa*, ed. Peter U.C. Dieke (New York: Cognizant Communications Corporation, 2000), p. 238.

132. Tourism Concern, "The International Network on Fair Trade in Tourism," www.tourismconcern.org.uk (accessed March 4, 2004).

133. Lara Marsh, Tourism Concern. "Corporate Social Responsibility," *Fair Trade in Tourism Bulletin* 2 (Autumn 2000), www.tourismconcern.org.uk (accessed October 2, 2004).

134. Deborah McLaren, *Rethinking Tourism and Ecotravel*, 2nd ed. (Bloomfield, CT: Kumarian Press, 2003), p. 27.

135. Pierre Encontre, "Tourism Development and the Perspective of Graduation from the LDC Category," in Diaz Benavides and Perez-Ducy, "Background Note."

136. Linda Richter, "After Political Turmoil: The Lessons of Rebuilding Tourism in Three Asian Countries," *Journal of Tourism Research* 38 (1999), pp. 41–45.

137. Reid, *Tourism, Globalization and Development,* p. 70.

138. A. Mathieson and G. Wall, *Tourism: Economic, Physical and Social Impacts* (Harlow: Longman, 1982).

4

Migrants and Immigrants

The town of Puerto Morelos is home to the service workers of Cancun, a prime tourist destination in Mexico. Although Puerto Morelos is bursting at the seams, it lies hidden from the sheltered tourist who does not seek out local flavor. Maun is less obviously poor and suffocating, although it serves the same purpose as Puerto Morelos—it has developed as a hub town for safaris and adventure travel in northern Botswana. Similarly, Manaus serves as a gateway for foreign tourists heading into the Brazilian Amazon. All three towns offer accommodations, travel agencies, and airports, but the tourist is never meant to linger. No fancy Western shops line the streets; no cafés for leisurely people-watching dot the sidewalks. Ultimately utilitarian towns, they are populated by those who work in the tourist industry.

And there are many such workers and a lot of work to do. As Thea Sinclair noted, "Underlying the images of hedonism and leisure which are commonly associated with tourism is a *large amount of work* [italics mine]."[1] That work is the focus of this chapter, along with the workers who perform it and the labor markets of which they are part. This chapter then turns to the second link in the circular flow of population movements, namely, the movement of workers who have responded to the labor requirements of the changing economic activities associated with tourism. I first present observations on the size of the tourism workforce and the nature of employment in the tourist industry, specifically with respect to job creation, skill requirements, and wages. Second, I discuss labor migrations associated with the spatial redistribution of economic activity in tourist destinations. In the end, I present an overview of the macroeconomic costs and benefits of labor movements in the tourist sector.

Employment in the Tourist Industry

In the aggregate, job creation from tourism has been remarkable. Studies by the WTTC have claimed that tourism is the world's largest generator of jobs. It accounted for 10 percent of total employment in 1997. It created jobs for about 230 million in 1998 and was expected to reach 328 million by 2010.[2] Donald Lundberg, Mink Stavenga, and M. Krishnamoorthy claimed that tourism is a great job stimulator and that for every $1 million of revenue generated, 20,000 new jobs are created.[3] According to the International Finance Corporation, for every hotel room, one to two jobs are created.[4] In the Virgin Islands, 50 percent of all employment came from direct and indirect work in the tourist sector; in Jamaica it was 37 percent and in the Bahamas 35 percent.[5] In Latin America, tourism is very important in employing people, as 54 million international visits per year translate into 2.5 million jobs, roughly 15 percent of the region's workforce.[6] M. E. Bond and J. R. Ladman found that the economic impact of tourism development in Mexico was as follows: forty-one jobs were created by an investment of $80,000, twenty-five more than by the same investment in the petroleum industry and twenty-six more than in metals.[7] In fact, worldwide, the economic literature on the impact of tourism on employment—by both independent economists and international organizations—overwhelmingly points to a stimulating effect.[8] Thus, when it comes to employment, tourism has proven to be a serious economic activity that generates jobs, not a candyfloss (cotton candy) industry (the term comes from the title of A. M. Williams's and G. Shaw's paper, "Tourism: Candyfloss Industry or Job-Generator?"[9]). By comparison with other industries, Brian Archer, Chris Cooper, and Lisa Ruhanen claimed that *"tourism seems to be more effective than other industries in generating employment and income* in the less developed, often peripheral, regions of a country where alternative opportunities for development are more limited [italics mine]."[10]

The positive perspective presented above is based on an overall, global assessment. Not all countries and not all regions in those countries have experienced significant job creation in the tourist industry. Just how much tourism employment is there in developing countries?

Table 4.1 contains data on employment in the tourist industries of developing countries grouped into categories A, B, and C (as in Table 1.1, countries are grouped by the percentage of their GDP derived from travel and tourism). Employment in the travel and tourism industry is listed as a percentage of total employment. As one might expect, countries in Group A have larger proportions of their labor force employed in the tourism industry than countries in Group C. Within Group A, the more GDP comes from tourism, the greater the labor force employment in the sector (witness, for example, the difference between the Virgin Islands and Dominica). A similar pattern can be observed within Groups B and C (with one exception: countries in the two top subgroups of Group B have very similar employment data—7.8 and 7.9 percent of their employment is in the tourist sector).

In all countries, employment in the tourist industry is determined by supply and demand. These are discussed throughout this chapter, but a few introductory words about demand are warranted here. Demand for labor is a derived demand in the sense that it exists only as long as there is demand for the service or product that is produced. Such derived demand takes several forms.[11] *Direct demand* for workers comes from tourists' expenditure on facilities such as hotels, air travel, rental cars, golf courses, and so on. Even when a package is prepaid and the foreign tour operator is the principal beneficiary, workers are needed to service the airport, clean the rooms, and cook the meals. Even when the infrastructure of tourism is imported from elsewhere, local workers are hired to build the hotels and sew the curtains and frame the windows. *Indirect demand* for labor comes from tourist expenditure on businesses outside of their package, such as local transport, handicrafts, and banking. Finally, *induced demand* comes from the expenditure by local residents who have earned income from tourist jobs and are now spending it. They purchase bicycles and motor scooters; they buy haircuts and medical services. In other words, they create the domestic demand essential for sustained economic development.

These three types of labor demand are linked through ever-expanding cycles of economic activity during which additional jobs are created. Indeed, as part of the linkages of tourism, initial expenditure by tourists causes a ripple effect in employment. Arrival of foreign tourists will stimulate the construction of roads, hotels, restaurants, and shops. It will also stimulate jobs creating locally produced furniture and decorations. Workers will provide textiles to lodges and hotels, sell beverages and snacks, produce handicrafts to sell to tourists. They will

Table 4.1   Travel and Tourism Industry Employment (as % of total) in Country Groups A, B, and C, 2004

% GDP	Group A	Average % N
70–100	Anguilla (31.6), Antigua and Barbuda (34.8), British Virgin Islands (38.3), Maldives (36.6)	35.3
50–69.9	Aruba (26.2), Bahamas (26.0), Barbados (19.8), Macao (32.8), Seychelles (38.2), Vanuatu (18.7)	27.0
30–49.9	Cayman Islands (18.0), Jamaica (10.7), Mauritius (16.2), St. Kitts and Nevis (9.0), St. Lucia (16.5), St. Vincent and Grenadines (9.2), Virgin Islands (12.3),	13.1
25–29.9	Dominica (7.7), Dominican Republic (7.7), Fiji (10.8), Grenada (8.2), Guadeloupe (8.2), Kiribati (8.2)	8.5
	Average for Group A	21.0
	Group B	
20–24.9	Angola (2.4), Bahrain (10.6), Belize (9.4), Gambia (8.6)	7.8
15–19.9	Cape Verde Islands (8.5), Egypt (6.7), Jordan (6.5), Morocco (7.7), Tunisia (10.0)	7.9
10–14.9	Brunei (4.2), Cambodia (3.0), China (2.0), Comoros (3.8), Costa Rica (4.8), Cuba (3.9), Ethiopia (4.2), Gabon (4.0), Guyana (3.1), Indonesia (3.2), Kenya (4.1), Lebanon (3.5), Malaysia (4.9), Oman (3.1), Panama (4.8), Papua New Guinea (4.3), Qatar (5.1), Solomon Islands (2.4), Sri Lanka (3.7), Thailand (4.3), Tonga (4.5), Trinidad and Tobago (2.6), Turkey (3.1), United Arab Emirates (1.6)	3.7
	Average for Group B	6.5
	Group C	
8–9.9	Bolivia (2.3), Botswana (5.7), Democratic Republic of Congo (1.9), Ecuador (2.3), Ghana (3.8), Honduras (2.5), Kuwait (2.6), Laos (3.4), Libya (2.2), Martinique (2.6), Mexico (2.4), Namibia (4.9), Nepal (3.1), Peru (3.1), Saudi Arabia (2.3), Singapore (1.6), Sudan (1.0), Tanzania (3.1), Uganda (3.5), Uruguay (3.8), Venezuela (2.1), Vietnam (1.6)	2.8

continues

lead botany tours, teach bush survival training, lead bird-watching tours, participate in music and dance performances, and guide tourists around the village.[12] As transport and telecommunications are needed, jobs are created to provide them; as cash and credit are needed, jobs in

Table 4.1   Continued

% GDP	Group C	Average % N
5–7.9%	Algeria (1.8), Argentina (2.9), Benin (2.2), Brazil (2.8), Burkina Faso (1.7), Cameroon (1.4), Chad (0.8), Chile (2.3), Colombia (2.1), Curaçao (3.0), El Salvador (2.2), Guatemala (2.0), Iran (2.8), Korea (2.4), Lesotho (1.7), Madagascar (1.6), Malawi (2.3), Mali (2.0), Nicaragua (2.2), Nigeria (1.0), Pakistan (1.8), Paraguay (1.3), Philippines (3.0), Reunion (2.3), Rwanda (2.5), São Tomé and Principe (2.9), Senegal (2.3), South Africa (3.0), Swaziland (2.6), Syria (2.4), Yemen (1.3), Zambia (1.9)	2.1
<4.9	Bangladesh (1.1), Burundi (1.9), Central African Republic (1.8), Congo (Zaire) (1.1), Côte d'Ivoire (1.2), Guinea (1.5), Haiti (1.2), India (2.6), Myanmar (1.5), Niger (1.3), Sierra Leone (0.8), Suriname (1.9), Togo (1.3), Zimbabwe (1.8)	1.5
	Average for Group C	2.1

Source: World Travel and Tourism Council, *Travel and Tourism—Forging Ahead*, the 2004 Travel and Tourism Economic Research Country League Tables (Madrid, 2004), Tables 46, 52.

Notes: Group A countries derive 25–100 percent of their GDP from travel and tourism; Group B countries 10–24.9 percent; Group C countries 0–9.9 percent. Numbers in parentheses following country names indicate the percentage of GDP derived from travel and tourism for the individual countries.

financial services spring up. Linkages to agriculture lead to the creation of jobs that provide food to the hotels and restaurants as well as to jobs in fisheries and food processing.

Just how large is the employment effect of all this spin-off economic activity? M. Thea Sinclair and Mike Stabler have used the Keynesian multiplier model to answer this question. The value of the multiplier is calculated as the ratio of the value of income or employment generated to the initial change in tourist spending or investment (this has been done for Antigua, Bahamas, Bermuda, Mauritius, and the Seychelles).[13] Not all types of tourism lead to the same job creation. It has been found that more jobs are created when the destination breaks out of enclave-type tourism. Indeed, if tourists come on package trips and are limited to a resort, then those wishing to sell to tourists can only hawk at the enclave entry and exit point, leaving little opportunity for economic exchange and therefore for lucrative work. A similar effect is achieved by cruise ships and all-inclusive packages. According to H.

Goodwin, cruise ship tourists spend an average of $0.03 in the local economy, package tourists spend $52.50, and independent travelers spend $97.40.[14] Clearly, expenditure by independent travelers will result in the most job creation.

Also, more jobs are created when strong linkages exist between sectors so that the demands of the tourist sector are more easily met by local suppliers. Countries with few economic linkages between tourism and other sectors will have low employment multipliers and low job creation. These countries often must resort to imports of goods for tourists' use. This is especially true in small island states. In Jamaica, for example, government policy has concentrated on strengthening the links between agriculture and tourism, thereby reducing the need for food imports for tourism.[15]

Irrespective of the size of the employment multiplier, tourist jobs share two characteristics. First, they tend to be labor intensive, making tourism a people-centered activity not only in terms of output but also in terms of inputs. According to the WTO, tourism is more labor intensive than manufacturing, although not as much so as agriculture.[16] Labor-intensive production is due to the very nature of the hospitality industry insofar as it is fundamentally the provision of a personal service (such as serving in restaurants, guiding tours, folk dancing in theaters, and so on). It is also due to the fact that labor is the abundant factor of production in most developing countries. As such, it is a cheap input into production. This does not mean that capital is not employed in tourism. To be sure, capital inputs are necessary in several phases of tourist product production (for example, computerized reservation systems, airplanes and other transportation vehicles, television sets in hotel rooms, and so on). Small-scale capital inputs are used by small producers of tourist services: In Kerala, houseboat tourism has generated much employment, as it uses as a principle factor the traditional rice boats that are in abundant supply.[17] In Panama's San Blas Islands, it is the dugout canoes; in Bukada (Turkey), it is the horse and buggy.

The above examples lead to the second characteristic of tourist jobs, namely that they tend to be housed in small enterprises. Although there are undoubtedly many huge hotels and airlines in third world destinations, they do not employ the largest proportion of tourist workers. Indeed, the tourism labor force tends to work in small- and medium-sized enterprises. These are often independent operators who rely on family labor. Tourism has offered creative and entrepreneurial locals a stage on which to apply their efforts. As in Europe, such entrepreneurial efforts are most evident in the accommodations sector in developing countries.

There, some 70 percent of total tourist accommodation capacity in Europe is provided by small- and medium-sized entrepreneurs; in developing countries this number might be as high as 85 percent.[18]

Carrying Capacity and Tourist Industry Employment

In one of the most visited cities of the world, Venice, there are twice as many tourists as residents (over the course of a typical year, six million tourists will spend at least one night in Venice and an additional fifteen million will come in for a day, whereas only 70,000 people live there).[19] The proportion is similar in Borocay (in the Philippines), where a population of some 8,000 people sustains a tourist accommodation capacity of some 1,500 rooms that sleep four people.[20] In Alaska, Arctic tourism during three summer months brings in four times as many people as the size of the local population. How do these tourist destinations, and others like them, survive the onslaught of visitors? To answer that question, scholars have looked at a region's carrying capacity, namely, how much tourism a region can absorb.[21] It is necessary to determine a country's carrying capacity in order to adjust supply and avoid potential overuse and destruction of natural resources. Each country has different conditions, so the impact of visitors will differ from place to place. For this reason, Philip Pearce suggested that all data on tourist arrivals must be placed in the particular context of the receiving countries.[22] In other words, some destinations can easily absorb an onslaught whereas others cannot. How can we identify which can and which cannot? David Harrison proposed several methods of inquiry.[23] Tourist intensity rates compare annual tourist arrivals with domestic population size, and tourist penetration rates measure the duration of tourist stays by comparing the nights tourists spend to nights spent in the country by all residents. There is also the tourist density ratio, which looks at the ratio of tourist nights to the area of the region. Finally, the concentration ratio indicates the percentage of tourists received from a country's three most important sending regions.

Tourist intensity rates are relevant for this chapter because they measure the influx of tourists relative to a host population; these rates in turn are related to employment capacity. Indeed, the greater the ratio, the greater the employment demands the destination's tourist sector will experience. Tourist intensity rates are presented in Table 4.2.[24] The tourist/resident ratio is highest in Group A countries, followed by Groups B and C (2.2, 0.6, and 0.1, respectively). This is to be expected, as tourist-dependent countries by definition have adjusted their capacity in order

Table 4.2 Tourist/Resident Ratio in Country Groups A, B, and C, 2002

% GDP	Group A	Average
70–100	Anguilla (4.1), Antigua and Barbuda (2.4), Maldives (1.6)	2.7
50–69.9	Aruba (10.0), Bahamas (5.1), Barbados (1.7), Seychelles (1.6), Vanuatu (0.3),	3.7
30–49.9	Cayman Islands (9.8), Jamaica (0.5), Mauritius (0.6), St. Kitts and Nevis (1.9), St. Lucia (1.7), St. Vincent and Grenadines (0.6)	2.5
25–29.9	Dominica (1.0), Dominican Republic (0.3), Fiji (0.5), Granada (1.4), Kiribati (0.1),	0.7
	Unweighted Average for Group A	2.2
	Group B	
20–24.9	Angola (0.01), Bahrain (4.0), Belize (1.0), Gambia (0.1),	1.3
15–19.9	Cape Verde Islands (0.3), Egypt (0.1), Jordan (0.3), Morocco (0.1), Tunisia (0.6)	0.3
10–14.9	Cambodia (0.1), China (0.02), Comoros (0.03), Costa Rica (0.3), Ethiopia (0), Gabon (0.1), Guyana (0.2), Indonesia (0.02), Kenya (0.03), Lebanon (0.3), Malaysia (0.6), Panama (0.2), Papua New Guinea (0.01), Solomon Islands (0.1), Sri Lanka (0.02), Thailand (0.2), Tonga (0.3), Trinidad and Tobago (0.3), Turkey (0.2), United Arab Emirates (1.6)	0.2
	Unweighted Average for Group B	0.6
	Group C	
8–9.9	Bolivia (0.04), Botswana (0.7), Democratic Republic of Congo (0.01), Ecuador (0), Ghana (0.02), Honduras (0.1), Kuwait (0.04), Laos (0.03), Mexico (0.2), Namibia (0.4), Nepal (0.02), Peru (0.03), Saudi Arabia (0.3), Singapore (1.2), Sudan (0), Tanzania (0.01), Uganda (0.01), Uruguay (0.6), Venezuela (0.02)	0.2

continues

to accommodate tourists. In some island countries, such as Aruba, the influx is up to ten times the number of the local residents.[25]

Skills

The tourist industry necessitates a wide range of skills that are not distributed along a bell-shaped curve but rather are concentrated at the two

Table 4.2   Continued

% GDP	Group C	Average
5–7.9	Algeria (0), Argentina (0.1), Benin (0.02), Brazil (0.03), Burkina Faso (0.01), Cameroon (0), Chile (0.1), Colombia (0.01), El Salvador (0.1), Guatemala (0.8), Iran (0.02), Korea (0), Lesotho (0.1), Madagascar (0.01), Malawi (0.02), Mali (0.01), Nicaragua (0.1), Nigeria (0.01), Pakistan (0), Paraguay (0.1), Philippines (0.02), Rwanda (0.02), São Tomé and Principe (0.05), Senegal (0.04), South Africa (0), Swaziland (0.3), Syria (0.1), Yemen (0), Zambia (0.1)	.08
<4.9	Bangladesh (0), Burundi (0.01), Côte d'Ivoire (0.02), Guinea (0), Haiti (0.02), India (0), Niger (0), Sierra Leone (0), Suriname (0.1), Togo (0.01), Zimbabwe (0.2)	.03
	Unweighted Average for Group C	0.1

Source: World Travel and Tourism Council, *Travel and Tourism—Forging Ahead,* the 2004 Travel and Tourism Economic Research Country League Tables (Madrid: 2004), Tables 46, 52; calculated from country tables in World Tourism Organization, *Compendium of Tourism Statistics* (Madrid: 2003); World Bank, *World Development Indicators.*

Notes: Group A countries derive 25–100 percent of their GDP from travel and tourism; Group B countries 10–24.9 percent; Group C countries 0–9.9 percent. There were no comparable statistics for the following countries: British Virgin Islands, Macao, Guadeloupe, Qatar, Cuba, Libya, Martinique, Curaçao, Oman, Brunei, Chad, Vietnam, Reunion, Central African Republic, Myanmar, and Congo (Zaire). These countries were not counted in the averages. The numbers in parentheses following country names indicate the tourist/resident ratios for the individual countries.

ends. The result of this bipolar distribution is a sharply segregated dual labor market. At one end lie the highly skilled, multilingual, and westernized resort managers, in all likelihood holding business degrees and well versed in hotel management. They embody the human capital that is the backbone of large-scale, organized resort tourism. At the other end lie the unskilled and uneducated local populations with few employment alternatives. With respect to sheer numbers, most employment in the labor-intensive tourist industry tends to be low skilled, where the barriers to entry are minimal and worker turnover is high. With respect to income earned, the advantages are in favor of the highly skilled workers.

Which workers are more important for the development of tourism? Some scholars claim it is the highly skilled workers in whose absence tourism would not get off the ground. Indeed, it has been claimed that African countries have not realized their tourism potential because they lack general economic management skills and, in particular, specific management skills within the tourism sector.[26] Others focus on the low skilled, claiming that without the chambermaid there is no one to clean the guest rooms. Clearly workers at both high and low levels of skills are necessary for the functioning of the tourist sector. A more relevant question might be: just how skilled do the unskilled and skilled workers really have to be?

With respect to the unskilled workers, do the chambermaids who clean the guest rooms need to have numeracy skills? Indeed, if tourists are flocking to a resort for its natural beauty, then are the language skills of local waiters relevant? Although literacy, for example, is not strictly a precondition for serving roasted chicken, familiarity with table settings as well as service-friendly attitudes has played a big role in the attraction of repeat visitors.

With respect to skilled workers, do they have to hold foreign graduate degrees and have years of international experience? Different businesses operating in the tourist industry have answered that question for themselves in different ways, depending on the type of tourism that prevails. The fact is that when appropriately skilled labor is available locally, then the number of expatriate workers can be reduced. This benefits the local population in the form of increased employment, and for foreign companies it represents a cost-saving measure.

It is interesting to note that locals in developing countries have become more skilled *as tourism has developed.* In other words, skills that did not exist a priori come into existence concurrently with tourism. At higher skill levels, tourism is a conduit for the introduction of modern management techniques and technologies. Across the LDCs, there are increasing opportunities for staff training and the development of transferable skills. In the Brazil tourism effort, skill building at the municipal level is one of the cornerstones of the National Tourism Municipalization Program.[27] In Malaysia, the strategic vision of developing rural tourism includes providing training in the key aspects of accommodation, catering, customer care, and safety standards as well as visitor attractions development, presentation, and marketing.[28] Even for low-skilled jobs, tourism is a conduit for basic skills. The stellar example of the Nusa Dua Resort in Bali is a case in point. The resort is located adjacent to two fishing villages and is surrounded by scattered farm settlements.[29] While the resort was still in the developmental stages, the question of integrating these villages into resort activities was addressed. As the residents were mostly uneducated, low-income wage earners, it was necessary to train them. They were first given the opportunity to work on the construction of the project, and later they were trained at the hotel and tourism training center that evolved in the resort. Given the overall low level of education, remedial courses were necessary before they could enroll in regular courses. Financial assistance was provided to students so they could attend these courses.

Wages

The dual labor market in the tourist industry fosters a supporting dual wage system that percolates into other price distortions. Highly skilled workers, often foreign, receive wages competitive with those in their home countries and usually in a desirable foreign currency, in addition to a package of benefits to offset the discomfort of expatriate life in an LDC resort.

By contrast, low-skilled workers have paltry wages and no benefits. Those wages are inconsistent, as their jobs have no security. Although there are variations among low-skilled wages both within a tourist destination as well as among destinations, usually these are insufficient to alleviate poverty in any meaningful way. Indeed, as Donald Reid pointed out, "it is often the poorest people living in these already underprivileged circumstances who provide labor to the tourism industry across the globe. *Employment in tourism provides a meager living to its workers*, rarely allowing them to lift themselves beyond conditions of social marginalization and poverty [italics mine]."[30]

Income of tourism workers is often so low because the services they sell are seasonal. In tropical tourist destinations, seasonality is governed by northern holidays as well as by local climate. In the Caribbean, the peak tourist season is when it is cold in the north and there is no hurricane season. In Africa's game parks, it has to do with mosquito seasons, and in the Pacific, cyclone seasons. (This cyclical pattern occurs even in Western resorts: in the Portuguese resort of Faro, there is a 30 percent increase in employment during summer[31]). Hotels are empty during the off-season, and employees are often jobless. Only when the region's economic base is well developed do workers have other options. Successful marketing of destinations in off-season times (that is, northern lands during winter, Caribbean during summer, and so on) have alleviated this problem.

The wages of unskilled workers are further eroded by inflationary pressures emanating from elevated tourist demand. Although everyone's purchasing power is undermined, it is the low-skilled workers that are most affected.

All in all, the welfare implications of tourism employment are not always positive: in the Maldives, 30 percent of the local children are malnourished because the produce goes to feed the tourists in hotels. In Peru, porters who assist tourists to climb Machu Picchu were found to be undernourished and abused.[32]

Efforts to introduce livable or fair tourism wages have been sparse in developing countries. In rare instances, local unions are strong enough to ensure wages are high. This is the case in Bermuda, where the Bermuda Industrial Union has kept wages high above the poverty line by a variety of measures, including, for example, imposing a mandatory 15 percent gratuity on all hotel and restaurant charges. It is more common for developing countries to rely on international rules concerning wages, such as Fair Trade in Tourism, a voluntary concept developed by Tourism Concern, that states that wages and working conditions in developing countries must reflect international labor standards with regard to national minimum wages, freedom of association, health and safety, no child or slave labor, and no discrimination, within the context of the UN Declaration on Human Rights.[33]

* * *

In conclusion, low wages, low skill levels, and underemployment are all tied together. In the words of James Mak, "lower pay in the tourism industries is generally attributed to a number of factors, among them the high percentage of unskilled jobs and the prevalence of seasonal, casual, part-time, transitory, and female employment."[34] Because wages are so low for unskilled workers, employment in the tourist industry has become part of a poverty reduction strategy in many developing countries. According to Odette Likikouet Bako, the Côte d'Ivoire's minister of tourism and handicrafts, "for many developing countries, such as the Côte d'Ivoire where most of the population lives in rural areas, tourism—especially ecotourism—constitutes a social and economic solution that is a *vital element of poverty-reduction strategies* [italics mine]."[35] The WTO has suggested maximizing employment of locals in tourism as a priority in enhancing benefits of tourism for local communities as well as for alleviating poverty.[36] In this way, tourist jobs can be sustainable substitutes for livestock grazing or subsistence agriculture in poverty-stricken regions. The creation of tourist jobs as alternatives to preexisting work has been a goal of numerous tourist destinations. The Gudigwa Safari Camp has been particularly successful in this way. It is an ecotourism venture owned entirely by the Bushmen and established in collaboration with Conservation International and Wilderness Safaris.[37] All proceeds are channeled into development projects that give community members sustainable alternatives to livestock grazing.

In addition to being substitutes for traditional economic activity, tourism jobs can be complements. In these cases, tourism projects are developed with the goal of offering comprehensive job opportunities to the communities. These commonly include the following employment-creating alternatives: agroforestry activities and village community forests for the production of medicinal plants, fruits, and firewood; development of irrigated rice farming; creation of fishponds and livestock farms to provide sources of protein as an alternative to the meat obtained from poached game, supporting the creation of nonagricultural employment activities in rural areas.[38] An apt example of this is the Parkside Area Programme, implemented in nine tourism activity centers around the Tai National Park in Côte d'Ivoire.[39] There, locally recruited (and trained) activity hosts work to inform and raise awareness of residents regarding sustainable development alternatives.

Labor Migrations and the Tourist Industry

Tourism services have to be consumed in situ—in other words, they cannot be transferred elsewhere, nor can their consumption be deferred.[40] It follows that the tourism labor force must be located in the place of consumption and available at the time of consumption, with few exceptions. If there are insufficient local workers to satisfy tourism demand, then labor migrations take place to fill the void. Indeed, if the expanding tourist destination is unable to provide appropriate labor, it will of necessity have to come from elsewhere. As noted in Chapter 2, labor migration is the adjustment to the new spatial distribution of economic activity induced by the localized growth of the tourist sector. Where mass tourism exists, the demand for workers, especially low skilled, is large, so migration occurs. Allan Williams and C. Michael Hall expressed this aptly: "In-migration is most likely to occur under conditions of mass tourism development whereas some of the smaller scale rural, cultural and urban tourism forms *may be able to meet most or even all labour from within the local labour market* [italics mine]."[41] Labor migration also happens for niche tourism, when the local labor market cannot supply the specialized skills that are needed (such as trained instructors in sports tourism). As suggested in Chapter 2, the more tourist oriented the country, the greater the labor adjustment of its population and the greater the inflows of foreign and domestic workers. To the extent that this does not happen, it is because of artificial constraints imposed on migration flows. These constraints, discussed in

Chapter 6, include work permits, citizenship rights, and laws pertaining to property ownership by foreigners. The research by Williams and Hall also pointed to the important role played by such constraints. They claimed that there is no definitive link between tourism and inmigration and no automatic translation of tourism growth into migration growth because of the institutional constraints that form barriers to migration.[42]

The next section is a discussion of the principal forms of voluntary migration associated with third world tourism that were presented in Chapter 2: immigration of foreign workers, immigration of domestic workers, and outmigration of domestic workers. Each of these refers to the tourist destination region and is discussed with particular reference to duration and choice. Empirical evidence is not presented because there are no comparable statistics by tourist region, by country, and by industrial sector. As Nazli Choucri noted, the actual numbers of cross-border migrations are difficult to determine, and counting them is "an exercise in statistical ambiguity."[43]

Inmigration of Foreign Workers: Voluntary/Temporary and Voluntary/Permanent

Foreign workers who move to an LDC tourist destination do so voluntarily. There is no doubt about their choice in the matter and the outcome of the personal cost/benefit analysis they perform. Some stay temporarily; others move with permanence in mind. It is likely that the temporary migrants are the highly skilled (usually) Western nationals who take managerial-level positions, whereas migrating workers who favor permanence tend to be less skilled and from other developing countries. They are immigrants. Given their skill levels, they have a lot in common with domestic voluntary workers; given their foreign passports, they have commonalities with skilled foreign workers. Their foreign passports necessitate contact with the home country's immigration laws. Most developing tourist-friendly countries have constraints on foreign nationals that vary in depth and breadth. International tourist sector businesses must work with the system in order to obtain work permits for their expatriate staff. Immigration authorities are less likely to grant such permits for workers who do not bring skills.

Whether they have skills or not, foreign migrants reinforce the duality of the labor market. In the ensuing discussion about skills, the focus is on migrant workers whereas earlier in the chapter it was about skills in general.

Voluntary/temporary: skilled foreign workers. Skilled tourist workers represent human capital, and as do other forms of capital, they flow across international borders in response to demand. This flow occurs mostly at the level of senior managers and mostly in terms of intracompany transfers and intercompany career moves. According to Williams and Hall, "the growth of transnational tourism capital has been highly uneven between sectors and across space . . . but is particularly strong in the international hotel sector, in franchised restaurant chains and—to a lesser extent—tour operators."[44] Indeed, across developing countries, international hotel chains will not get involved unless their personnel are in place. Their personnel form an invaluable link to the company. Moreover, their personnel are likely to have high labor productivity (according to Lundberg, Stavenga, and Krishnamoorthy, in many developing countries, "two employees are needed to perform the work of one elsewhere"[45]). For these reasons as well as others, foreign companies prefer to see their people, expatriates, manage resorts.

What exactly is it that the foreign skilled national brings to a developing country? In their discussion of the foreign migrant, C. Aitken and C. M. Hall highlighted the relevance of skills for the tourism industry.[46] P. Dawkins, S. Kemo, and H. Cabalu listed a set of foreign skills valued by local tourism employers: foreign language proficiency, having lived or worked in a foreign country, contacts with foreign people, specific cultural knowledge, knowledge of foreign business ethics, and formal study of a foreign country.[47] These skills then become part of the technology transfer that occurs to the benefit of the host country's tourist industry. This much touted positive externality can, in theory, provide much-needed managerial skill and expertise in developing local enterprises. Sometimes this transfer is not successful, however, and when foreign workers leave, there is nothing left. L. J. Lickorish and C. L. Jenkins noted that when the foreign consultant leaves, often those who stay behind have not acquired sufficient skills to take over.[48]

To increase the chance of successful skill transfer, some foreign tourist companies provide training programs for local staff. Chain hotels, for example, often provide extensive training programs that can, according to the World Bank, "stimulate the entire sector to greater competitiveness."[49] Such investment in training local tourist workers also comes from outside the hotels themselves, as in Kenya, where a group of Swiss specialists, with the aid of a Swiss grant, helped the government open a hotel school. Alternatively, foreign nationals come as advisers, responsible for setting up an entire tourist program. For example, in the development of village tourism in Senegal, it was an international specialist who provided technical advice (together with an international agency that provided start-up financial assistance[50]). Some scholars have claimed that these efforts are not altogether necessary. Valene Smith said that tourism is no longer so exotic that labor cannot be found: she claimed that "models of success where local employees obtained positions of considerable responsibility can be found in many tourist areas." Also, if qualified workers are not available at one site, she claimed, they can easily be recruited from another.[51]

Voluntary/permanent: unskilled foreign workers. Mauritanians seek jobs in the booming Senegalese tourist industry, and Zimbabweans flock to the tourist areas of South Africa. These immigrants then compete with local unskilled workers migrating to the tourist destinations in search of employment. In this competition, these immigrants have the disadvantage of bureaucratic controls on their labor. To the extent that they have working permission, they can compete. Without it, they fall into the casual worker pool, functioning in the underground economy at lower wages and in working conditions inferior to those of domestic migrants.

Competition among immigrants and locals is not limited to the tourist industry. Malaysia reported that workers from Indonesia who entered the country on two-week tourist visas would then disappear to remote plantations in the interior. There they could work illegally without being found by authorities.[52]

Sometimes competition between immigrants and locals does not occur. Where tourism is not the principal industry, tourist sector jobs are readily left to the newcomers. An example of this is Trinidad, where immigrant workers do not compete with locals in the tourist industry because the locals prefer to work in the thriving petroleum industry. The work opportunities in tourism are luring people from other parts of the Western Hemisphere, and Spanish-speaking immigrants from Venezuela and Colombia have recently moved to fill service jobs in restaurants, among others.[53]

Inmigration of Domestic Workers: Voluntary/Temporary or Voluntary/ Permanent

Like inmigrating foreign workers, domestic workers migrate into tourist destinations voluntarily. Also, like foreign workers, their migration can be temporary or permanent, although the initial intention is often blurred and is prone to change. The similarity stops there, however. Domestic migrants usually speak the language of the resort and do not have citizenship or working papers to contend with. They also rarely have the high skills that their foreign counterparts bring. In fact, most come from the rural areas where the lack of employment prospects pushed them off the land. Those who speak the language of the tourists are likely to become tour guides and agency representatives. If they have computer skills, they may work in reservations. The lower their skill levels, the more menial their employment. Also, the more menial their job, the lower the barriers to entry and the higher the labor turnover. This turnover is especially poignant in single-peak seasonal destinations and is a draw for the low-skilled migrants who expect ample employment opportunities.

There is a difference among male and female migrant workers with respect to how they fare in tourism employment. Without a doubt, tourism absorbs women, although the percentage of female employment varies—in Bolivia it is 60 percent, whereas in Muslim countries it is less than 10 percent.[54] There is also no doubt that tourism has provided women with new opportunities (in fact, Thea Sinclair claimed it gave women greater opportunities for paid work and higher earnings than they had had before[55]). Women tend to be in informal commerce, hospitality, and menial service work. They are nightclub workers, dancers, hair braiders, and basket weavers. Prostitution offers an especially lucrative source of income, as sex tourism has become more pervasive and more open.[56] Although these are undoubtedly low-prestige jobs, they are often better and there are more of them than what women had before. In addition, immigrant women encounter obstacles that men do not simply because they are female. Williams and Hall called this the "dual obstacles of their gender and their migrant status."[57] The gender obstacles include the fact that women as the prime childcare providers are tied down by their children (there is evidence that families with young children are the least mobile sociodemographic group[58]). Another obstacle is that some jobs are viewed as obviously male or female. This gendered segregation of the tourist labor market is often the reflection of gender inequalities in the society and the household. Sinclair reported that in the Caribbean, men perceive women's participation in the tourist accommodation sector in the context of their domestic roles.[59] In Greece, also, women undertake tasks in the tourist industry that they tend to do at home, such as making beds and cleaning.[60] An extension of this is women in prostitution.[61]

Outmigration of Local Workers:
Involuntary/Temporary and Involuntary/Permanent

Tourism accounts for 70 percent of the economy of Venice, Italy. Those businesses that do not benefit from tourism, such as cinemas and supermarkets, are closing down, and the workers employed therein become unemployed.[62] Such displacement of nontourist economic activity also occurs throughout tourist destinations in developing countries.

As a region becomes a tourist destination, the very foundations of economic activity begin to shift in a particular direction. The nature of output changes as producers respond to incentives to produce tourist-related goods and services. This change in demand translates into a change in derived demand for workers in the tourist industry, and those who previously were employed in another sector become displaced. Such displacement by economic development·may be gradual, owing to market forces, or it can be artificial, finite in time and space, and government-sponsored (the third type is discussed in Chapter 5). Either way, the move is involuntary, as workers do not choose to leave their jobs or their land. Some displacements are temporary, as workers leave a location only to later return to participate in the growing tourism industry; other displacements are permanent, as people relocate to destinations that may be inside or outside the country.

As Peter Penz noted in his study of displacement by development, there are no statistics on the numbers worldwide who have been displaced in this way. Evidence from the World Bank suggested that some ten million people per year were being displaced by large infrastructure projects such as the construction of roads, railway lines, dams, canals, mines, harbors, industrial plants, urban expansion, and so on.[63] This is obviously an underestimate of the total because it is limited to a particular size and type of project. Whatever the number of displaced people worldwide, it is a fact that, as Penz stated, "we are so accustomed to economic change that we take the losses and misfortunes of the victims of development as natural."[64] And so, when people are forced to move because of development efforts, they are rarely compensated. If they are, it is rarely sufficient.

What happens when the development of tourism displaces old forms of employment, when the land used for plantation agriculture is taken over by a hotel enterprise, when water for herded animals is diverted for swimming pools, and when subsistence fishing is disrupted by yachts and water scooters? Sometimes this occurs when the demand for labor in a sector shifts over to tourism, as in the Canary Islands, where fishing and tomato growing were displaced by tourism. In St. Lucia, the lucrative banana crop died out because of labor shortages that occurred when workers migrated to the tourist destinations.[65] Sometimes displacement occurs as a result of permanent environmental restructuring, including the building of an airport, that takes land away from agricultural production. In the Maldives, tourism took off after a large landing strip enabled large-bodied airplanes to land, but agricultural workers were displaced in the process. In these cases, without being formally evicted or forcibly resettled, people are forced to move because their livelihood is undermined and their physical habitat becomes unviable.

Such displacement of traditional industries is not necessarily a smooth process, and local workers often put up a fight in their clash with developers. They reject the encroachment of tourism that clashes with their livelihood. Four examples across the globe illustrate this struggle: the Galapagos Islands of Ecuador, Jordan, East Africa, and Vietnam. In each case, tourism, economic development, and conservation all mix in the displacement.

In the Galapagos, the fishing and the tourist industries have mutually exclusive goals. Conservation efforts promote tourism on the islands, but those same efforts restrict fishing activities. As a result, local fishermen, concerned about their fishing rights, standards of living, and displacement from traditional work, have clashed with government and international conservation efforts. For years they have encroached on the protected waters, and lucrative catches have doubled the number of fishermen to around 1,000. At the same time, some of the 18,000 residents are involved in the tourist industry that depends on conservation. In an effort to strike a balance between the needs of the fishermen, conservation efforts, and economic development, in 1998 the Ecuadorian government declared the Galapagos to be a marine reserve to be managed by a committee on which conservation bodies, tourist firms, government ministries, and fishermen are all represented. This inclusionary step did not stop the disagreements, and in 2004, a group of fishermen held thirty scientists hostage, demanding the right to use semi-industrial techniques in the protected waters.[66] In 2005 a new source of dispute emerged, namely shark fishing. It is illegal in the marine reserve, but shark fetches a high price when sold in Asian markets.[67]

In Jordan, the communities living around the Dana Reserve were engaged in ecologically damaging economic activities that impaired the development of tourism. As a result, a program was set up in 1994 to build on local skills and develop alternative forms of income generation.

Small business were set up to supply handcrafted silver jewelry, medicinal and culinary herbs, jams, and other tourist souvenirs.[68] Also, jobs in tourist facilities were generated, including tour guides and services in campsites and lodgings. By 1998, fifty-five full-time jobs had been created, providing direct and indirect tourist economic benefits for over 800 people. This job creation subdued the clash between locals and tourist developers.[69]

In East Africa, the livelihood of people in human settlements in safari destinations has been negatively affected because tourism encourages the growth of big game animals, especially elephants. Those animals then compete with cattle and farm animals for watering holes and grazing lands.[70]

Finally, in Vietnam's Babe National Park, the government is involved in a project, started in 1999, aimed at conservation in order to develop ecotourism.[71] The local villagers nevertheless continue with their lifestyle practices of clearing forests from mountainsides for agriculture and timber exploitation (thus reducing the wildlife habitats), wildlife hunting, harvesting of forest products for home construction, the traditional practice of fish bombing, and so on. These activities threaten the biodiversity of the park and have resulted in a decrease in wildlife. Although the government promises that the tourist industry will provide employment for the village population, many remain unconvinced, and the two sides remain pitted against each other.[72]

Sometimes populations are dislocated by secondary effects of tourism rather than by structural unemployment. They may move because of high rents and land prices. As Archer, Cooper, and Ruhanen pointed out, land prices in particular are affected by the development of tourism: as tourism grows, the demands for land rises. The result, they claimed, is that "farmers and other local landowners are encouraged to sell, with the result that, although they may obtain short-term gains, they are left landless with only low paid work available."[73] In addition, tourist demand causes demand-pull inflation that makes the cost of living prohibitively expensive, inducing locals to move away (as has occurred in Hawaii). Tourist-induced inflation does not occur when guests purchase goods and services that locals do not consume. Indeed, the tourist demand for suntan lotion, gambling, and expensive dining is unlikely to produce inflation that spills over into the rest of society. The demand for land on which the shops, casinos, and restaurants are built adds to the rise in property values, however, which affects local populations. In Uruguay's Punta del Este resort, property values have been driven up by wealthy Argentines buying vacation homes; in Swaziland's Ezulweni Valley, land prices rose owing to South African investors and speculators.

Another secondary effect of tourism that displaces local workers results from Western volunteerism. When youth groups travel to developing countries with altruistic goals of helping others by building homes and clearing bushes, they upset the local labor market. They pay to do what locals do for pay. Volunteer travel does not cause displacement if it involves work locals do not perform.[74]

Irrespective of how displacement occurs, its welfare implications are not negligible. Although the net effect is not the same across developing countries, more often than not the standards of living are low as involuntary displaced people are crowded into slum dwellings where they often have no jobs or sanitation (such is the reality for the thousands of Dayaks of Sarawak, forced off their land and into towns).[75] Donald Reid spoke to the issue of employment and said how depressing the tourism industry is to a local worker who "lost a lucrative, unionized forestry job and replaced it with a seasonal job in the outdoor adventure tourism sector, or who has opened up his or her private dwelling as a bed and breakfast."[76] Brian Copeland also discussed the welfare implications when tourism leads to the contraction of the manufacturing sector, especially if the potential trade effect of expansion of industry is greater than the benefits generated by tourism.[77] If the development of tourism fails in Canada or New Zealand, there is a safety net of social services to receive the workers left without jobs or income. Such safety nets are rarely available in developing countries, neither de jure nor de facto.

The Costs and Benefits of Labor Movements in the Tourist Sector

Even though large waves of economic migrants have enabled economic development in host regions, including the United States, the Middle East, and Western Europe, losing states have suffered from the loss of human capital. Although there is no doubt that population movements have economic, political, and demographic implications for both the host and home regions, there is disagreement as to their net effect. According to the World Bank, "migration is usually beneficial to both sending and receiving countries."[78] This optimistic view is not shared by those who argue that outmigration hurts home regions by stripping them of human capital while serving the interests of international capital.[79]

Others simply claim that the effect of migration is too complicated and unresolved to make a clear assessment.[80]

During the circular flow of populations, workers migrate in response to spatial changes in economic activity stimulated by tourist demand. As workers migrate in order to participate in this growing sector, losing regions incur costs and reap benefits and so do receiving regions.[81]

The benefits of inmigration to tourist destinations are derived from the inflow of both skilled and unskilled workers. In the case of the former, the resulting brain gain (which complements the losing region's brain drain) is a result of the fact that the training of the migrants took place at the expense of another government.[82] Often the benefits of skilled migrants extend beyond their earning and productive capacity to the work ethic they bring with them (as often migrants are self-selected by their drive and adaptive ability). Receiving regions reap benefits even when immigrant workers are unskilled, since they are often willing to perform undesirable and dangerous tasks, many of which are shunned by indigenous populations (for example, the western Chinese cities along the old Silk Road are growing exceptionally fast; migrant labor from the rest of China is moving to Xinjiang to fill an employment void, as many locals do not want to perform the "dirty, hard and tiring work"[83]).

Receiving regions also benefit from the inflow of financial assets that often accompanies the arrival of a new population. If these migrants have personal assets, they will be spent, saved, or invested in the host country.

Lest too rosy a picture is depicted for the receiving tourist destinations, the incurred costs must be discussed. Direct costs include those associated with resettlement and integration: housing, education, policing, transportation, water and health controls, and so on. Over time, indirect costs become evident, including the social ramifications of local perceptions that their livelihood is threatened, living costs are rising, and the competition for scarce resources has been unfairly sharpened.

What about the benefits and costs experienced by the losing regions in which the migrants originated? The principal benefit accrues when a region reduces its surplus of labor and thus relieves the demand for employment while arresting the downward pressure on wages and the strain on infrastructure. For this reason, regions with high population densities and insufficient opportunities for their workers encourage outmigration. This is often supported by the central government as part of a regional policy (as in Mexico and the Philippines).

Losing regions incur a high cost of emigration because they lose the employment and productivity that the migrant would have contributed. In addition, they lose the migrant's taxes (resulting in a decrease in government revenue), savings (resulting in a decrease in the rate of investment), and fertility (resulting in a decrease in the future human capital pool). But the most pronounced long-term cost associated with outmigration is the loss of human capital. Although scholars disagree as to how to measure the magnitude of such brain drain,[84] they do agree that the price a losing region pays in terms of economic growth potential is great. Losses are incurred when a region pays for education and training of migrants who then move before they make a contribution to the economy. The more trained the migrant, the greater the loss.

These costs and benefits of population movements and displacement of workers (and traditional work) in tourist destinations have implications for development policy. When LDC leaders promote tourism, they rarely consider that the concomitant labor migration puts additional pressures on them to provide infrastructure of a type that is not necessarily paid for by the international organizations such as IMF and World Bank. For instance, it is not just the unregulated waste from the resorts that is polluting the towns but also the waste from the migrant labor. Governments cannot claim ignorance, as the costs and benefits of population movements are increasingly receiving media attention. Also, scholars have provided evidence for policymakers to reflect on.[85] International organizations such as Tourism Concern have also become involved. The World Bank, in its project proposal for Morocco's coastal regions, specifically noted that developing a tourist project would necessitate the need to "reconcile the spatial claims of a quality international resort, sprawling urbanization and consequent migration of population towards the coast and land and infrastructure needs of other economic sectors."[86] In other words, the World Bank highlighted the repercussions on the agricultural and fishing communities by incoming migrants.

In response to this information, some LDC authorities have readjusted their development policies. Sometimes they aim to preserve traditional livelihoods and thus protect people from displacement. In Bali's Nusa Dua resort, mentioned earlier, "*in order to maintain the fishermen's livelihood*, those places on the beach used by the fishermen for launching and storing their boats were reserved for that purpose, and access was provided through the resort via pedestrian corridors to the boat storage areas [italics mine]."[87] Alternatively, they aim to keep people from migrating to work in tourism by bringing tourism to their villages. For example, in Senegal, authorities wanted to offer something other than beach hotels. In the 1970s, they set out to develop village tourism, thereby distributing tourists to all regions of the country and, most important, stemming the flow of migration into the urban areas.[88]

In addition to government policy, the drive to control population movements sometimes comes from the tourist destination itself. In Nunavut, the Inuit people have lived as subsistence hunters and gathers for millennia. Even though tourism was welcomed as a source of employment and income, it was feared because it would draw migrants. Based on a community survey in the village of Pangnirtung, "it was decided to develop tourism *gradually* in order to prevent *overcrowding of the village* [italics mine]."[89]

Notes

1. M. Thea Sinclair, "Issues and Theories of Gender and Work in Tourism," in *Gender, Work and Tourism,* ed. M. Thea Sinclair (London: Routledge, 1997), p. 1.

2. Studies by the WTTC cited in World Bank Group, "World Bank Revisits Role of Tourism in Development," *World Bank News* 17, no. 12 (1998).

3. Donald Lundberg, Mink Stavenga, and M. Krishnamoorthy, *Tourism Economics* (New York: Wiley, 1995), p. 3.

4. IFC cited in World Bank Group, "World Bank Revisits."

5. World Tourism Organization, "Contribution of the World Tourism Organization to the SG Report on Tourism and Sustainable Development for the CSD 7 Meeting," "Addendum A: Tourism and Economic Development," April 1999, p. 5.

6. World Tourism Organization, Tourism Policy Forum, "Tourism's Potential as a Sustainable Development Strategy," (October 19–20, 2000) Washington, DC, p. 2.

7. M. E. Bond and J. R. Ladman, "Tourism: A Strategy for Development," *Nebraska Journal of Economics and Business* (1972), pp. 37–52, cited in Lundberg, Stavenga, and Krishnamoorthy, *Tourism Economics*, p. 141.

8. M. Thea Sinclair, ed., *Gender, Work and Tourism* (London: Routledge, 1997), pp. 9–10.

9. A. M. Williams and G. Shaw, "Tourism: Candyfloss Industry or Job-Generator?" *Town Planning Review* 59 (1998).

10. Brian Archer, Chris Cooper, and Lisa Ruhanen, "The Positive and Negative Impacts of Tourism," in *Global Tourism*, 3rd ed., ed. William Theobald (Amsterdam: Elsevier, 2005), p. 82. Not everyone agrees with this

positive view. In his study of the Kenyan tourist industry, John Akama said, "Kenya's tourism activities are spatially constrained to a few locations in the popular wildlife parks. The majority of Kenyan people in most regions of the country do not receive any form of direct monetary benefit from the industry. Furthermore, few people who live at or near tourist attractions and facilities receive jobs, even relatively lowly ones, in local tourism and hospitality establishments." John S. Akama, "Neocolonialism, Dependency and External Control of Africa's Tourism Industry," in *Tourism and Postcolonialism*, ed. C. Michael Hall and Hazel Tucker (London: Routledge, 2004), p. 149.

11. John Lea, *Tourism and Development in the Third World* (London: Routledge, 2001), p. 46.

12. Selling handicrafts continues to be popular because of the universal desire by tourists to bring home souvenirs—something tangible after spending money on intangibles such as travel.

13. M. Thea Sinclair and Mike Stabler, *The Economics of Tourism* (London: Routledge, 1977), p. 141.

14. H. Goodwin, "Tourism and Natural Heritage: A Symbiotic Relationship," in *Environmental Management and Pathways to Sustainable Tourism*, ed. M. Robinson et al. (Sunderland, Tyne and Wear, England: Business Education Publishers, 2000), pp. 97–112, cited in "Background Note by the OMT/WTO Secretariat," *Tourism in the Least Developed Countries*, ed. David Diaz Benavides and Ellen Perez-Ducy (Madrid: World Tourism Organization, 2001).

15. World Tourism Organization, "Contribution of the World Tourism Organization," p. 4.

16. Diaz Benavides and Perez-Ducy, "Background Note."

17. World Tourism Organization, *Enhancing the Economic Benefits of Tourism for Local Communities and Poverty Alleviation* (Madrid: 2002), p. 29.

18. Diaz Benavides and Perez-Ducy, "Background Note."

19. *New York Times*, June 10, 2004.

20. Sylvia Chant, "Gender and Tourism Employment in Mexico and the Philippines," in Sinclair, *Gender, Work and Tourism*, p. 156.

21. For an overview of the literature on carrying capacity, see Peter Williams and Alison Gill, "Addressing Carrying Capacity Issues in Tourism Destinations Through Growth Management," in *Global Tourism*, 3rd ed., ed. William Theobald (Amsterdam: Elsevier, 2005).

22. Philip Pearce, "The Role of Relationships in the Tourist Experience," in *Global Tourism*, 3rd ed., ed. William Theobald (Amsterdam: Elsevier, 2005), p. 103.

23. David Harrison, "International Tourism and the Less Developed Countries: The Background," in *Tourism and the Less Developed Countries*, ed. David Harrison (London: Belhaven Press, 1992), p. 11.

24. More countries are listed in Group A here than in Chapter 1 because more countries have reported these data.

25. There are countries with extraordinarily high numbers of tourists per capita that could not be included here because of the unavailability of expenditure data. According to the World Travel and Tourism Council, they include

Saba (6.00), St. Maarten (5.76), North Mariana Islands (5.69), and St. Eustatius (4.04), among others (World Travel and Tourism Council, *Travel and Tourism—Forging Ahead*, the 2004 Travel and Tourism Economic Research Country League Tables (Madrid: 2004), Tables 46, 52.

26. Erik Holm-Peterson, "Institutional Support for Tourism Development in Africa," in *The Political Economy of Tourism Development in Africa*, ed. Peter U.C. Dieke (New York: Cognizant Communication Corporation, 2000), p. 195.

27. World Tourism Organization, *Enhancing the Economic Benefits of Tourism*, p. 36.

28. Ibid., p. 39.

29. Ibid., p. 42.

30. Donald Reid, *Tourism, Globalization and Development* (London: Pluto Press, 2003), p. 2.

31. World Tourism Organization, "Contribution of the World Tourism Organization," p. 5.

32. *CondeNast Traveler*, November 2004, pp. 85–108.

33. Tourism Concern, "The International Network on Fair Trade in Tourism," www.tourismconcern.org.uk (accessed March 4, 2004).

34. James Mak, *Tourism and the Economy* (Honolulu: University of Hawaii Press, 2004), p. 120.

35. World Tourism Organization, Enhancing the Economic Benefits of Tourism, p. 48.

36. Ibid.

37. Press release, Conservation International, April 2, 2003.

38. World Tourism Organization, *Enhancing the Economic Benefits of Tourism*, p. 47.

39. Created in 1972, Tai National Park is west Africa's largest tropical rain forest. It was designated by UNESCO as a Biosphere Reserve in 1978 and as a World Heritage Site in 1982; tourists come there to watch chimpanzees that, unlike those in other African parks, use tools to break the nuts they eat. Ibid.

40. See John Urry, *The Tourist Gaze: Leisure and Travel in Contemporary Societies* (Newbury Park, CA: Sage Publications, 1990).

41. Allan M. Williams and C. Michael Hall, "Tourism, Migration, Circulation and Mobility: The Contingencies of Time and Place," in C. Michael Hall and Allan M. Williams, *Tourism and Migration, New Relationships Between Production and Consumption*, ed. C. Michael Hall and Allan M. Williams (Dordrecht, The Netherlands: Kluwer Academic Publishers, 2002), p. 22.

42. Ibid., p. 23.

43. Nazli Choucri, "Cross-border Movements of Population in a 'Fair Globalization,'" *Development* 48, no. 1 (2005), p. 44.

44. Williams and Hall, "Tourism, Migration, Circulation and Mobility," p. 24.

45. Lundberg, Stavenga, and Krishnamoorthy, *Tourism Economics*, p. 18.

46. C. Aitken and C. M. Hall, "Migrant and Foreign Skills and Their Relevance to the Tourism Industry," *Tourism Geographies: An International Journal of Place, Space and the Environment* 2, no. 3 (2000), p. 66–86.

47. Cited in Williams and Hall, "Tourism, Migration, Circulation and Mobility," p. 30.

48. L. J. Lickorish and C. L. Jenkins, *An Introduction to Tourism* (Oxford: Butterworth-Heineman, 1997), p. 179.

49. World Bank, "Tourism in Africa," Findings Report #22617, *Environmental, Rural and Social Development Newsletter,* July 2001.

50. World Tourism Organization, *Enhancing the Economic Benefits,* p. 40.

51. Valene Smith, *Hosts and Guests: The Anthropology of Tourism,* 2nd ed. (Philadelphia: University of Pennsylvania Press, 1989), p. 7.

52. Some 90,000 Indonesians have thus been reported "missing," aided by some twenty syndicates who cater to the demand. Y. Sulaiman, "Some 90,000 Indonesian Tourists Reported Missing," www.eTurbonews.com (accessed October 14, 2004).

53. *New York Times,* October 13, 2004.

54. Diaz Benavides and Perez-Ducy, "Background Note."

55. M. Thea Sinclair, "Gendered Work in Tourism: Comparative Perspectives," in Sinclair, *Gender, Work and Tourism,* p. 232.

56. There is a vast literature on sex tourism. See, for example, Barbara Ehrenreich and Arlie Russell Hochschild, eds., *Global Women: Nannies, Maids, and Sex Workers in the New Economy* (New York: Metropolitan Books, 2003).

57. Williams and Hall, "Tourism, Migration, Circulation and Mobility," p. 29.

58. Ibid., p. 1.

59. M. Thea Sinclair, "Issues and Theories of Gender and Work in Tourism," in Sinclair, *Gender, Work and Tourism,* p. 5.

60. Ibid., p. 4.

61. C. M. Hall, "Gender and Economic Interests in Tourism Prostitution," in *Tourism, A Gender Analysis,* ed. V. Kinnaird and D. Hall (Chichester, UK: Wiley, 1994); W. Lee, "Prostitution and Tourism in South-east Asia," in *Working Women, International Perspectives on Labour and Gender Ideology,* ed. N. Redclift and M. T. Sinclair (London: Routledge, 1991).

62. In order to offset that trend, the mayor is preparing a project to attract small businesses by offering them space in a less developed part of town called Arsenale (there will, however, be no tax breaks). *New York Times,* June 10, 2004.

63. Peter Penz (in collaboration with Jay Drydyk and Pablo Bose), "Population Displacement by Development, Justifiability and Wrong-Doing" (paper presented to the International Studies Association Annual Convention, Honolulu, Hawaii, March 1–5, 2005), p. 3. World Bank statistics were used by Penz.

64. Ibid.

65. G. Young discussed the case of St. Lucia in the Caribbean, where labor migrated into the tourist industry and abandoned the lucrative banana industry, which until then had been the chief source of foreign income. The banana crop subsequently failed owing to labor shortages and low productivity of those remaining, and food had to be imported, straining the balance of payments.

Tourists, Migrants, and Refugees

Tourism did not offset that strain. G. Young, *Tourism, Blessing or Blight?* (Harmondsworth, UK: Penguin, 1973).

66. *Economist*, March 6, 2004, p. 34.

67. *Economist*, March 26, 2005, p. 40.

68. World Tourism Organization, *Enhancing the Economic Benefits of Tourism,* p. 50.

69. It was so successful that the experience was replicated in other sites, with the funding of the US Agency for International Development (USAID) and other donors.

70. Reid, *Tourism, Globalization and Development*, p. 74.

71. World Tourism Organization, *Enhancing the Economic Benefits of Tourism,* p. 45.

72. The project has a training program for tour guides and service employees. It also provides incentives to farmers to concentrate their agricultural activities on flatlands instead of mountain slopes. In that way the mountains will regain their natural forest cover, and the flatlands, where productivity is higher anyway, will supply the food for the local population as well as the tourists. With respect to wood for house construction and other purposes, villagers will obtain that from outside the park. Ibid.

73. Archer, Cooper, and Ruhanen, "The Positive and Negative Impacts of Tourism,"p. 83.

74. For example, in the Caribbean the St. Croix Leatherback Recovery project allows tourists to help out with the turtles, finding, recording, and ultimately helping hatchlings make their way to sea. This volunteer project is less damaging since it is unlikely that a local person would be hired to perform the job. *American Way*, May 15, 2004, p. 27.

75. Since the 1970s, Malaysian tourism as well as development in the form of logging, mining, dam construction, and oil palm plantations has taken lands away from the Dayaks of Sarawak. *Survival* reports that they now have poor nutrition, lack employment, and live in appalling sanitation. "Tribes Defy Loggers," *Survival, 1998.*

76. Donald Reid, *Tourism,Globalization and Development,* p. 11.

77. Brian Copeland, "Tourism, Welfare and De-Industrialization in a Small Open Economy," *Economica* 58 (November 1991), p. 527.

78. World Bank, *World Development Report, 1995* (New York: Oxford University Press, 1995), p. 68.

79. See, for example, Stephen Castles and Mark J. Miller, *The Age of Migration: International Population Movements in the Modern World* (London: Macmillan, 1993), p. 65.

80. R. Appleyard, "International Migration and Development—An Unresolved Relationship," *International Migration* 30, no. 3-4 (1992).

81. This has huge implications for policy. Indeed, the relative importance of these costs and benefits underlies migration, immigration, and emigration policies of countries. When the pain associated with inflows of migrants becomes too high, countries alter their immigration policies to stop the flow. Al-

ternatively, when the benefits exceed the costs, immigration policies become more receptive.

82. Indeed, countries such as the United States and Switzerland have been absorbers of qualified workers for decades: it is estimated that the United States saved some four billion dollars in training costs of its labor force from World War II until the 1960s. D. N. Chorafas, *The Knowledge Revolution* (New York: McGraw Hill, 1968), p. 56.

83. *Miami Herald*, September 26, 2004.

84. T. W. Shultz estimated losses on the basis of educational costs, whereas Gary Becker, Jacob Mincer, and Mary Jean Bowman emphasized internal rates of return. For a discussion of these, see Robert Myers, *Education and Immigration* (New York: David McKay, 1972), p. 178.

85. Among others, see Melanie Smith, *Issues in Cultural Tourism* (London: Routledge, 2003), p. 121.

86. World Bank, "Sustainable Coastal Tourism Development," Project Appraisal Document, Report no. 20412-MOR (June 16, 2000), p. 28.

87. World Tourism Organization, *Enhancing the Economic Benefits of Tourism,* p. 42. This program of integrating local communities was so successful that it was then applied to resort development in other parts of the Indonesia.

88. Authorities developed developed accommodations in the traditional styles, built of indigenous materials. Local cooperatives are responsible for the operation of the camps and the allocation of the profits. The Lower Casamance region was chosen for this project because the distance between villages is quite small and the local culture is colorful. Villages were invited, not forced, to participate. (Ibid., p. 40.)

89. Ibid., pp. 54–55.

5

Refugees and Internally Displaced Peoples

A wilderness safari company offers a three-day stay with the Kalahari Bushmen in their natural environment. For a whopping fee, tourists can witness meal preparation, participate in hunting and gathering, and enjoy flavorful local storytelling (and then retreat to their luxury tents that deny few Western comforts). In the hills of Bolivia, families offer simple accommodations to their visitors as well as the opportunity to witness household members engage in their daily chores.

Visiting villages and homes to observe social customs and traditional occupations is, according to Deborah McLaren, "one of the fastest growing segments of the consumer travel market."[1] The importance of this so-called ethnic or indigenous tourism is so great that governments have recognized the economic potential of exotic ethnicities and are promoting them. Cultures once forgotten and looked down upon are now being touted as exotic and unique. This occurs in Western countries such as Australia and New Zealand, where B. Kirschenblatt-Gimblett showed that in national marketing campaigns, indigenous peoples were becoming more prominent in tourist destinations.[2] In the United States, cultural activities such as hula dancing greet tourists at the Hawaii airport even though such dancing was banned when the islands were first annexed.[3] Tej Vir Singh described the collaboration between the Sheraton Resort in Phoenix and the Maricopa and Pima tribes that offer visits to the Gila River Indian Reservation.[4] Developing countries are not oblivious to this new trend. Indeed, in Indonesia, the Toraja house was chosen as the design on the 5,000 rupiah bill after decades of shunning of the Torajan culture.[5] Authorities in Namibia are urging the indigenous populations in the Spitzkoppe Community Tourist Rest Camp to share their knowledge with visitors through cultural performances and guided tours around the region.[6] Part of the Vietnamese Babe National Park Ecotourism project entailed "encouraging the park villages to maintain their traditional architectural styles and the villagers to retain their mostly traditional customs, which are of interest to tourists, and maintain cultural identities of the ethnic groups."[7] In Paraguay, authorities promote indigenous culture, and the official tourist board brochures offer tours that bring tourists in close proximity to such cultures.[8]

Touting indigenous cultures for the purpose of luring tourists is potentially a minefield. Indeed, what happens when prime beach properties or land with the best game are inhabited by indigenous tribes that are largely outside the mainstream economy or have no desire to perform for the tourists? As noted by Deborah McLaren, "the problem is that tourist businesses often do not own what they sell."[9] That includes the land where tribes reside as well as their cultures and traditions. Even though some LDC governments may attempt to secure the cooperation of indigenous populations and to find workable solutions, more likely than not they will simply uproot targeted peoples and relocate them elsewhere. As Melanie Smith noted, "in many cases, tribal groups have been forcibly moved from their homeland so that a national park, hotel complexes or golf-courses can be developed."[10] In other words, to maximize potential revenues from golf courses, safari camps, and sprawling hotels, entire tribes and communities are displaced. This scenario became a reality in western Nepal, where people were moved from their lands to make space for Lake Rara National Park; in Penang, Malaysia, where fishing communities were displaced by beach hotels; and in Kenya and Tanzania, where the Maasai were excluded from essential grazing lands by the creation of game parks.

One might shrug and ask, what is new about that? Involuntary migrations have been a part of history, ongoing since time immemorial. As noted in Chapter 2, no historical period and no continent have escaped them. The population displacements under discussion in this chapter did not occur because of political upheavals, wars, or revolutions, however, but for the development of tourism.

There are two reasons, both based on economic incentives, why such displacement occurs. The first has to do with the opportunity cost of the land inhabited by the indigenous population and the economic incentives that governments have for realizing that land's potential on the market. In order for a government to care sufficiently about a tribal population to displace them, there must be economic interest in the land they inhabit. Thus, it is a matter of overriding economic incentives on the part of the leadership. The second economic reason for displacement of indigenous groups is their potential for disrupting tourism, either as an eyesore or because they pose a threat of belligerent behavior (political unrest and interethnic conflict).

This chapter contains a discussion of the last of the three population flows that are an integral part of the circular flow of populations. Involuntary dislocations occur in response to tourist demand, as did the labor migrations discussed in Chapter 4. This chapter describes how dislocations occur, both with respect to the actual mechanics of removing people from their homes and to the justifications in which perpetrators cloak their actions. Then the two economic reasons for tourist-related population displacements noted above are linked to ethnicity. This chapter will revisit the relationship between growth and interethnic competition by indicating how tourism represents the potential for growth that induces economic competition to take place along ethnic lines. The chapter ends with a discussion of the negative implications of displacement for the very tourist industry that LDC authorities want to promote.

Unfortunately, supporting data were hard to come by because governments do not publicize how many people they have displaced. Instead, their actions are monitored and scrutinized by various international bodies. As noted in Chapter 3, numerous NGOs act as watchdogs and publicize their findings so that incidents of population displacement for the expansion of tourism have become well documented. As a result, this chapter relies on information from NGOs, the organization Survival, and *New Internationalist.*

Population Displacement: Definitions

In contemporary international jargon, several terms pertaining to displaced peoples convey information about their host destination, their international status, and the proximate push that induced them to move.

Refugees have been defined as those individuals who flee from man-made disasters. The most commonly used definition is that of the 1951 UN Convention on Refugees, according to which refugees are "people who are outside of their own country, owning to a well founded fear of persecution, for reasons of race, religion, nationality, membership of a particular social group, or political opinion."[11] Leon Gordenker amplified this by defining refugees as "persons who have left their customary homes under the pressure of fear for their present or future lives, because of immediate, overt threats or—more comprehensively—clear denials of basic human rights whose enjoyment is required for continued life over a short or longer period."[12]

Irrespective of the precise reason for their displacement, refugees cross international borders. They then also become broadly classified as immigrants, asylum seekers, and/or undocumented persons.

If displacement occurs within state boundaries, then it is called internal displacement. Internally displaced people are forced to migrate but remain within the state and therefore within government jurisdiction. A large-scale study undertaken by Roberta Cohen and Francis M. Deng highlighted the magnitude of such migration.[13] They found that the number of internally displaced people across the globe was significantly higher than that of refugees—some thirty million, compared to some twenty-three million refugees in 1994. Although China had the largest number of internal migrants, the Sudan had the largest internally displaced population. By some accounts Turkey ranked second in the world, with three million displaced at the end of 1997.[14]

Despite their greater number, internally displaced persons fail to receive the world attention given to refugees. Indeed, international organizations, media, and governments focus their efforts on the plight of refugees more than that of internally displaced persons. This happens for two principal reasons. First, there is less information about internally displaced persons because they are monitored by the home state. Therefore, it is the home government that controls information and its uses. Second, international law covers refugees but does not cover internally displaced persons. The comparison of refugees and internally displaced peoples pivots on one aspect of their definitions, namely the existence or lack of a border crossing.[15] The reason why this detail is of paramount importance is that it determines the international protection and aid for which people are eligible. According to UN covenants, refugees are entitled to specific protection and aid.[16] Thus, even though international organizations can operate within a receiving host country to ensure that refugees get what they are entitled to, they have no comparable rights within the home state. This distinction is most evident when it comes to human rights. According to Luke Lee, "although refugees and internally displaced persons are entitled to the same basic human rights, international protection of the latter poses the question of its compatibility with the traditional concepts of national sovereignty and non-interference in the internal affairs of a state."[17] In other words, organizations have no legal basis for operation within borders of sovereign states, especially when uninvited by host governments (sometimes host states allow operations but impose restrictions, such as a tax on the wages of aid workers or some proportion of aid supplies).

One subset of internally displaced peoples consists of so-called native or indigenous peoples. These are longtime residents of a territory that has been claimed and settled by colonial newcomers. Although such occupations have taken place in several ways, the result has always been the dislocation of the native population.[18] As a result, there are currently several Western democracies that house native peoples whose ancestors occupied the land before Europeans arrived. These are Canada and the United States (home to the Inuit and other native peoples), New Zealand (the Maoris), Australia (the Aborigines and the Torres Strait Islanders), Japan (Ainu), and Greenland (Inuit).[19] Indigenous populations also exist in South and Central America and in Africa. It is also erroneous to think that only whites displaced indigenous populations: for example, in Rwanda, it was the Twa (Pygmies) who inhabited the land before the Tutsis and the Hutus arrived. Although involuntary displacement of these indigenous populations occurred for economic reasons, those did not include tourism (indeed, it is unlikely that the architects of the reservations systems of the twentieth century ever imagined someone would pay to visit them, as they do in the twenty-first).

Population Displacement for the
Expansion of Tourism: The Mechanics

In the aftermath of the tsunami of 2004, refugee fishermen in the Thai province of Phangnga rushed home from the shelters because they feared their land would be taken over by the authorities and turned into tourist resorts.[20] They do not legally own the land. They occupy it with official squatters' rights. It would not be the first time that these people lost land they had used throughout their lifetimes, all for the sake of tourism.

This happens because tourism development requires land, be it beachfront property, jungle, desert, or sacred sites. It also requires access to water. As noted above, sometimes those resources are controlled by people who have no interest in developing tourism. In that case, more often than not authorities remove the impediment to development—in other words, they remove the resisting populations.

In an earlier study, I identified two ways of executing this removal, direct and indirect.[21] The direct way is simply to physically remove peoples from their residences using force; the indirect way entails harassment and pressures that cause people to leave (including the denial of rights, employment restrictions, confiscation of land, and so on). In theory, there is a difference between the loss of property rights and physical removal at gunpoint. In practice, however, the border between them is slippery owing to the lack of clearly defined property rights, legal recourses, and human rights in many developing countries. In cases of dealing with indigenous populations who are out of the mainstream, governments have not let the indirect means take their courses but rather have chosen the more direct path.

Forced population displacements are fundamentally different from the displacement of labor discussed in Chapter 4, in which people become structurally unemployed and their lack of livelihood indirectly induces them to leave. Those people are neither singled out by ethnicity nor physically removed from their homes.

Direct Population Expulsion

In an expulsion, individuals or entire communities are simply given a time period during which they must vacate their homes. Often they are forced at gunpoint to collect their belongings while their homes are destroyed, their farms bulldozed, and their crops burned. Examples abound. In Guatemala, 300 campesino families were evicted in 1996 to make way for a tourist complex.[22] They were told they had no claims to the land and thus the burning of their homes was justified. Padaung communities in Myanmar were forcefully displaced to make way for large-scale ecotourism facilities.[23] In west Nepal, the Chhetri people were moved from their lands for the development of tourism at Lake Rara National Park. In Sri Lanka, the hunting-gathering Wanniya-laeto were evicted from Madura Oya National Park in 1983 and forced to become rice-cultivating peasants (those who stayed behind were abused because their activities were against park regulations).[24] In Thailand, villagers were evicted so that foreign investors could expand tourist facilities.[25]

Indirect Population Expulsion

Land provides the principal source of sustenance for a large portion of LDC populations. It is a source of employment, income, livelihood, status, and pride. As a result, regulations that determine rights to land ownership and/or use are by definition a sensitive matter. If indigenous people do not have those rights in a world where a Western system of land rights reigns, then they cannot sell their land, lease it, use it for collateral for a loan, or pass it on as inheritance. It cannot be a source of income. Thus, when a segment of the population is prevented from using its land to start a new business or apply for agricultural credit, they have an inducement to seek greater opportunities elsewhere.

In many developing countries, especially in Africa, the question of land ownership is complicated because land is often held communally. This type of social organization relies on tradition that dictates the economic activities of the tribal members as well as the space in which they are performed. David Weaver, in his study of tourism and communal ownership, discussed Malawi, where two-thirds of the land is owned communally.[26] There, people work on the land on which their forefathers worked. Like the feudal lords of Europe, the chief holds land in trust for the tribe. When developers want to buy land in order to build on it, they have to work through the chief. But there are no papers, as agreements historically tended to be verbal. This unclear and potentially unstable situation makes foreign investors nervous. For this reason, it has been said that the communally held lands participate only marginally in tourism, whereas the privately held lands have sophisticated tourism sectors.[27] To rectify this imbalance, LDC authorities are motivated to dismantle what they view as archaic forms of land use. The governments of Kenya and Tanzania provide an example: they tried to obliterate the Maasai system of shared access to land and tried to impose collectives, such as group ranches in Kenya and pastoral associations in Tanzania.[28]

Even if land is communally owned and owners have no formal deeds, authorities can make people's presence on the land illegal simply by withdrawing the right of usage. By doing so, they are indirectly inducing people to migrate. The example of the Samburu herdsmen in Kenya's Shaba Reserve clearly illustrates this indirect pressure. Water that was previously used for cattle was diverted to fill the swimming pool of the Sarova Shaba Hotel.[29] As a result, the herdsmen had to leave their land and seek livelihood elsewhere. Similarly, when the Sariska National Park was created in Rajasthan (India) in 1984, tribal people inhabiting twenty-four villages were made illegal residents and thus were indirectly forced to vacate.[30] These examples of indirect population expulsion show how the loss of control over resources essential to the survival of the population, such as watering holes for animals and grazing lands for cattle, induces people to move.

One might wonder how such behavior goes unnoticed by international organizations that monitor behavioral transgressions. Indeed, how do LDC authorities expropriate land and resources for the sake of tourism without sparking the ire of watchful human rights activists? They do so by being ingenious. They do so by finding acceptable ways of achieving their goals. One of these ways entails the conversion of communal lands into private lands, followed by a purchase for tourism development. For example, when governments in Tanzania and Kenya subdivided communal ranges into private plots, some Maasai acquired good land and then sold it to developers. A similar pattern was evident in Panama in 2004. The proposed expansion of the Panama Canal, necessary to accommodate tourist demand as well as modern cargo ships, would devastate some jungle villages. In one of these, San Pedro, part of the Indian village would become a lake, and thousands would be forced off their land. Under the auspices of campaigning activists and church groups, the local population had come to suspect that none of the $6 billion renovation project would go to build the schools and hospitals that they desire. To circumvent the mounting local resistance (as well as the international uproar generated when news of the plan became public), the authorities gave out land titles to the populations along the waterways with the hope that at least some inhabitants would be lured into selling their land.[31]

Whatever the means by which expulsion occurs, the end result may not be what was hoped for. Indeed, the curtailment of indigenous livelihood activities by the authorities sometimes backfires and leads to poorer populations and no additional tourists. The example of Pretorius Kop is a case in point. In this region of South Africa's Kruger National Park, one effect of the park's enclosure was to prohibit the tribal populations from burning soil and grazing cattle.[32] As a result, thick brush grew, changing the wildlife population from large savannah species to smaller, less easily seen forest animals. But visiting tourists want to see large game (namely, the big five: elephants, lions, rhinoceroses, water buffalo, and leopards), so it led to the decrease in popularity of that section of the park.

Direct and Indirect Population Expulsion: The Case of Botswana's Bushmen

The Bushmen of southern Africa represent a well-documented illustration of contemporary population displacement.[33] As they have become the darlings of Survival, an international watchdog organization supporting indigenous rights, their plight has been brought into the limelight. Consequently, the Bushmen have received media attention shared by few other disadvantaged groups. A commercial film about their lives was so successful that it generated a sequel; a novel about an anthropologist studying their customs won the National Book Award.[34]

Who are these people? The nomadic Bushmen, numbering some 90,000,[35] are not a single homogeneous entity but rather encompass numerous groups that speak different languages (although they all use the distinguishing click). They were the first inhabitants of southern Africa, their territory stretching from Angola to Zimbabwe and reaching well into Namibia, Botswana, Zambia, and South Africa. As the agricultural Bantu peoples arrived from the north, the Bushmen were slowly pushed into less fertile land. Later, white farmers pushed them farther into marginal land. In order to survive, they became adept at exploiting scarce resources such as vegetation and animals. They are the only people known to be able to survive without surface water.

The experience of Botswana's Bushmen (most of whom belong to the San subgroup) began to diverge from that of the others when in 1961 the government created the Central Kalahari Game Reserve (CKGR). At some 20,800 square miles (52,000 square kilometers) in size, it was the third largest in Africa. It was originally intended for the Bushmen and the wildlife they hunted. At the time, the San population in the reserve was about 5,000 (others lived outside the reserve). By 2001, it had dwindled to 1,000–1,400. What had happened?

The number of inhabitants dropped largely as a result of the government efforts to transform the seminomadic San into sedentary farmers. These efforts began in the 1960s and picked up momentum during the 1980s, in the name of protecting wildlife and promoting tourism.

Several indirect methods of eviction were used. Authorities restricted the numbers of animals the San were allowed to hunt, making them dependent on government rationing. It was said that the authorities selectively enforced wildlife laws in an effort to intimidate. It was also claimed that some San were abused and harmed by wildlife officials for exceeding their hunting allowance.[36] In the late 1980s and early 1990s, the policy of "freezing" was adopted in the Kalahari reserve. Afrol News reported: "When the borehole at !Xade, the largest community in the reserve, broke down, it took months before it was fixed. Buildings and roads were not maintained in the reserve, except for those going to the Department of Wildlife and National Parks camps. Even drought relief feeding programs were slower in the Central Kalahari than elsewhere in Botswana, according to the American Anthropological Association."[37] Since the early 1980s, the government had been trucking water and mobile health clinics into the reserve. That was discontinued in 2002.[38] Government trucks arrived at the Kalahari reserve and dumped the community's water into the desert sand and then took away the tank. They also dismantled the people's thatched stick huts and loaded the people away to a resettlement camp ten hours away, called New Xade.[39] The government cited cost reasons, saying that the $9,500 per month for trucking in water and health clinics was too high (which Survival International spokesperson Fiona Watson dismissed, citing a grant for some $10 million to develop game parks and national reserves).[40]

Once relocated, the lives of the San did not improve. There are presently sixty-three resettlement villages where most of Botswana's 50,000 San people have been relocated. One of these, New Xade, is home to some 1,500 people. There is a school where children are taught classes in Setswana and English rather than the click tongue of the San. None of the graduates of the school has found a job. There are no traditional bush foods to gather. Most people, especially the young, sit around and do nothing but drink homemade beer. The government had made an offer to the displaced, that they would be given a concrete block houses and five head of cattle in order to start anew. Years later, people complained that their houses were unfinished and that lions had killed their calves.[41] There are no jobs, there is no grazing for goats and cattle, no veldt food to gather, no wild animals to hunt. The nearest town is more than 43 miles (70 kilometers) away, an expensive and difficult three-hour journey.[42] There are reports of some displaced people who were successful. They used an allocation of $3000 to buy a pickup truck and sell homemade beer and groceries.[43] Meanwhile, those who try to return to their old homes are met by guards blocking the entrance to the Kalahari reserve and are ticketed for failing to wear seat belts, for driving without a license, or for registration technicalities. Their vehicles are confiscated, thus preventing future attempts at return-migration.[44]

With dwindling hunting grounds, and reduced to subsistence and disenfranchised, the San Bushmen experienced textbook pressures to relocate. Indeed, many of the methods of indirect inducement described above were put to use in the Kalahari. Although government officials say the relocations were voluntary, San spokesmen have spoken of intimidation and forced relocation.[45] According to the organization Survival, the government methods to evict the San have included torture, intimidation, oppression, and starvation.[46] Almost half a century after the creation of the CKGR, there is no agreement as to the precise nature of the population evictions. That is but one of the reasons why the San Bushmen are pitted against the authorities. More important is that the two sides have fundamentally different goals. Those who speak in the Bushmen name claim that all they want is to be left alone, to pursue their hunting and gathering activities as they did before the creation of the CKGR. They want to protect their right to their resources (especially in light of efforts by the government to push a bill through parliament eliminating a key clause in the constitution that protects Bushman rights[47]). They want to preserve the bush skills they have honed for generations. They also want to be close to the buried souls of their ancestors.[48] Although it is possible, even likely, that some Bushmen would like to participate in the development of tourism and benefit from lucrative opportunities, their voices have not been the loudest.

The Basarwa and Khwe San peoples have organized protests by forming indigenous advocacy organizations (such as Kgeikani Kweni [First People of the Kalahari]). They lobby at the national and international levels and have support from organizations such as Amnesty International, Survival, and others. World consciousness was raised when supermodel Iman quit as the public face of DeBeers in protest over the company's diamond mining business on the lands of the Kalahari Bushmen (many believe that mining business was behind the government decision to evict the Bushmen).[49] They organized international solidarity so that the Innu Indians from Canada and the Maasai from Kenya together stood vigil in front of the Botswana High Commission to protest the eviction of Bushmen from their lands.[50] Even foreign governments have been pulled into the conflict, on the side of the Bushmen (or at least paying lip service to their cause). In its 2004 annual report on human rights, the US State Department condemned Bushman evictions.[51] Attention was further called to the San evictions when the outgoing US ambassador, John Lange, condemned the government action. After visiting the Gana and Gwi San communities and their resettlement camps outside the Kalahari Reserve, he stated that the conditions were "unsustainable" and that the Bushmen should be able to choose where they live.[52] Moreover, the case of the San evictions was discussed in the European Parliament, and a member of the European Parliament's development committee visited the reserve to get a first-hand overview of the situation.[53]

The other side of the conflict, namely Botswana's government, has used numerous justifications for its actions. Although denying the torture allegations, authorities have insisted that displacement of the San was necessary in order to promote economic development and protect the environment (these justifications and others are discussed in the next section). The former implies promoting diamond mining (the world's largest open pit mine for commercial diamonds, Juaneng, is located in the CKGR). The slogan Diamonds for Development has been the government's battle cry as it promoted this lucrative sector. Moreover, the development of wildlife tourism in the game parks has added to the inflow of foreign currency. As a result, Botswana had the highest rates of economic growth in the world in 2002, and that was certainly not due to the hunting and gathering activities of the Bushmen. Without a doubt, the central government will have to reach an understanding with the international organizations (which are both providing the capital for the development of Botswana's resources and monitoring human rights) that takes into consideration the role of indigenous populations in the promotion of tourism.

Displacement of Populations for the Expansion of Tourism: The Justifications

The justifications for population displacement have differed over time, as each historical epoch has been characterized by its own particular behavioral norms and cultural standards. When European settlers first came to Australia, Canada, and the United States, annexing native resource-rich lands was couched in terms of spreading superior civilization and saving souls, and thus was deemed acceptable. Today, population evictions for the expansion of tourism are not so blatantly ethnocentric, but nevertheless the underlying economic motivation of control over lucrative resources is couched in politically correct terms. For this reason, environmental considerations have been touted as sufficient justification for displacement, as have economic development and its concomitant improvement in the standard of living. After all, few voices would argue against the conservation of the habitat or the spread of health care and education to larger segments of the population. Some common justifications used by LDC governments and the international organizations (which alternately condone or resist the displacement) are discussed in the following sections. Given the economic bias of this study, questions of social justice and morality of population displacements are not considered.

Third World Governments

Uganda's president Idi Amin justified the expulsion of the Indian population by citing their disproportional presence in the economy—a presence he said was due to unfair advantage that needed to be corrected. It is noteworthy that he found it necessary to justify his actions. After all, he was a dictator and it was the cold war—it was not a time of democratization, globalization, and the protection of human rights. In the early twenty-first century, under the watchful gaze of powerful democratic trading partners, an alert media, and muckraking NGOs, authorities in tourist-friendly countries exert great care in how they present population displacement policies. In accordance with international behavioral norms, they have found ways to sugarcoat such policies and argue their necessity for the sake of national objectives. One of these objectives is economic growth. By citing the link between tourism and economic growth, they claim that benefits will trickle down to the entire population, even those who had to be displaced. Alternatively, authorities raise environmental concerns and explain the beneficial conservation measures that can accompany displacement. The involvement of communities in development and tourism is another justification, and that goal can be better achieved when populations are spatially concentrated (even if that requires displacement). Their local culture can also be preserved in that way. Development, environmental protection, democratization, and promotion of local culture—all four, which are discussed below, are hard to argue against.

Incidentally, not all LDC population displacements are scrutinized. Information is often impossible to obtain, as many of the victims are illiterate and have no access to modern means of information dissemination. They do not vote and cannot make themselves heard, so the usual political costs of displacing them are not incurred.

Economic development. In Chapter 4, economic development as the underlying cause of population displacement was discussed with an emphasis on workers and structural unemployment. Here the focus is on displacement of targeted populations so they can better reap the benefits of development. In speaking about the Bushman population, L. Boyce Sebetele, a member of the Botswana government, stated, "We would like the residents of the CKGR to become part of the mainstream population and *benefit from the socio-economic development being enjoyed by all Botswana* [italics mine]."[54] The government insisted that its motives were to ensure that the Bushmen were not left behind in the development process. Its goal was to reduce the region's 35 percent poverty rate. Major General Moeng Pheto, in charge of the San relocations, said, "As a country and as a people we all have to change with the times. *We cannot live the lives our forefathers lived* [italics mine]."[55] In other words, the Bushmen needed to be propelled into the twenty-first century. This justification for the displacement of the Bushmen invokes a politically correct national goal, namely economic development. Under the guise of national modernization goals, authorities justify assembling people where they can more effectively provide services such as health care and education. Such displacement is considered acceptable because it is assumed to be Pareto optimal so that the benefits to overall society will outweigh the costs. The facts that benefits and costs are borne by different people and that those who suffer most from them are usually the quietest are often disregarded.

Environmental concerns and conservation. In order to enhance tourism, countries have taken steps to preserve their physical environment—that is, after all, what tourists come to see. The creation of national parks and wildlife reserves is part of this conservation effort, as described by John Lea.[56] To ensure good management of protected lands as well as the environment in general, authorities have introduced regulations and controls they deem to be essential. Among these is the restraint on selected traditional economic activities deemed harmful to the environment (such as fishing, hunting and gathering, grazing, and so on). When controls have proved difficult to enforce, authorities have displaced the populations whose lifestyles clash with conservation goals. The Maasai of Kenya were displaced to preserve land for game parks. In Uganda, in order to conserve the mountain gorilla, over 1,300 people were displaced.[57] In Jordan, the nomadic Bedouin were displaced for the sake of tourism because of the impact of their livestock grazing on biodiversity in Wadi Rum.[58]

The response to population displacement in order to conserve the environment has been strong. C. Deihl said that it is ironic "that one of the first steps in establishing a national park is to rid the region of its original caretakers."[59] In the same vein, Martin Mowforth and Ian Munt pointed out, "it is difficult to escape the realization that wildlife and the pastoral activities of the Maasai have managed to co-exist in the region for many centuries and that the landscape . . . was the product of their grazing and burning practices."[60] According to *Survival*, conservationists believe that to protect nature one must create wilderness where no humans live. Yet these very areas have been inhabited by human beings for thousands of years. "This idea of nature as wilderness provides a convenient cover for government programmes of forced assimilation."[61] Despite such verbal protests, third world governments continue to use the key words *conservation* and *environment* when they vacate indigenous lands.

Community involvement in tourism. When the British colonials expropriated African lands to dedicate them to wildlife preserves, they took the best land, replete with wetlands and water holes. The local Maasai were outraged, and they threatened to kill game if the issue was not resolved. In the absence of game, a wildlife preserve is not a wildlife preserve. Such pressure led to a compromise that entailed involving the local population in tourism, in other words, giving the Maasai a stake. Today, the Kenya Wildlife Service, together with the Kenyan government, enjoys a partnership that takes into account communities adjacent to wildlife parks as well as the private sector and landowners that might be affected. Anyone with a stake in the land and tourism has the right to be heard.

Community participation in conservation and tourism development on communal land has become a frequently invoked goal by LDC authorities. International organizations such as the WTO have also promoted the idea of empowering communities by giving them rights over wildlife and tourism.[62] Social scientists have also supported it: for example, Donald Reid offered a proposal for tourism planning that is community based, takes into consideration the local culture, and maintains the value system of the local community.[63] All this support of community involvement is based on the idea that it will lead to local empowerment and democratization. Who can argue against democracy?

But do empowerment and democratization of indigenous populations justify their displacement? For example, were the authorities justified in removing the Maasai from their land because they have since experienced local empowerment through the development of cultural Bomas?[64] To the extent that there has been increased democratization and that displaced people are given some measure of control over resources, are all sins then forgiven? Those who agree would take the argument one step further and state that this decentralization of power and the ensuing democratization would have been impossible without relocation. Although such an argument has been made by LDC authorities, its validity can only be determined on a case-by-case basis. The examples of the Iban and Kuna peoples illustrate such case-by-case examinations.

In Sarawak, Borneo (Indonesia), the largest ethnic group, the Iban, have been hosting tourists since the 1960s. Decisions pertaining to tourism are decentralized, giving rise to a multitude of arrangements at the local level. Indeed, the community's level of involvement ranges from supplying services to tour operators to controlling all tourism and accommodation facilities. In some cases, the community has also formed partnerships with ecotourism companies.[65] The Iban offer accommodation to tourists in their traditional longhouses for which tour operators pay a fee (determined by the tribal headman or elder). Others offer their labor, as tourism has increased the diversity of options they now have. They transport and work as jungle guides; they are cooks and cultural performers. According to Melanie Smith, "Iban people are allocated certain tasks or roles which are organized on a roster basis."[66] She concluded that, on the whole, Iban community tourism appeared to be managed fairly and effectively.

On the other side of the globe, some 30,000 Kuna Indians inhabit Panama's San Blas Islands (now renamed Kuna Yala). Their semiautonomous reserve consists of some fifty communities engaged in subsistence economic activities, including coconut trading, textile production (especially molas), commercial fishing, and migrant wage labor. Increasingly, tourism is adding to the cash economy. The region is unique insofar as the residents have retained control and major financial interest over their tourism industry.[67] Decisions pertaining to tourist projects, foreign investment, and local development rights are made by the chiefs and a select group of elders. My research visit to Kuna Yala suggested that, despite the increase in the number of tourists and the increased role of tourism in the local economy, little had changed in the decisionmaking process.[68]

Promotion of local culture. Another justification for tourist-induced population displacements is the preservation of indigenous cultures. The rationale is based on the view that without the tourist demand for exotic cultures, there would be no organized supply of such cultures, and over time, they would not sustain themselves. Local cultures would die out when they came into contact with the globalizing international economy and its homogenizing trends. Thus tourism helps maintain and preserve traditions that might otherwise be lost. Examples in support of this view abound. Among the Kuna Indians, Margaret Byrne Swain found that tourism had served to regenerate traditional industries by providing a market for the molas, as tourist demand had turned local culture into a lucrative business.[69] Balinese fishermen had a similar experience. As noted in Chapter 4, when the Nusa Dua Resort in Bali was developed, the fishing boats were not moved for fear of disrupting the villagers' livelihood. These fishing activities, so tied up with the Balinese culture, became of interest to tourists staying in the resort. This led to a new economic activity: taking tourists out for excursions and touting the role of fishing for Balinese culture.[70] Finally, among the Australian Aborigines, locals are perpetuating traditional art by producing sand paintings for lucrative export.[71]

In addition to empowering the local population through income-earning opportunities, the promotion of local culture through tourism also empowers people through a new appreciation of their history and roots. In her study of Eskimo peoples, Valene Smith showed how tourists have "contributed to the renaissance of Eskimo culture as they have shown the Eskimo that their culture is of great interest to tourists who are prepared to pay substantial sums to visit the arctic to see the Eskimo life-style. This reaffirms the sense of ethnic self-worth that had been eroded in the early years of [the twentieth] century by missionary, health and school personnel."[72] Melanie Smith described a similar renaissance taking place among the Samis of Lapland and northern Finland, the Maoris of New Zealand, and the Inuit of Arctic Canada.[73]

This promotion of local culture has led scholars to diverse conclusions. R. K. Hitchcock noted that tourism has "done more to promote hunting and gathering than all the efforts of anthropologists put together."[74] Theron Nunez pointed out an irony: "In order to survive and perpetuate their cultural integrity and identity, . . . traditional cultures . . . encourage and invite the most successful agents of change," namely, the tourists.[75] Meanwhile, third world governments continue to use the promotion of local cultures as a justification for displacing populations into a new location, more convenient for tourism.

International Community

As noted in Chapter 3, the international community is involved with LDC tourism not only by providing capital but also by setting guidelines, promoting trade of services and other economic activities, and overseeing progress in the development of the industry. The politics of the laws and their implementation are complicated, so a very simple overview is presented here, enough to provide a background to local and global activism on tourism issues.

When it comes to involuntary displacement of populations, international organizations have mostly played the role of watchdogs. They are also known to have been indirect perpetrators, however. As a result of these contradictory positions, sometimes one agency has butted against another in promoting mutually exclusive goals.

The World Bank, the European Union, and other multinational development agencies often underwrite mining, agroindustrial activity, roads, dams, and other projects. Such projects have had a negative affect on many people in developing countries, as Linda Richter noted.[76] Indigenous populations in particular are hurt. In the Philippines, since the 1970s, the World Bank has sponsored large infrastructure projects on tribal lands. Sacred sites have been defiled, and key agricultural areas have been destroyed by the construction of hydroelectric dams and geothermal power stations.[77] In Indonesia, the World Bank funded numerous transmigration policies that entailed sending millions of people to West Papua to relieve the overcrowded islands.[78] The private arm of the World Bank, the International Finance Corporation, is funding the BHP Billiton, the world's biggest mining company, in exploring the Kalahari Reserve for diamonds, without the consent of the traditional inhabitants.[79]

In addition to enduring the negative externalities of these development projects, indigenous populations are sometimes hurt even by international humanitarian efforts. Such efforts, aimed at coming to the rescue of one disadvantaged group, end up hurting another. Namibia provides a good example. There, the UN High Commissioner for Refugees (UNHRC), together with the Namibian government, was constructing a refugee camp in 2001 for 17,000 Angolans in the resource-scarce environment where the !Kung San lived.[80] The 6,000 !Kung of the Tsumkwe District West, a remote part of Namibia, were overwhelmed by the sheer size of the refugee camp. In order to survive, camp inhabitants supplemented their rations by foraging, hunting, engaging in petty commerce, and using firewood. Not only did such activities have grave environmental consequences, but they sharpened competition for scarce resources.

Are international organizations aware of the population displacements that sometimes occur in order to support their projects? Evidence indicates that they are. For example, the World Bank's assessment of pilot projects and future investments for tourism development entails checking off whether there was involuntary resettlement or not.[81] The WTO, the world's leading tourism organization, also recognizes that displacement occurs: "Tourism imposes substantial non-economic costs on the poor, *in terms of displacement,* lost access to resources, and cultural and social disruption [italics mine]."[82] International organizations know about the displacement because sometimes they participate in the cleanup (as in Uganda, when displaced villagers were compensated by funds from the US Agency for International Development (USAID)[83]).

That is when other Western organizations, both governmental and nongovernmental, step in to act as watchdogs, monitor behavior, and offer suggestions. They do so in the context of international law that prohibits the involuntary movement of people. They cite the Nuremberg Charter of 1945, for example, which makes mass deportation a crime against humanity, and the 1949 Geneva Convention Relative to the Treatment of Civilians in Time of War, which also prohibits forcible transfers, mass or individual.[84] Even the forced return of refugees, known as *refoulement,* is now illegal by international conventions.[85] Moreover, the UN Universal Declaration on Human Rights states that everyone has the right to leave any country and to return to his or her own country. Although this was adopted the year after the partition of Palestine into a Jewish and Arab state, its relevance has extended since then to many crisis spots in the world, including Rwanda and Bosnia. It can also be applied to involuntary migration due to tourism.[86]

Among the primary NGOs involved with issues of population displacement, indigenous land, conservation, and tourism are Survival, Tourism Concern, Rethinking Tourism Project, Center for World Indigenous Studies, and Cultural Survival. It has long been the contention of Survival that conflict between indigenous peoples and conservation forces can be avoided if people stop creating protected areas on indigenous territory and if they recognize tribal land rights. Increasingly this is happening in Brazil, Colombia, Ecuador, Peru, and Bolivia, where more land is now recognized as indigenous territory than as protected area.[87] Tourism Concern has been very involved with Fair Trade in Tourism (described in Chapter 3) according to which local stakeholders, namely the populations that inhabited the land before the onset of tourism, receive a fair share of its benefits.[88] The World Wide Fund for Nature (WWF) in 1996 adopted a statement of Principles on Indigenous Peoples and Conservation in which it recognized indigenous peoples' land rights and their right to control their resources, the need for informed consent for projects on their land, and the right to self-identification as peoples.[89]

Governmental organizations have also offered suggestions. The WTO General Assembly adopted the Global Code of Ethics for Tourism. Its Article 5 stated: "Local populations should be associated with tourism activities and share equitably in the economic, social and cultural benefits they generate."[90] Also, "tourism policies should be applied in such a way as to help raise the standards of living of the populations of the regions visited."[91] In its discussion of local communities, the WTO encourages governments to spread tourism development and, therefore, its benefits geographically. Thus, the Global Code of Ethics for Tourism sets a frame of reference for the responsible and sustainable development of world tourism.

The Effect of Displaced Peoples on the Expansion of Tourism

According to the United Nations, there are over one million displaced people in Darfur and over 100,000 of them have sought shelter in Chad.[92] What effect does the existence of these refugees have on tourism? Chad is not a major tourist destination, despite attaining the world's highest growth of the travel and tourism industry in 2004 (see Table 1.1). Chad has neighbors that are actively promoting desert tourism, however. Graphic images of hungry and ragged refugees in tent cities cannot but affect the Western traveler contemplating a vacation in nearby Mali and Niger.

The intersection of tourists and refugees is not unique to West Africa. So far we have looked at the displacement of peoples in order to make way for tourism; here the effect of displaced people on tourism is addressed. In other words, do Western tourists care if the water in their swimming pool has been diverted from a herding well on indigenous land and, as a result, hundreds of people have had to leave their homes? Do they care enough to decrease their demand for travel to a particular destination? Or do they only care when the displaced peoples are belligerent and their exodus mired in conflict and violence that pose a personal security risk?

Contradictory evidence exists in answer to these questions. There are numerous examples of displacement, whether for tourism or other reasons, which did not dampen the demand by visitors. The most blatant and large-scale case of displacement is that of South Africa: the Land Act of 1913 prevented blacks from owning land outside of a few arid, worthless parcels, thereby allotting 90 percent of the territory to whites. It resulted in the segregation and forced resettlement of blacks on ten ethnic reserves, where since 1960, 3.5 million blacks have been resettled.[93] Despite this obvious and large-scale discrimination, black homesteads such as Soweto have become tourist attractions sought out by Western tourists.

Similarly, Rio de Janeiro's travel agencies offer half-day trips into the Favelas where migrants from the rural areas eke out a living. Tourists visit refugee camps of the Saharawis in Algeria. Noble refugees and glorified aid workers have become the focus of commercial films starring high-profile actresses such as Angelina Jolie; refugee camps were the topic of a bestseller by the author of *Bridget Jones's Diary*.[94]

These examples are exceptions rather than the rule. In most cases the presence of refugees and internally displaced peoples, whether displaced for tourism or other reasons, has a negative affect on tourism. This is because the existence of refugees is usually associated with ethnic conflict, civil war, and terrorism. To the extent that the displaced pose a threat to order, then they are viewed as a security risk, and concomitant bad publicity further repels the tourist. Terrorist activity, with or without roots in population displacement, is focused on tourists who, as Michael Hitchcock pointed out, are soft targets for terrorists.[95] Among the goal of terrorists is the destablization of regimes dependent upon tourism receipts (such as Morocco and Kenya, as well as Spain and Turkey).

Tourists back away from destinations even when threats are not related to tourists. In Zimbabwe, Western tourists are turned off by government measures to confiscate white-owned land without compensation.[96] Similarly, tourists avoid the highly policed Isla Fuerteventura in the Canary Islands because it has become the point of illegal entry into the European Union.[97]

More often than not tourists have no sense of the conflict brewing and/or taking place behind the scenes. Authorities do their best to conceal it, and displaced populations are too marginalized to effectively reveal it. Therefore, most tourists who climb Ayers Rock are not told that they are violating Aborigine ancestral grounds; the guests in Goa's hotels do not know that there is conflict over water distribution to the local population. When tourists do not know that people have been displaced in order to accommodate them, they are unknowing participants in the process, since their demand reinforces the rationale of the perpetrating leaders. The call for responsible tourism is in part an effort to educate the tourist.

Interethnic Differences in Tourist-Friendly Countries

Traditionally, priorities of tourism development were the contribution to GNP, foreign exchange earnings, and employment. As a result, performance was measured by growth in arrivals and foreign exchange revenue.

Those measures ignore the distribution of tourist-generated benefits, however. To the extent that the rich benefit and the poor do not, tourist income serves to widen the schism between income groups. Brian Copeland showed numerous conditions under which the welfare loss associated with tourism outweighed the benefit to the local population.[98] More precisely, Reiner Jaakson said, "tourism may well increase the overall welfare in a country, but the direct benefits from tourism often accrue to only a small percentage of the population. Elites in developing countries consistently gain disproportionately more from tourism development, as for example through soaring land values and from favouritism in the participation in investments from abroad."[99] David Harrison cited numerous studies that show that multinational organizations and expatriates are the principal benefactors. He added that when domestic entrepreneurs arise, they tend to be from the preexisting business community, the one that is poised to make the most of the new opportunities tourism provides.[100] In other words, tourism enables the rich to get richer, which is what has occurred in Indonesia, where a significant portion of the economic benefits of Balinese tourism are passed to Javanese business interests that own much of the beachfront land.[101] Moreover, when the rich are also part of the governing elite, then control of tourism interests is consolidated within one group. This is the situation in Tonga, where the monarchic structure controls tourism,[102] and in Thailand, where the royal family (together with the Chinese commercial class and multinational investors) dominates tourism.[103]

In multiethnic states, in addition to a division between rich and poor, tourism also accentuates preexisting differences among ethnic, race, and linguistic groups. To the extent that the costs and benefits of tourism are borne by different segments of the population, the negative effects are especially acute for these minority ethnic groups (as was the case in Fiji in the 1980s). Tourism thus widens the bifurcation of society, forming a chasm between the empowered and the marginalized, the black and the white, the core and the periphery. This is the result of the interethnic struggle for economic and political power that occurs in multiethnic states (as discussed in Chapter 2).

Applied to tourism, this demographic struggle for power results in the following: those who benefit most from tourism's engine of growth and those who benefit least are of different ethnic groups. There is much support of this contention from scholarly literature. C. Michael Hall and Hazel Tucker claimed that "concepts such as gender, class, ethnicity and race become a ground for 'internal colonialism' in which identities are constrained and oppressed and selectively represented."[104] Thea Sinclair said that "the tourism labour force in destination areas is clearly segmented by gender and race."[105] She went on to say that, in fact, the entire tourism industry is characterized by subdivisions among workers in the form of gender and race. "While not as evident as those between tourism consumers and producers, such divisions are significant not only for the operation of tourism but for the relative incomes, status and power of those involved in it."[106] Cynthia Enloe also contributed to the literature on race, gender, and class divisions in tourism. Airlines, she argued, took their cues from the longer-established ocean liner companies in which a racial (and gendered) division of labor was used. "Initially, ocean-liner crews were male, ranked by class and race. The white officers were to exude both competence and romance for passengers. The Indonesian, Filipino and other men of color serving in the dining rooms and below deck reflected a comforting global hierarchy while permitting the company to pay lower wages."[107] Finally, Sinclair reported how racial divisions in the labor force became clear in the distribution of jobs within the luxury hotels, usually those owned by foreigners.[108] This is further accentuated in destinations where colonial structures have been inherited, namely structures that promote one group and deny rights to another. A study by Rosemary Jommo found that indigenous investors in hotels catering to international tourism went bankrupt, whereas those who were previously in the domestic tourism market succeeded.[109] As in many developing countries, the economic elites and politically powerful ethnic groups formed an alliance with foreign capital.

This racial and ethnic schism in the benefits of tourism is evident across the third world in countless examples. In Cameroon, the Bamileke, a rich tribal group, controls the luxury hotels.[110] In Bali, the higher-paid and higher-status occupations are not in the hands of locals.[111] In Java, there is evidence that ethnicity and tourism entrepreneurship are clearly related.[112] In Fiji, there is a discrepancy between ethnic groups when it comes to participation in the tourist industry, as the newcomer Indians are in low-status "laboring" jobs, whereas the indigenous Fijian populations hold the more prestigious jobs (waiters, receptionists, security guards).[113] Among local tour operators in Kenya, it was whites or Asians who succeeded, and souvenir shops, restaurants, and entertainment were all in the hands of nonblack Africans.[114] Similarly, in Trinidad there is at least the perception (if not the fact) that the benefits of development are unevenly divided between people of African and Indian descent.[115]

It therefore seems that in multiethnic states, participation in the tourist industry is somehow related to ethnicity. To the extent that membership in an ethnic group predisposes individuals to certain jobs and skills, affects their access to credit and capital, and ultimately determines their income, then interethnic competition is taking place. As proposed in Chapter 2, the greater the role of tourism in the economy, the more acute the interethnic competition for its benefits and for the control of tourist-related resources.

Adding involuntary population displacement into the mix highlights the interethnic schism because those who are displaced and those who displace belong to different ethnic groups. Indeed, it is not the dominant, high income, and privileged ethnic groups that get displaced to make space for tourism. Rather, it is the poor, illiterate, less modern, and more marginalized peoples who are involuntarily displaced. To the extent that displacement occurs for the sake of tourism development, disadvantaged ethnic groups bear most of the negative costs.

The Paradox of Indigenous Tourism

Cultural tourism, also known as indigenous tourism or ethnic tourism, occurs when visitors to third world countries seek out indigenous populations to fill their travel experience. According to S. Harron and R. Weiler, such tourism is based on direct contact with host cultures and environments.[116] J. Seabrook said that such tourism is undertaken to broaden horizons, whereas K. Kutay called such tourists "peace corps–type travelers looking for a meaningful vacation."[117] Whatever their emphasis, scholars agree that these tourists have the following common denominator: they seek an experience that is authentic, exotic, and different. In other words, these tourists want to experience the real; they want to sense the genuine (even if, as David Harrison noted, the authenticity that tourists seek, if found, will inevitably be lost for future tourists[118]). For that reason, they reject make-believe foreign cultures such as Disneyworld, Williamsburg, Hawaii's Polynesian Cultural Center, and Fiji's Orchid Island.[119] They have an anthropological desire to learn about other cultures—they are cultural voyeurs. Local culture becomes the end in itself. These wannabe anthropologists are travelers who want to break out of the usual tourist bubble. They are not mass or mainstream tourists. They are not drawn to Paris or London but rather to the hill tribes in Thailand and the Bushmen in Botswana. Irrespective of whether they choose rudimentary or luxury accommodations, it is the exotic that they seek. This drive to seek differentiation of the tourist experience is reflected in the title of a paper by Nina Prebensen, Svein Larsen, and Birgit Abelsen: "I'm Not a Typical Tourist."[120]

The supply response to this particular tourist demand has been quick and eager. Tour operators are offering "alternative format" tours that enable an authentic experience, including a one-to-one relationship between hosts and guests. They include overnight stays in authentic local homes and meals at the table with the hosts. Tourists get to observe and even participate in daily activities ranging from hunting to meal preparation. LDC governments, in planning tourism, consider the demand for tradition. Across Africa they sponsor wildlife parks dotted with indigenous villages. In Mexico's Baja California, they retained the sleepy provincial feel of colonial San Jose Cabo by keeping cruise ship visitors away (immediately adjacent is Cabo San Lucas for tourists who like large hotels and made-in-the-USA chain eateries, underscoring the difference between tourists at the two destinations).

Even though the supply response by tour operators and governments is straightforward, resting as it does on perceived demand and potential profits, the response by the local indigenous populations is uneven and complex. Some welcome tourism with open arms, hoping for money and what it buys; others resist change and cling to tradition.

Those who respond rationally to economic incentives supply their culture to Western tourists. In the process, they must deal with the changes in their culture brought about by tourism. Such change is inevitable. The engine of growth becomes an agent of change as job opportunities, rising incomes, and labor mobility alter traditional ways of doing and being. Indeed, although cultural tourists pride themselves on being subtle and leaving no footprint, their very presence is a footprint. Their demand alters preexisting markets, and thus foreign visitors become active participants in the structural transformation of LDC destinations. Under these circumstances, what are indigenous populations to do when their main tourist attraction, namely their traditional culture, is slipping away? The response differs from culture to culture and from one developing country to another. In some destinations, locals fake the authentic experience. As Paul Beedie said, they choreograph the tourist experience.[121] The Western tourists' demand for the exotic, Hall and Tucker said, "may lead to the invention of traditions and heritage for external consumption that meet visitor conceptions of the other."[122] Because ethnic tourism promises to show how people live, locals exaggerate traditions for greater impact. They contrive local dance performances, enhance rituals, and highlight traditional foods. In other words, they add color where it might have faded.

In her study of hill tribe trekking in Thailand, Melanie Smith described the lengths indigenous peoples will go to supply Western tourists with what they want: "Tourists assume that they are going native, staying in accommodation that is typical of the local style, eating basic foods, and are cloistered from the trappings of the material world. It is only when you venture further afield that you realize that some of the villagers are actually living in brick houses down the road with satellite television and well-stocked local grocery stores!"[123] Mowforth described a similar situation in a Bushmen camp in remote Botswana. When the residents see a tourist Jeep arriving, they drop whatever they are doing and quickly pull off their T-shirts, trousers, and cotton dresses and begin to dance.[124] R. K. Hitchcock found a similar situation: tourist demand in the Kalahari Desert led to the creation of inauthentic villages where Bushmen activities included what tourists wanted to see but few Bushmen actually did anymore.[125]

Not all indigenous populations want to be ogled and photographed; not everyone wants their daily life put under a microscope. In ethnic tourism, the people and their lifestyles become commodities, as interesting as their landscapes.[126] Culture and wildlife are tied together in the tourist's mind because traditionally the animals and the indigenous populations inhabited the same land. This has led to the complaint that people are not accorded the respect that humans deserve, that there has been a zooification process.[127] In the words of Nobel Prize winner Rigoberta Menchu, a Guatemalan Quiche Indian, "what hurts Indians most is that our costumes are considered beautiful, but it's as if the person wearing it didn't exist."[128] Donald Reid found that "except when quaint displays of local culture in the form of traditional song and dance are of interest to the visitor, tourism businesses prefer the local population to remain invisible."[129]

The invisibility of the locals has received less attention than the fact that tourists rarely pay for the privilege of watching local culture in action. Watching an economic activity take place in a village is not the same as buying tickets to watch a traditional ballet. In the latter case, tourists are buying a service. In the former, they are merely being voyeurs.[130] Reid pointed out how resentful Eskimos in Alaska had become because they were getting nothing from the tourists who came to see Eskimos doing Eskimo things (namely, living their lives in their traditional ways).[131] If culture were exchanged in the market, many indigenous populations would be less resentful. Alas, as Davydd Greenwood noted in his discussion of cultural commoditization, local culture has been considered as a natural resource by tour operators as well as tourists and thereby part of the land factor, or simply part of the "come-on."[132]

Poverty and Underdevelopment in the Tourist Demand Function

The contrast-seeker tourist, a name coined by Reiner Jaakson, is one "for whom erosion of difference affects negatively their touristic experiences, and who seek[s] aggressively destinations and experiences which provide a high degree of contrast."[133] Such travelers shun mass tourism because they do not wish to be around others like themselves. They delve further and further into developing countries in order to experience the difference. In doing so, they seek out unspoiled landscapes. Unspoiled means untouched—untouched by other tourists but then also untouched by the global economy, even the nation's urban economy. Where there is no commercial activity and no monetary network, development will not occur. That translates into poverty. Untouched landscapes, then, are characterized by poverty: as Cynthia Enloe said, "to be a poor society in the late twentieth century is to be 'unspoilt.'"[134]

Does it follow that Western tourists who seek out unspoiled cultures and landscapes are in reality seeking out poverty? To the extent that Western tourists are in pursuit of contrast, extreme poverty is the single greatest difference between the Western tourist's home and the tourist destination. It is as though poverty is more authentic than development. Given the expense of long-distance travel and safaris, it seems as though there is an inverse relationship between level of development and how much people will pay to see it. Indeed, cultural tourists are not attracted to Bermuda, whose historic town of St. George's has been designated a world heritage site by UNESCO, where people look like westerners, and there are no visible signs of poverty. Tourists do, however, travel to the middle of Algeria to visit the Saharawi refugee camps. They do so because refugee camps represent the epitome of scarcity, and living conditions are imagined to be squalid. In fact, conditions are not as bad as tourists would like them to be, and camp residents, like other indigenous populations, have come to supply the demanded attraction. According to Mowforth, "the tents of the drought-stricken refugees are normally covered with plastic sheets—only when the tourists arrive are the old coverings of animal hide brought out."[135]

It is not just poverty that attracts the Western tourist, however, it is exotic poverty (Americans are not interested in seeing black slums in Chicago, and Europeans do not visit gypsy encampments on the outskirts of Paris). This attraction to exotic poverty led Pratap Fughani to speak of "famine pornography," induced by brochures picturing indigenous populations that "are obscene if not vomitorial."[136]

The Overdevelopment of Underdevelopment

The above discussion points out two contradictory and mutually exclusive efforts by authorities promoting LDC tourism. On the one hand, they are involuntarily moving indigenous populations in order to build resorts or create parks and conservation areas. In other words, they pursue a policy of *moving people* to *attract people*. On the other hand, they are promoting indigenous cultures, complete with their traditional ways and their lack of modernization. The mixed messages that these two efforts convey to workers in the tourist industry, perceptive and prospective tourists, and Western watchdog organizations are both confusing and infuriating. But most important, the contradictory policies may backfire if authorities find themselves obliterating the very people tourists come to see. Western tourists do not travel to the far ends of the third world to photograph evidence of modernization.

In addition to indigenous populations, wildlife has also been affected by confused policies. On the one hand, animal viewing is in demand, and promoting it has resulted in lucrative economic activity in many LDC destinations. On the other hand, too much animal viewing disrupts animals and thus will have negative repercussions on future earning capacity in the future. Evidence of wildlife tourism externalities abound. Across Africa, large animals have reduced their rate of breeding because of tourist intrusions.[137] It has been found that when tourist minibuses approach to view cheetah families, vultures and lionesses are not far behind, causing cheetahs to abandon their babies.[138] In Uganda, crocodile nests viewed by tourists are more likely to be destroyed by predator lizards than those not visited. Animals are becoming stressed out. Penguins are losing weight, polar bears are not hibernating peacefully, and dingos are becoming aggressive. All are susceptible to the transmission of disease as well as the disturbance of daily routines and breeding. According to the New Scientist, "in the long term the impact tourists are having could endanger the survival of the very wildlife they want to see."[139]

Contradictory policies pertaining to both populations and wildlife bring to mind the words of Pierre Encontre, who said that conventional tourism development policy has proven "its ability to bring about the early destruction of the very attractions that were the basis for its existence."[140] Indeed, the overdevelopment of underdevelopment raises questions about tourism as a strategy for development. Developing countries must figure out how to develop while preserving that which is a crucial source of development. With special reference to indigenous people, policies of involuntary population movements are counterproductive because they translate into the obliteration of the very exotic peoples that attract tourists. As stated in Chapter 2, such policies are shortsighted, based on short-term benefits without consideration of long-term consequences, and must be reassessed on economic grounds. Although a few LDC governments have understood these concerns and have begun to revise their policies (for example, in the Central African Republic, authorities are backtracking and scrambling to bring back the Pygmy population that they previously displaced from the Dzanga-Ndoki[141]), most have not, to the detriment of their development prospects.

Notes

1. Deborah McLaren, *Rethinking Tourism and Ecotravel*, 2nd ed. (Bloomfield, CT: Kumarian Press, 2003), p. 3.

2. B. Kirschenblatt-Gimblett, *Destination Culture: Tourism, Museums and Heritage* (Berkeley: University of California Press, 1998).

3. M. Trask, "Culture Vultures," in *Indigenous Peoples, Human Rights and Tourism*, Tourism Concern, *In Focus*, 29, pp. 14–17, 1998, cited in Melanie Smith, *Issues in Cultural Tourism Studies* (London: Routledge, 2003), p. 47.

4. Tej Vir Singh, "Tourism Searching for New Horizons: An Overview," in *New Horizons in Tourism*, ed. Tej Vir Singh (Cambridge, MA.: CABI Publishing, 2004), p. 1.

5. Eric Crystal, "Tourism in Toraja (Sulawesi, Indonesia)," cited in Melanie Smith, *Issues in Cultural Tourism Studies* (London: Routledge, 2003), p. 161.

6. World Tourism Organization, *Enhancing the Economic Benefits of Tourism for Local Communities and Poverty Alleviation* (Madrid: 2002), p. 53.

7. Ibid., p. 45.

8. "The New Imperialism," *Survival* (1998).

9. McLaren, *Rethinking Tourism*, p. 3.

10. Melanie Smith, *Issues in Cultural Tourism Studies* (London: Routledge, 2003), p. 119.

11. Richard Black and Vaughan Robinson, eds., *Geography and Refugees* (London: Belhaven Press, 1993), p. 7.

12. Leon Gordenker, *Refugees in International Politics* (New York: Columbia University Press, 1987), p. 63.

13. Roberta Cohen and Francis M. Deng, *Masses in Flight* (Washington, DC: Brookings Institution Press, 1998); Roberta Cohen and Francis M. Deng, eds., *The Forsaken People, Case Studies of the Internally Displaced* (Washington, DC: Brookings Institution, 1998). UNHCR reported in 2006 that the number of refugees—9.2 million—is now the lowest in 25 years; but there are an estimated 25 million internally displaced people. http://www.unhcr.org/cgi-bin/texis/vtx/news/opendoc.htm?tbl=NEWS&id=4445f6334. (accessed May 25, 2006).

14. Bill Frelick, *The Wall of Denial: Internal Displacement in Turkey* (Washington, DC: US Committee for Refugees, 1999), p. 1.

15. According to Luke Lee, the significance of crossing a border emerged for historical reasons. The distinction really became implemented at the time of the cold war, since border crossing became synonymous with persecution, namely from communism. Luke T. Lee, "Internally Displaced Persons and Refugees: Toward a Legal Synthesis?" *Journal of Refugee Studies* 9, no. 1 (1996), pp. 30–32.

16. This does not mean that UN covenants are always heeded. Although most signatory countries adhere to international laws pertaining to refugees most of the time, events do occur all too often that show disrespect for rules and norms. For example, in May 1991, the last Sudanese refugee camp in Ethiopia was attacked, and some 400,000 refugees were forced to trek back to Sudan. On the way, they were bombed by the Sudan Air Force. Thus, both the host and the home country broke international law pertaining to refugees. Hiram A. Fuiz, "The Sudan: Cradle of Displacement," in Cohen and Deng, *The Forsaken People,* p. 150.

17. Lee, "Internally Displaced Persons," p. 37.

18. Malcolm Shaw described several of these ways: effective occupation of *terra nullius* (when it is argued that non-Europeans inhabiting territories had no sovereign rights over those territories), cession (according to which European powers entered into bilateral treaties to acquire territory from local sovereigns), and conquest (taking possession of territory through war). Malcolm Shaw, *Title to Territory in Africa: International Legal Issues* (Oxford: Clarendon Press, 1986), pp. 31–46.

19. Ted Robert Gurr, *Minorities at Risk* (Washington, DC: United States Institute of Peace, 1983), p. 162.

20. Eliza Griswold, "Postcard from Thailand," *New Yorker*, January 24 and 31, 2005, p. 36.

21. Milica Z. Bookman, *Ethnic Groups in Motion: Economic Competition and Migration in Multiethnic States* (London: Frank Cass, 2002), chap. 5.

22. M. Flynn, "Report on Guatemala," *Mesoamerica* 15, no. 8 (1996), p. 4, cited in Martin Mowforth and Ian Munt, *Tourism and Sustainability: New Tourism in the Third World*, 2nd ed. (London: Routledge, 2003), p. 237.

23. Martin Mowforth and Ian Munt, *Tourism and Sustainability: New Tourism in the Third World,* 2nd ed. (London: Routledge, 2003), p. 237.

24. "Parks and People," *Survival* (1998).

25. David Harrison, "Tourism in Less Developed Countries: The Social Consequences," in *Tourism and the Less Developed Countries*, ed. David Harrison (London: Belhaven Press, 1992), p. 24.

26. David Weaver, "Tourism and Land Tenure in Sub-Saharan Africa: The Expansion of the Modern Space Economy," in *The Political Economy of Tourism Development in Africa*, ed. Peter U.C. Dieke (New York, Cognizant Communications Corporation, 2000), p. 260.

27. Ibid., p. 260.

28. "Cattle People," *Survival* (1998).

29. "Survival International Tourism and Tribal Peoples Information Sheet," 1995, cited in Mowforth and Munt, *Tourism and Sustainability*, 2nd ed., p. 51.

30. "Parks and People," *Survival* (1998).

31. *New York Times*, May 27, 2004.

32. John Lea, *Tourism and Development in the Third World* (London: Routledge, 2001), p. 57.

33. See, for example, Laurens Van Der Post, *The Lost World of the Kalahari* (New York: Morrow, 1958); Rupert Isaacson, *The Healing Land: The Bushmen and the Kalahari Desert* (New York: Grove Press, 2001); Kenneth Good, *Bushmen and Diamonds,* Discussion Paper no. 23 (Uppsala, Sweden: The Nordic Africa Institute, 2003); Sidsel Saugestad, *The Inconvenient Indigenous* (Herndon, VA: Stylus Publishing, 2001).

34. The films were *The Gods Must Be Crazy* I and II. The novel, *Mating*, was written by Norman Rush.

35. The Bushmen are spread out as follows: 8,000 in Angola; 45,000 in Botswana; 33,000 in Namibia; 2,500 in South Africa; 1,500 in Zambia; and 500 in Zimbabwe. "Hunters Facing Change," *Survival* (1998).

36. Afrol News, June 1, 2001.

37. Ibid.

38. Afrol News, August 28, 2002.

39. *Chicago Tribune*, October 7, 2002.

40. "Botswana Cuts Bushman Services," *BBC News*, January 2002.

41. *Chicago Tribune*, October 7, 2002.

42. *BBC News*, March 18, 2002.

43. www.Philly.com (accessed April 12, 2002).

44. *Chicago Tribune*, October 7, 2002.

45. Afrol News, August 28, 2002.

46. Ibid.

47. News release, Survival International, April 11, 2005.

48. www.Philly.com.

49. Press release, Survival International, May 7, 2004.

50. Ibid., May 4, 2004.

51. www.state.gov/g/drl/rls/hrrpt/2004/41589.htm (accessed November 29, 2004).

52. Afrol News, August 28, 2002.

53. Ibid.

54. *Chicago Tribune*, October 7, 2002.

55. Ibid.

56. Preservation includes the rehabilitation of existing buildings and historic sites (such as Ankor Wat in Kampuchea, Ayudhya in Thailand, and Borobudur in Indonesia) as well as the transformation of old buildings to new uses (such as making princely palaces throughout India into hotels). Lea, *Tourism and Development,* pp. 54–55.

57. Mowforth and Munt, *Tourism and Sustainability*, p. 240.

58. Numerous scholars have discussed the environmental and tourism concerns in Wadi Rum and Wadi Dana. See, for example, Laurie Brand, "Development in Wadi Rum? State Bureaucracy, External Funders, and Civil Society," *International Journal of Middle East Studies* 33 (2001); Geraldine Chatelard, "Conflict of Interests over the Wadi Rum Reserve: Were They Avoidable?" special issue, Proceedings of the Dana Conference on Mobile Peoples and Conservation, *Nomadic Peoples* 7, no. 1 (2003).

59. C. Deihl, "Wildlife and the Maasai," *Cultural Survival Quarterly* 9, no. 1 (1985), p. 37.

60. Mowforth and Munt, *Tourism and Sustainability*, p. 238.

61. "Parks and People," *Survival* (1998).

62. World Tourism Organization, *Enhancing the Economic Benefits*, p. 52.

63. Donald Reid, *Tourism, Globalization and Development* (London: Pluto Press, 2003).

64. Smith, *Issues in Cultural Tourism Studies,* p. 60.

65. Ibid., p. 125.

66. Ibid.

67. Margaret Byrne Swain, "Gender Roles in Indigenous Tourism: Kuna Mola, Kuna Yala and Cultural Survival," cited in Smith, *Issues in Cultural Tourism Studies*, p. 85.

68. I conducted interviews while on a research visit to Kuna Yala in March 2005.

69. Swain, "Gender Roles," pp. 83–104.

70. World Tourism Organization, *Enhancing the Economic Benefits*, p. 42.

71. This demand by tourists has pushed locals to figure out better ways of production. John Lea described how Aborigine populations in northern Australia have adapted the use of acrylic paints and canvases to make a lucrative export of ancient sand painting. Lea, *Tourism and Development*, p. 71.

72. Valene Smith, *Host and Guests?* p. 78.

73. Melanie Smith, *Issues in Cultural Tourism Studies,* pp. 123–124.

74. R. K. Hitchcock, "Cultural, Economic and Environmental Impacts of Tourism Among Kalahari Bushmen," in *Tourism and Culture: An Applied Perspective*, ed. E. Chambers (New York: State University of New York Press, 1997).

75. Theron Nunez, "Touristic Studies in Anthropological Perspective," p. 267.

76. Linda Richter, *Land Reform and Tourism Development in the Philippines* (Cambridge, MA: Schenkman Publishing, 1982); Linda Richter, *The Politics of Tourism in Asia* (Honolulu: University of Hawaii Press, 1989).

77. "Many Islands, Many Peoples," *Survival* (1998).

78. After pressure from Survival and other organizations, the World Bank stopped funding these programs. The Amungme representatives are suing a US company, Freeport, in the US courts for $6 billion in damages. "A Multitude of Peoples," *Survival* 1998.

79. International news release, Survival, March 22, 2005.

80. Afrol News, January 18, 2001.

81. World Bank, "Project: Transfrontier Conservation Areas and Tourism Development Project," Integrated Safeguards Data Sheet no. 25633, July 1, 2003.

82. David Diaz Benavides and Ellen Perez-Ducy, eds., "Background Note by the OMT/WTO Secretariat," *Tourism in the Least Developed Countries* (Madrid: World Tourism Organization, 2001).

83. Mowforth and Munt, *Tourism and Sustainability*, p. 242.

84. Donna E. Arzt, *Refugees into Citizens* (New York: Council on Foreign Relations, 1997), p. 67.

85. Countries have been getting around the law against *refoulement* by creating safe havens in the countries of conflict. For example, the international community did so in Iraq with the Kurds and thus allowed Turkey to close its border to them. The United States did something similar with the Haiti population and created a safe haven within the island as well as on its base in Guantanamo Bay in Cuba.

86. In 1993, the Arusha Accords, signed between the president of Rwanda, Juvénal Habyarimana, and the Rwanda Patriotic Front, brought the war between the Hutus and the Tutsis to an end and ensured the right of those who had been displaced to return home. The right to return is a cornerstone of the Dayton Peace Accords that ended the war in Bosnia. The right of return remains a crucial issue in the peace negotiations between Israel and the Palestinian Authority.

87. "Parks and People," *Survival* (1998).

88. The goal is to reduce leakage and increase linkages. These involve a fair price, fair competition between foreign and domestic investors, fair distribution of tourism revenues, use of local products and materials where appropriate, compliance by foreign investors with destination's tax regulations, and respect for cultural assets. TourismConcern, "The International Network on Fair Trade in Tourism," www.tourismconcern.org.uk/downloads/pdfs/fairtrade-introduction.pdf (accessed March 4, 2004).

89. The WWF takes no position on restoring land to those from whom it was taken. "Parks and People," *Survival* (1998).

90. World Tourism Organization, *Enhancing the Economic Benefits.*

91. Ibid., p. 21.

92. *New York Times*, May 4, 2004.

93. Ibid., May 31, 1994.

94. Jolie starred in *Beyond Borders.* The book was *Cause Celeb,* by Helen Fielding.

95. Michael Hitchcock, "Tourists as Political Targets: Reflections on the Bali Bombings" (paper presented to the International Studies Association Annual Convention, March 1–5, 2005, Honolulu, Hawaii).

96. *Economist*, February 19, 2000, p. 45.

97. *Miami Herald*, February 14, 2004. The island is called the golden trampoline because of the facility with which people are smuggled into Europe. First the Moroccans used it as an entry point and now they smuggle Africans from Sierra Leone, Côte d'Ivoire, and the Democratic Republic of Congo.

98. Brian Copeland, "Tourism, Welfare and De-Industrialization in a Small Open Economy," *Economica* 58 (November 1991).

99. Reiner Jaakson, "Globalization and Neocolonialist Tourism," in *Tourism and Postcolonialism*, ed. C. Michael Hall and Hazel Tucker (London: Routledge, 2004), p. 170.

100. Harrison, "Tourism in Less Developed Countries," p. 22.

101. World Tourism Organization, "Contribution of the World Tourism Organization to the SG Report on Tourism and Sustainable Development for the CSD 7 Meeting, April 1999," "Addendum A: Tourism and Economic Development," p. 5.

102. S. Britton cited in Harrison, "Tourism in Less Developed Countries," p. 24.

103. Meyer cited in Harrison, "Tourism in Less Developed Countries," p. 24.

104. C. Michael Hall and Hazel Tucker, "Tourism and Postcolonialism: An Introduction," in *Tourism and Postcolonialism*, ed. C. Michael Hall and Hazel Tucker (London: Routledge, 2004), p. 10.

105. M. Thea Sinclair, "Gendered Work in Tourism: Comparative Perspectives," in *Gender, Work and Tourism*, ed. M. Thea Sinclair (London: Routledge, 1997), p. 230.

106. M. Thea Sinclair, "Issues and Theories of Gender," in *Gender, Work & Tourism,* ed. By M. Thea Sinclair (London: Routledge 1997), p. 1.

107. Cynthia Enloe, *Bananas, Beaches and Bases: Making Feminist Sense of International Politics* (London: Pandora, 1990), p. 33.

108. Sinclair, "Gendered Work in Tourism," p. 225.

109. Rosemary Jommo cited in Harrison, "Tourism in Less Developed Countries," p. 23.

110. Amy Chua, *World on Fire: How Exporting Free Market Democracy Breeds Ethnic Hatred and Global Instability* (New York: Anchor Books, 2004), p. 111.

111. Sinclair, "Gendered Work in Tourism," p. 225.

112. M. Hitchcock, "Ethnicity and Tourism Enterpreneurship in Java and Bali," *Current Issues in Tourism* 3, no. 3 (2000).

113. John Samy cited in Harrison, "Tourism in Less Developed Countries," p. 23.

114. Jommo cited in Harrison, "Tourism in Less Developed Countries," p. 23.

115. *New York Times*, October 13, 2004.

116. S. Haron and B. Weiler, "Ethnic Tourism," in *Special Interest Tourism*, ed. B. Weiler and C. M. Hall (London: Belhaven Press, 1972), cited in Smith, *Issues in Cultural Tourism*, p. 117.

117. J. Seabrook, "Far Horizons," *New Statesman and Society*, August 11, 1995, p. 23; K. Kutay, "The New Ethic in Adventure Travel," *Buzzworm: The Environmental Journal* 1, no. 4 (1989), p. 35, cited in Mowforth and Munt, *Tourism and Sustainability*, p. 55.

118. David Harrison, "Tourism in Less Developed Countries," p. 19.

119. Smith, *Issues in Cultural Tourism Studies*.

120. Nina K. Prebensen, Svein Larsen, and Birgit Abelsen, "I'm Not a Typical Tourist," *Journal of Travel Research* 41, no. 4 (2003).

121. Paul Beedie, "Mountain Guiding and Adventure Tourism: Reflections on the Choreography of the Experience," *Leisure Studies* 22, no. 2 (2003), pp. 147–167. The literature on staged authenticity and constructed realities is vast. See Dean MacCannell's pioneering work, *The Tourist: A New Theory of the Leisure Class*, 3rd ed. (Berkeley: University of California Press, 1999). See also, among others, Julie A. Lacy and William A. Douglass, "Beyond Authenticity: The Meanings and Uses of Cultural Tourism," *Tourist Studies* 2, no. 1 (2002); and E. Hobsbawm, "Introduction: Inventing Traditions," in *The Invention of Tradition*, ed. E. Hobsbawm and T. Ranger (Cambridge: Cambridge University Press, 1983).

122. Hall and Tucker, "Tourism and Postcolonialism, An Introduction," p. 12.

123. Smith, *Issues in Cultural Tourism*, p. 130.

124. Mowforth and *Munt, Tourism and Sustainability,* p. 247.

125. Hitchcock, "Cultural, Economic and Environmental Impacts of Tourism Among Kalahari Bushmen," p. 96.

126. Mowforth and Munt, *Tourism and Sustainability,* p. 58.

127. Ibid., p. 246.

128. "The 'New Imperialism,'" *Survival* (1998).

129. Reid, *Tourism, Globalization and Development,* pp. 12–13.

130. Davydd Greenwood, "Culture by the Pound: An Anthropological Perspective on Tourism as Cultural Commoditization," cited in Smith, *Issues in Cultural Tourism*, p. 173.

131. Reid, *Tourism, Globalization and Development,* pp. 49, 63.

132. Greenwood, "Culture by the Pound," p. 172.

133. This category is as opposed to the contrast-indifferent or the contrast-avoider tourist. Reiner Jaakson, "Globalization and Neocolonialist Tourism," p. 175.

134. Enloe, *Bananas, Beaches and Bases,* p. 31.

135. Mowforth and Munt, *Tourism and Sustainability,* p. 247.

136. Cited in McLaren, *Rethinking Tourism and Ecotravel,* pp. 21–22.

137. Reid, *Tourism, Globalization and Development,* p. 74.

138. Lea, *Tourism and Development,* p. 58.

139. Scientists are worried about the massive growth of ecotourism, which is increasing at 10 to 30 percent per year. Indeed, now one in five tourists worldwide is an ecotourist. "Massive Growth of Ecotourism Worries Biologists," NewScientist.com (accessed March 4, 2004).

140. Pierre Encontre, "Tourism Development and the Perspective of Graduation from the LDC Category," in Diaz Benavides and Perez-Ducy, "Background Note by the OMT/WTO Secretariat," p. 1.

141. "Peoples of the Forest," *Survival* (1998).

6

The Circular Flow
of Populations and
the Global Economy

Throughout this book, descriptions of tourist destinations in developing countries have often mirrored the pattern of population movements observed in the Caprivi Strip (as described in Chapter 1). In such destinations across the globe, when tourists do what tourists usually do, the host economies respond: they build hotels and train guides; fishermen market their catch; and people move or are moved. Tourists, workers, and involuntarily displaced peoples are all in motion, not necessarily aware of each other yet highly dependent on each other. Each is an instigator and an enabler of the others. In the absence of their cumulative movements, there would be none of the consecutive cycles of economic activity that are associated with development.

Chapters 3, 4, and 5 each focused on a single population movement; this chapter returns to the broader macrolevel perspective described by the concept of the interdependent circular flow of populations. Such a macroperspective is useful for many kinds of analyses, including the determination of whether a tourist-led development strategy is a panacea for developing countries. The previous three chapters highlighted microlevel reasons why it is not, and this chapter offers national- and international-level considerations that further argue against the universal and unconditional pursuit of tourism.

One of these considerations is the global context in which tourists, migrants, and refugees coexist. In the twenty-first century, that context can be described by one word, *globalization,* a term that has a multitude of meanings and elicits highly divergent and loaded responses from scholars, policymakers, and activists. The study of population flows and how they affect and are affected by globalization is crucial to an understanding of the costs borne by the developing countries when they promote a tourist-led development strategy, whether they are in county groups A, B, or C. Indeed, given that globalization provides an environment conducive to the spread of cultural, economic, and political ideas whenever populations travel, authorities are careful to assess their demonstration effect on host populations.

In addition to the spread of ideas associated with globalization, tourist-friendly developing countries also consider their escalating dependency on MDCs, the principal source of their tourists and thus their engine of growth. Such dependency, although arguably different from its monocrop variety of the colonial era, nevertheless raises potential problems for countries that pursue a growth strategy based on the volatile demand of Western tourists.

Finally, this chapter also looks at impediments to the circular flow of populations. These occur when authorities inside and outside the tourist-friendly country erect barriers that alter or prevent population movements. Such impediments decrease the potential of tourists to be engines of growth, of workers to respond to economic incentives, and of displaced peoples to participate in interethnic economic competition. They prevent the circular flow of populations from occurring side by side with the circular flow of economic activity in self-perpetuating ways.

Globalization, dependency, and impediments to the circular flow are all part of the global reality in the twenty-first century and must be considered by authorities when developing a tourist-led development strategy. Indeed, policymakers in country group B, as well as in groups A and C, must consider not just the microaspects of developing tourism, such as the building of casinos and the staffing of rental car agencies, but also the macroconsiderations at the national and international levels. Together, the micro- and macrolevel concerns indicate that placing all development eggs in the tourist basket is far more complex than it may initially seem, and the conditions under which the eggs break are more numerous than most eager tourist-friendly governments at first realize.

Population Movements and Globalization

The tsunami disaster of 2004 highlighted the complex relationship among tourism, population displacement, ethnicity, and employment. It also underscored the role of the global environment both before and after the disaster. That environment, partially described by the concept of globalization, is essential in any assessment of population movements in the twenty-first century. To the extent that globalization entails increased economic activity across national boundaries, then the population movements studied in this book, namely tourists, workers, and involuntarily displaced ethnic groups, represent globalization par excellence. They are an integral part of transnational economic activity that is remarkable for its breadth and speed: people trade goods and services across borders and invest capital in faraway places, labor travels to jobs in distant locations, jobs travel to workers in places near and far, ideas flow easily across the globe, and cultures seem to converge. Efficient advances in transportation and communication systems, coupled with the universal penetration of the Internet, have revolutionized movements of labor, capital, goods, and ideas. Thus, it is globalization that enables population movements while concurrently those same population movements reinforce globalization.

In developing countries, it is tourism that is most closely associated with globalization. According to Frances Brown, tourism is one of the main forces *driving* globalization; Donald Reid argued instead that tourism is one of the main products *being* globalized.[1] In either case, there is consensus in the social science literature that the link between tourism and globalization is strong. According to Cynthia Enloe, "from its beginnings, tourism has been a powerful motor for global integration. Even more than other forms of investment, it has symbolized a country's entrance into the world community."[2] John Lea wrote, "there is no other international trading activity which involves such critical interplay among economic, political, environmental and social elements as tourism."[3] Melanie Smith said that "the majority of developing countries are afforded few opportunities to play their part in the global economy, except perhaps through tourism."[4] Thus, through consumption, production, and investment of tourist goods and services, even the poorest third world countries become linked to the global economy.

At the global level, the role of foreign tourists goes beyond providing convertible currencies and a market for local tourist services. In fact, tourists participate in the globalization process by bringing with them an abundant supply of ideas that inadvertently rub off on receptive locals. The tourists' political views, economic assumptions, and behavioral norms are all put on display when they travel. This demonstration effect of Western tourists in developing countries is huge. Whether they are bikini-clad Scandinavians or do-good ecotourists, all leisure travelers are vessels of globalization. And they are not alone. Migrating workers and involuntarily displaced people are also vessels because they too spread foreign cultures, ideas, and values. In addition, these people in motion have the potential to spread interethnic tolerance and peace simply by doing what they do: namely, circulating the globe in ever-expanding waves of population flows.

Globalization I: Population Movements and the Homogenization of Culture

When populations move from one location to another, they carry with them their cultural baggage. Since globalization entails the increased flow of tourists, migrants, and refugees into all corners of the world, it follows that more people are exposed to more foreign cultures. The opportunity for those cultures to take root and/or consolidate is also increased. Indeed, with increased contact among diverse cultures, borrowing from each other may occur, leading to changing social identities, lifestyles, and aspirations through an acculturation process.

When tourists flow into less developed countries, however, it is unclear just how much two-way borrowing takes place. Many scholars view the process as a one-way transfer, in which the weaker host cultures absorb the dominant Western cultures. This leads to a standardization and homogenization of local cultures. Fast food, action films, and disposable utensils are all too easily absorbed by locals who associate those goods with the intoxicating wealth and power that foreign tourists seem to have. The local culture becomes a commodity purchased by tourists rather than an equal partner in the acculturation process. In the words of Donald Reid, "tourism is a dynamic force homogenizing societies and commodifying cultures across the globe."[5] Jaakson said that tourist destinations have become a blend of local and global.[6]

By contrast, other scholars have claimed that there is, in fact, a two-way flow of cultural influence. Peter Burns claimed that a fusion of histories takes place, preventing us from observing tourism simply in a binary form (namely consisting of passive consumers [tourists] and congenial locals).[7] J. Beynon and D. Dunkerley argued that "ethnicity no longer resides in the narrowly local, as witnessed in the proliferation of ethnic cuisine, ethnic fashion, ethnic holidays and ethnic music. All over the globe there has been an indigenization of music, art, architecture, film and food, and what was feared by many (namely, western cultural domination) is becoming less likely."[8] Indeed, there are few major cities of the world that do not have a plethora of Indian and Chinese restaurants.

The disagreement in the scholarly literature about the cultural spread associated with globalization is mirrored in LDC policies. Some leaders embrace the westernization trend and the modernization it implies. The king of Bhutan, for example, promotes the introduction of US basketball and Spice Girl T-shirts. He is purported to have said that gross national happiness is more important than gross national product. Most people, however, focus on the negative effects of cultural homogenization. Even though they welcome the infusion of capital and job opportunities that tourism brings, they resent the changes in their culture. In particular, they focus on the liberal Western attitudes toward homosexuality and promiscuous behavior. They also focus on the increased demand for child prostitution and the proliferation of AIDS. This leads some countries, such as Saudi Arabia, Malaysia, and Indonesia, to attempt to limit the demonstration effect on local populations. They encourage enclave tourist destinations and discourage intermixing between hosts and guests. In order to counter the influence of foreign cultures, some countries intensify the promotion of their own. In Iran, an important objective of tourism is to introduce westerners to the local culture. The chairman of Iran's Touring and Tourism Organization, Mohammad Moezzeddin, listed his first priority in tourism development as being to "increase and maintain awareness of the Islamic Republic of Iran's heritage and Islamic culture."[9] On the other side of the globe, the president of Peru, Alejandro Toledo, said that "tourism is an industry that will allow us to become part of the global economy *while preserving our cultural roots* [italics mine]."[10] He would like foreign tourists to appreciate those roots.

Irrespective of how much cultural homogenization has occurred and how much LDC authorities are resisting it, the fact is that not all differences in cultures have been obliterated. If they were, there would be less tourist demand, especially from those who travel long distances in search of something different. As Allan M. Williams and C. Michael Hall pointed out, it is differences between places that induce tourism and migration ("place differences shape both the origins and the flows of mobility").[11]

Globalization II: Population Movements and Spread of Market Economics

Those scholars who advocate globalization do so primarily because they believe that open markets, the free flow of resources, and the international pursuit of profits bring economic benefits.[12] Increased migration and immigration, embodied in the larger category of population movements, are evidence of the mobility of human capital that responds to the changing spatial distribution of economic activity across the globe. The earlier quote by Hall and Williams ("place differences shape both the origins and the flows of mobility") also refers to labor. Namely, if prices, working conditions, and opportunities were the same everywhere, there would be no inducement for workers to move from place to place. Yet that is not true. We know that there is in fact a steady increase in worker movement from place to place.

Just as migrants and immigrants embody globalization, they also spread economic values. They demonstrate that by migrating they are doing a rational cost/benefit analysis and maximizing their utility. Immigrants send a particularly strong message to their former home countries. As members of the diaspora who have made it outside the country, they instill hope in those left behind. Also, workers in the diaspora are motivated to see their former home countries grow and modernize. To that end, they are likely to invest money in businesses, purchase property, and send remittances to family and friends. According to Yossi Shain, the remittances sent home by diasporic groups such as the Koreans, Greeks, Mexicans, Arabs, and Israelis in the United States play a major role in the economic development of their home countries.[13] Similarly, in South African townships, C. M. Rogerson and Em. M. Letsoalo found that the principal source of household income was the remittances of long-term labor migrants.[14] That income in turn is used to participate in economic activities that stimulate economic development in the homelands.

Tourists, in their casual interaction with local LDC populations, also convey an economic culture that is often as foreign to the local economy as McDonalds is to the local cuisine. Western economic culture in the twenty-first century has come to embody market economics, resource mobility, and free prices—all intangible values that fill the Western tourists' luggage. The mere fact that they had the freedom of choice among millions of travel destinations illustrates to the local population the Western concept of consumer sovereignty and the individual right to go, to do, to buy. Raoul Bianchi wrote of the culture of mobility that has become an integral part of westernized societies. It is a part of globalizing mobile consumers and the faith in free markets and open borders.[15] Moreover, price determination by supply and demand is conveyed to the local population through tourists' consumptive behavior. For example, when in Sri Lanka children who beg at airports are able to earn more cash in one day than their farmer-fishermen parents earn in one month,[16] a lesson is learned in market economics. Another way in which market values are conveyed is through the tourist-induced readjustments in the language hierarchy. As English has become the lingua franca of global tourism and of computers and media, it has come to be associated with growth and development (and therefore, as Thomas Friedman noted, the demand for English language studies is ferocious[17]). Thus, those locals who are competent in the language have an advantageous skill over others, as noted by Friedman in his study of globalization. Indeed, there are more Chinese learning English than there are Americans. As a result, they have greater opportunities to work as interpreters, waiters, clerks, police, tour guides, and so on, and they earn a higher wage in the labor market. Finally, the presence of the Western tourists may have a demonstration effect on the local populations that stimulates the economy by increasing productivity. Locals may think that if they work harder, they might achieve the way of life of the tourists.[18]

Globalization III: Population Movements and the Spread of Democratic Values

Globalization has come to be associated with what in the West has been called universal values. These broadly include respect for the individual and for private property, as well as democratic principles. Leading Western states have introduced legislation that protects individual and human rights and have encouraged other countries to uphold their principles and laws. In this way, the Western world, spearheaded by the United States, has transformed its views on individual rights into a set of "universal values" that it asserts is not location specific. With the cold war over, Western states have been able to tout (and even impose) their values as well as their view of governance without worrying about the nonaligned or socialist states.[19]

Moving populations carry in their luggage the political culture that is an integral part of who they are. This is true for tourists, who assume respect for human rights is transferable across borders (and then get in trouble with the law in countries such as Iran, Turkey, and Malaysia). It is also true of immigrants who bring with them assumptions that they must then shed in order to assimilate in foreign lands. Last, it is also true of refugees whose political values continue to guide their behavior in host countries' camps (for example, the Hutu/Tutsi views on interethnic relations held strong in neighboring Congo). The most important spread of Western political/universal values occurs through the cross-border movements of tourists and immigrants. These are discussed in the following sections.

Tourists. It has been said that, not having found weapons of mass destruction, President George W. Bush waged war in Iraq in order to spread democratic values. Critics have suggested it would have been more effective to send busloads of tourists. This view of tourism as a vessel of democratization is not new to the academic literature. The spread of Western values occurs unintended, without a specific aim. Tourists do tourist things, and their search for experiences creates externalities (positive or negative, depending on one's point of view). Those who are inclined toward natural or ecological or cultural travel are a self-selected cohort that tends to be sensitive and politically correct. Often they believe in the rule of law and personal rights, and they treat their hosts, who are often less politically correct than they, with sensitivity.

Tourism, especially cultural tourism, has the effect of empowering local populations. As noted in Chapter 5, the mere demand by westerners for indigenous cultures raises awareness within host government circles and leads to an improvement in their status. The income generated by Western demand increases the leverage of indigenous peoples. To the extent that their activities have an effect on tourism, local indigenous populations are listened to. A recent example from Bolivia illustrated such empowerment. Five provinces adjoining Lake Titicaca formed an alliance to promote tourism. The Indian populations requested aid money from the government for small-scale tourism projects. As the money was not forthcoming, they created roadblocks and protests that trapped some tourists. That got the attention of the authorities (and the Indians received the aid).[20]

Indigenous populations are not the only ones empowered by tourism. Politically correct and sensitive tourists have the power to affect events in LDC countries by voting with their feet. Although most tourists do not know the politics of their destination in advance of their travel, those who do know then choose their destinations on the basis of the forms of government (they avoid dictatorships) and/or social issues (they avoid countries that condone child prostitution). Jaakson referred to this as the "untapped political power in an activist tourism, waiting to be implemented for the betterment of the world."[21] A travel boycott sends a message to the authorities. The opposite message is sent by a travel endorsement.

Western tourists to developing countries also convey their belief in personal freedom. As Jozsef Borocz pointed out, international travel is viewed as a civic liberty, and countries that prevent it curtail freedoms.[22] When people travel, they indicate that they are free to do so. The message by diasporic tourists is especially potent. Indeed, when immigrants and migrants travel to their home states for vacation or to visit friends and family, they represent a living example of the benefits of open markets. By going back and forth between home and host countries, they carry back to their roots the new values they have picked up.[23]

Immigrants. It has been said that "you can take a Palestinian out of Palestine but you can't take Palestine out of a Palestinian." This phrase, applicable to every ethnic group, explains the emotional bond between people and their ancestral territory that survives both temporal and spatial distance. Indeed, both voluntary and involuntary migrants retain ties to their lands over time and across continents. As a result of this bond, diasporas can be a conduit for the spread of universal values.[24] That conduit is explained below.

With voluntary and involuntary migrations across borders on the rise in the current era of globalization, there has been an increase in diasporas of virtually all ethnic groups (since 1959, the diaspora of Rwandan Tutsis has grown to one million; some 800,000 Tamils are estimated to be in the diaspora; nearly three million Palestinians live in Arab countries, Europe, and the Americas). This increase in their numbers has helped diasporas expand their role. They now affect policies in both home and host states, and they play an important role in promoting political and economic change. Diasporas residing in the West can spread Western values pertaining to rule of law, and they can pressure multiethnic countries across the globe to adopt minority rights.[25] They are able to promote Western values to their home countries because they "speak both languages." This nonliteral interpretation of language encompasses all aspects of culture. Since diasporas have sensitivity to home cultures, they are better positioned to guide the penetration of Western values. As Yossi Shain has shown, diasporas residing in the United States have long been instrumental in bringing Western ideas pertaining to democracy, human rights, and respect for minorities back to their home countries.[26] Functioning as a conduit, these former immigrants can help transform interethnic relations in their home countries and, in the process, promote interethnic harmony (for example, Palestinians in the diaspora have provided political support for their encamped co-nationals by forming lobby groups in host countries).

Has globalization affected the way in which diasporas interact with their home states and ethnic groups? The answer is unequivocally yes. Diasporas make use of the Internet, the telephone, the media, and inexpensive travel to keep up with events in their homelands.

Globalization IV: Population Movements and Peace

As just discussed, workers and immigrants in the diaspora spread Western values when they make tourist visits to their third world home countries. When they are not vacationing, however, but rather are engaged in their daily lives in the MDCs, these same immigrants spread international understanding. This happens because contemporary immigrants live with one foot in one country and the other in their home state. They are not the immigrants of old, who never set foot on their home soil after leaving and who forbade their children to speak their native tongue in order to speed up integration into the host culture.

This modern diaspora has loyalties in both locations and participates in the economy and the political system in both locations. Its people perceive themselves as nationals of the home state and citizens of the host country. In other words, when immigrants become citizens of their new country, they do not leave their nationality behind. When they acquire host country citizenship, their sense of belonging to the state increases, as does their capacity and incentive to participate in its culture.

They also want to exert their power, express their opinion, and influence policy. The electoral system, newly opened to naturalized immigrants, allows them to do this. The evidence from the United States is clear: the newly empowered groups using the electoral system to exert their influence include the Cubans, Haitians, Koreans, Chinese, Vietnamese, Dominicans, and Mexicans (they supersede the traditional groups, namely the Italians, Poles, Greeks, Jews, and Germans). According to Yossi Shain, these groups have been successfully empowered: "One of the signs that an ethnic group has achieved a respectable position in American life is its acquisition of a meaningful voice in U.S. foreign affairs."[27]

Despite such involvement in their host states, immigrants do not forget their home country and kin. Their concern with both countries motivates them to become ambassadors of peace. As already noted, the Internet allows them to stay in touch with their home countries, and it further strengthens their ability to promote peace between their home and host states. Several scholars have found that the Internet promotes peace. Nicholas Negroponte has said that children of the future will not know what nationalism is because their primary loyalties will lie with the international community that they access through the Internet.[28] For the same reasons, Michael Detrouzos has said that the Internet will spread computer-aided peace across the globe.

In addition to immigrants, tourists also spread peace across the globe. Dawid de Villiers, the deputy secretary general of the World Trade Organization, wrote that "three of the most immediate and urgent problems that African leaders will have to address are first, to establish peace, security and stability; second, to deal with poverty and create jobs; and third, to preserve the environment. It is important to note *that tourism is directly linked to all three of these major challenges* [italics mine]."[29] Although de Villiers was referring to Africa, his words are applicable throughout the third world, as everywhere tourism has the potential to foster understanding among different cultures and traditions and to develop mutual acceptance and tolerance. Tourism, he concluded, is a powerful tool for peace.

De Villiers is not alone in his view. The International Institute for Peace Through Tourism is based on the premise that international understanding can be fostered by the movement of tourists who act as ambassadors for peace and promote understanding.[30] James Mak said that "many in the tourist industry also believe that tourism can foster global peace by reducing world poverty and promoting cross-cultural understanding."[31] After Jordan and Israel signed a peace treaty in 1994, the promotion of tourism was viewed as a starting point in the regional economic cooperation that would, according to Shimon Peres's vision, create the *new* Middle East.[32] Scholars have studied peace ramifications of tourism across demilitarized zones in places such as Cyprus and North and South Korea.[33] At a less ambitious level, Eastern European Holidays has launched trips to Bosnia in order to "educate ignorance." Australian-born company owner Ben Robinson recognizes the role of tourism in the revitalization of the entire region and cites as the objectives of the trips the dispelling of illusions, the spread of information and education, and even the rebuilding of the country.[34] Similarly, tours into Brazilian *favelas* and the more recent tours of Villas Miserias in Buenos Aires are said to be aimed at striving for international understanding and raising consciousness by exposing poverty.[35] Even the apartheid government of South Africa encouraged tourism as evidence of international legitimacy and a vehicle for spreading information; in the words of David Weaver, this was "disseminating the best possible image."[36] In all these examples, the focus is on the broadening effect of tourism on tourists. Contact with local populations, it is believed, broadens horizons and opens up new worlds. Tourists return home with a raised consciousness, and often they act on humanitarian urges that developed during their travels (this does not happen when tour packages bring mass tourism into isolated enclaves separated from the local population and when tourists rarely venture outside their self-contained bubbles).

Western tourists can be ambassadors of peace even in countries with ongoing wars. Afghanistan, for example, has emerged as a tourist destination owing largely to Western demand. Hinterland Travel, which also offers visits to Iraq, scheduled a few trips in 2005, and Travel Afghanistan is joining in. Lonely Planet, the guidebook, is putting its Afghanistan chapter online "due to overwhelming interest."[37]

Even domestic tourism plays a role in spreading peace. It was tourism that broke the barriers after World War II in the former Yugoslavia and enabled the diverse ethnic groups to overcome their war animosities. In India, a tour guide hoped that "domestic tourism by Indians traveling within their own subcontinent will eventually help break down the language disputes and provincialism that continue to fracture government efforts toward national consolidation."[38] According to Brian Archer, Chris Cooper, and Lisa Ruhanen, domestic tourism can "act as an integrating force strengthening national sentiment."[39] If peace is indeed promoted by increased domestic travel, then as incomes rise in developing countries, people will buy more leisure travel and so increase the chances for peace.

Although many believe in the virtues of tourism as a force of peace and global understanding, not everyone agrees that globalization and population movements bring about peace. Amy Chua has argued that exporting the free market to LDCs increases the possibility of conflict and increases income differences between groups and between rich and poor.[40] To the extent that tourism spreads market values, it follows that the result will not be increased peace. Similarly, Archer, Cooper, and Ruhanen pointed out that international tourism may cause problems because of the vast economic, political, and social differences between tourist and locals.[41] Some LDC governments join the ranks of scholars who think increased tourist exposure will not lead to peace but rather will be counterproductive. They fear that globalization and increased population movements, together with the concomitant increase in communication, have the effect of inciting ethnic sentiment, forming ethnic identities, and strengthening ethnic boundaries. Cellular telephones and email have indeed added to global communication possibilities that circumvent authoritarian controls. Because of their role in liberalizing uncontrollable communication, cellular telephones have been a frequent target of concerned governments (for example, the Moroccan government banned cell phone usage by the Sahawari ethnic group that sought independence of Western Sahara[42]).

Conclusions Pertaining to the Demonstration Effect

Population movements are vessels of globalization insofar as they transmit cultural, economic, and political ideas. They set examples both in their host and home regions. Just how many people must cross borders in order to set an example, to make an impact, to produce a demonstration effect? In other words, how many tourists, migrant workers, and refugees need to mingle with local populations for the flow of ideas to take place? The answer depends on the quantity of contact, the nature of the contact, and the national origin of the source of contact.

With respect to quantity, the more tourists travel to LDC destinations, the greater their aggregate impact. The effect of sheer volume is clear in Asia, where the influence of the Chinese has grown concurrently with their capacity and incentive to travel (they have more disposable income and fewer political impediments). More than twenty million Chinese traveled abroad in 2004, and by 2020, this number is expected to surpass 100 million.[43] A critical mass of immigrants also influences local populations. Indeed, Indians and Pakistanis living in London have changed the city's cultural landscape. With respect to displaced populations, the Iraqi refugees across the border in Iran and the Tibetan refugees in India have all left a footprint because they change the density and ethnic composition of the population.

The nature of the contact between moving populations and locals is also relevant in determining the impact of the demonstration effect. Much tourist contact is of short duration and involves minimal contact and therefore tends to be superficial. Indeed, cruise travelers who take a morning land excursion are unlikely to leave much of an impression on their hosts (unless they spread the Norwalk virus, as in years past). Longer stays by tourists who live, eat, and play among the locals are more likely to leave a mark. Some locals seek out such contact, wishing to absorb elements of foreign culture and otherwise profit from the contact. The demonstration effect of tourism is greatest in those countries in which there are the fewest restrictions on interaction with foreigners (as there sometimes are in Muslim or communist societies). As a result of their longer stays, migrants and immigrants are more likely to mingle with local populations. Given their desire to rapidly make a life for themselves, however, they seek to integrate into the host society, drawing values and ideas from it. Involuntarily displaced peoples are also more likely to try to assimilate to the host environment, especially if they view their stay as long term (and if they are given the opportunity).

The national origin of traveling populations is also relevant, since at any time in history, some cultures have more global influence than others. In the early twenty-first century, cultures grouped under the umbrella term *Western* are the most influential. The Western culture, although prevalent in Britain, France, Germany, and elsewhere, is dominated by its US version. Although only one in ten Americans has a passport,[44] the impact of their culture on LDCs is huge. Z. Sardar and M. Wynn Davis said that the United States is omnipresent, that it is inescapable: "The rest of the world is exposed to its politics, foreign policy, media and cultural products."[45] They go on to add that Americans are often less frequently exposed to foreign influence than are the citizens of any other nation.[46] They are also less absorbing of other cultures, in part because they have a strong sense of their values and believe they are superior. It is these values that, according to David Fisher, rub off on local populations when US tourists travel.[47] The fact that the language of Americans, namely American English, is the language of popular entertainment, technology, and finance at the global level only serves to reinforce the dominance of US culture.

Irrespective of the quantity of contact, the nature of the contact, and the national origin of the source of contact, it is likely that the impact of population movements on less developed host countries is inversely related to the duration of their stay and the freedom of choice in their travel. In other words, short-term, voluntary tourist visits affect society more than long-term movements of labor or refugees. Indeed, when people move with expectations of staying, they tend to assimilate or build enclaves to preserve their uniqueness. In either case, they do not produce a demonstration effect as significant as that of a wealthy Western tourist.

Dependency in Tourist-Friendly LDCs

After the link with the Soviet Union was severed, it was foreign tourists that kept Cuba afloat and provided a lifeline throughout the 1990s. Tourism averaged double-digit growth and earned 25 percent profits. In 2003, tourist industry sales of $2.1 billion provided almost half of Cuba's total hard currency revenues. In mid-2004, those numbers were up by 12 percent.[48] It seems obvious that Cuba's tourist industry is an engine of growth, yet Raul Castro, the defense minister, likened it to "a tree born twisted that must be uprooted and planted anew."[49] The main reason for the Communist Party's apprehension of tourist development has to do with the dependency on foreign markets that it fosters. Cuba's experience illustrates the sentiment shared by numerous leaders and scholars who find the dependency of LDCs on MDCs to be dangerous.

Although other moving populations, such as third world migrants and immigrants, also depend on Western markets, it is tourism that has borne the brunt of the contemporary dependency literature. S. Britton applied the original dependency theory of the 1970s to tourism, and C. Michael Hall and Hazel Tucker edited a volume on the contribution of postcolonialism to tourism studies.[50] The terms *neocolonialism* and *imperialism* have been used repeatedly in the literature. Both are embodied below in the discussion focusing on key issues of the dependency scholarship.

LDCs supply tourist goods and services to the global markets, where they are purchased mostly by MDCs. Thus, much of the economic activity generated both directly and indirectly by the tourist industry depends on foreign demand. According to Melanie Smith, "tourism is often described as the quintessential global industry, although it hardly needs to be pointed out that it is again a western-dominated phenomenon in which the only role played by 'peripheral' countries is that of host rather than generator."[51] To the extent that tourism plays an important role in a host economy, then the country's GDP is dependent on foreign demand (according to A. Mathieson and G. Wall, tourism fosters dependency because developing countries depend on tourism as a source of revenue[52]). Indeed, in tourist-dependent Group A countries as well as many Group B countries, a drop in tourist visits translates quickly into a drop in revenue. Even at the microlevel, tribal people who were once self-sufficient or used local trade to survive are now dependent on tourist income.

LDCs then are at the mercy of foreign demand for their tourism industry. This demand is inconsistent and volatile and can disappear overnight (both for any single third world destination and for developing countries in general). Such volatility brings to mind the disadvantages of monocrop economies that gave rise to the initial dependency literature of the 1970s. At the time, developing countries exported raw materials and crops despite decreasing terms of trade. To the extent that developing countries have replaced raw materials with tourism, they are no less dependent on the West than they were previously. According to Cynthia Enloe, "tourism is being touted as an alternative to the one-commodity dependency inherited from colonial rule. Foreign sun-seekers replace bananas. Hiltons replace sugar mills."[53]

Moreover, investment in the tourist industry tends to come from foreign sources, further fostering dependency (incidentally, these sources

are usually Western[54]). As a result of stipulations set by investors as preconditions to investment, repatriation of profits occurs. Indeed, as noted
by Mathieson and Wall, much of tourist expenditure and profit flows
back to foreign investors.[55] This results in high leakages that raise questions about who the beneficiaries of tourism really are.

Another type of leakage that fosters dependency has to do with the
importation of goods not necessary before the development of tourism.
As many Western tourists like the foods, media, and comforts associated with home, limited foreign currency in developing countries is ex-
pended in order to import them. But consumption is not limited to the
tourists. As a result of the demonstration effect, demand is created
among locals, further increasing dependency on imports (this is true for
Coca-Cola as well as for Western medicines to combat AIDS).

Another feature of dependency is the racial difference between the
local populations in developing countries and the tourists who come to
those countries. Generally, tourists are Western and white, whereas
local populations are neither. In Africa especially, tourism is clothed in
racial issues, as most arrivals are from former colonists (with the exception of Botswana, which gets most of its tourists from South
Africa). The French account for up to 40 percent of the tourists in West
African countries; the British and the Germans go to East Africa.[56]
Such evidence led David Harrison to associate tourism with white colonialism[57] and Robert Poirier to refer to tourism in Africa as Euro-
dependent because most tourists are European.[58] These racial differences between visitors and hosts have not been viewed positively in the
literature. Indeed, Harrison noted that because tourism was for a long
time associated with white colonialists, many were opposed to it as just
another form of underdevelopment.[59]

The racial issue is related to employment insofar as the nonwhite locals perform service tasks for the white visitors. Martin Mowforth and
Ian Munt claimed that modern third world travel was a form of neocolonialism because the Western, white visitors were pampered by poor
locals, as they were during colonial rule.[60] To the extent that whites do
the pampering, it is in their capacity as managers. Indeed, nonlocals are
employed in professional and managerial positions (this point extends
dependency theory beyond the tourist industry and includes transnational labor[61]). When senior positions in the tourist industry are filled
with nonnationals from countries of the former colonizers, then, as John
Lea stated, we can invoke the concept of neocolonialism.[62] Also related
to this are the enclave environments that develop across LDC tourist
destinations as foreign managers (as well as tourists) stay in contained

environments that are enclaves of Western society. This is not different from the enclave economies that existed in developing countries during colonialism.

The preceding discussion points to the issue of subordination in tourism and the consequent exploitation of local populations. Davydd Greenwood stated that with tourism, "local culture is in effect being expropriated and local people are being exploited."[63] In part this happens because, as Jean Holder noted, tourists are unable to distinguish between service and servitude.[64] In this vein, Mowforth and Munt stated that the former Ss of tourism (sun, sea, sand, and sex) have been replaced by subjugation, servility, and subservience.[65]

Such evidence of dependency has led some scholars to state that relations between Western states and developing countries are fundamentally no different from what they were two centuries ago. As stated by H. G. Matthews, "tourism may add to the numbers of jobs available and it may increase the trappings of modernity with modern buildings and new services, but if it does not contribute to the development of local resources, then *it differs little from the traditional agricultural plantation* [italics mine]."[66] It follows then that by putting all their development eggs in the tourism basket, third world countries are placing themselves in a position in which westerners are once again providing them with their engine of growth. For some countries this has policy implications as they attempt to prevent or control the tourist industry.

Impediments to the Circular Flow of Populations

In his study of Fiji, David Fisher noted that "while tourists may only visit for very short periods, their collective impact in terms of numbers and income to the community may be enormous."[67] His words extend beyond the confines of Fiji. As noted in Chapter 1, a westerner's frivolous demand for a leisurely week at a LDC beach resort, when summed across the market, has huge ramifications on the economies, societies, and politics of host countries. These tourists come for a temporary stay but in the process produce a cumulative effect that is all but temporary. Tourist visits activate new economic activity that is both high-impact and irreversible. They can also result in population movements and displacements that are high-impact and permanent.

This circular flow of populations has become an integral part of globalization in the twenty-first century. Although globalization touts open markets and the free mobility of resources over borders, the reality, however, is far from open and free. In fact, there are constraints that limit tourist travels, migration, immigration, and involuntary displacements. These constraints, both in home and host countries, shatter illusions about free global markets for resources. They are not universally uniform, so even though globalization touts freedoms, not all people are equally free. Some of these constraints are discussed below.

Tourists

Western tourists believe they have the right to travel and explore in LDCs at their whim, choose among destinations, and change their minds repeatedly. In reality, this right is sometimes constrained by prohibitions on where individuals are allowed to travel. When imposed by the home country, such constraints take the form of outright prohibitions (as when US citizens are prevented from traveling to Cuba) or strong cautioning (as when the US State Department issues warnings against travel to Iraq or Sudan). Laws in the tourist destinations also curtail the freedom of Western tourists by restricting entry (as in pretransition Albania) or, if they allow entry, by closely monitoring tourist movements and limiting their contact with locals (as in the former Soviet Union and in China). Moreover, the freedoms Western travelers do have rarely apply in reverse—in other words, there is rarely reciprocity. Although they often enter third world countries with only a passport, LDC citizens cannot visit Western countries so easily. Indeed, in order to visit the United States, Canada, Australia, or Europe, travelers from developing countries face strict visa obstacles that are overcome with much difficulty. Since September 11, 2001, the US authorities have made travel (and migration) into the United States even harder than before, effectively discouraging the tourist demand from developing countries. Some countries have fought back—Brazil, for example, fingerprinted Americans. Such retaliation had no effect on US policy, however.

Migrants

The choice to migrate does not translate into the choice of destinations to which to migrate. In other words, although migrants may exert their free will in the decision to move, constraints limit the countries or regions a migrant can aspire to reach or set limits on the activities he or she can pursue on arrival. These constraints limit the way in which workers can respond to changes in the demand for labor. Impediments within the labor market come from policy, institutions, infrastructure, and personal constraints. Each includes both push and pull forces that act on the employer and the worker in their respective attempts to maximize their profits or utility.[68] For the purposes of this chapter, it is policies related to immigration and emigration that constitute the greatest impediment to the circular flow of populations.

Immigration policies. At the turn of the twentieth century, people did not need passports to cross borders and set up residence outside their country of birth. Today, visas and work permits restrict mobility not only between MDCs and LDCs but also within each group of countries. The purpose of immigration policies is to manipulate mobility. To that end, most Western states have immigration policies that contain aspects of one or more of the following goals: social (that is, to reunify families), economic (that is, to improve incomes and satisfy manpower demands), cultural (that is, to increase diversity), moral (that is, to ensure human rights), and security (that is, to reduce illegal immigration).[69] Governments make choices among these goals, and they put them in the context of particular prevailing national conditions. In so doing, they also answer three basic questions in the formulation of immigration policy: who, how many, and from where.[70]

With respect to who is allowed to enter a country, the response depends upon the overriding objective of immigration policy, as stated above. To the extent that immigration policy entails the humanitarian objective and that refugees are accepted through some form of political asylum or resettlement program, it is people fleeing from oppressive regimes and interethnic conflicts that seek entry. Such a debate does not exist for economic immigrants, namely those who are selected because they have sought-after skills. Such workers usually have high levels of education, language proficiency in the local tongue, employment prospects, and earning capacity. They are unlikely to be a burden to the host country, as their contribution to the economy is expected to be high. In the United States, Canada, and Australia, immigration policies are increasingly skewed in favor of professional immigrants. Canada has a system that awards points for education and skills.[71] In 1997, of the 205,000 planned admissions, 113,000 were admitted under the "skilled category." In Australia, during 1998 and 1999, more than half came under the "skill stream." The United States is trying to go the same route, albeit with less success: the number of employment-based visas actually dropped in the 1993–1995 period from 147,000 to 85,000.

In answer to the question of how many, immigration policies must consider the country's absorptive capacity. Doing so entails paying attention to the labor market, population density, facilities (such as housing), and services (such as education). All of these will be strained by the inflow of migrants (especially since they tend to cluster in selected neighborhoods), and therefore domestic policy must be tied closely to immigration policy.

When discussing where migrants should come from, many national policies can be said to be ethnic policies. Until 1965, the United States (as well as many other Western countries) based the geographical distribution of their immigrants on their own societies. In other words, the formula was to mirror the ethnic composition of the domestic population. Those policies have been replaced with laws based on neutrality of country of origin, making the ethnicity of the newcomers irrelevant. Despite such laws, Myron Weiner found that ethnicity is "the most plausible explanation for the willingness of states to accept or reject migrants."[72] Immigration into developing countries is more openly restricted on the basis of national origin and ethnicity.[73]

Emigration policies. In addition to the immigration restrictions that affect inflows of populations into a host territory, countries also impose restrictions on the outflow of people. Emigration policies refer to restrictions on citizens' mobility across borders, and internal migration laws prevent the free flow of migrants within a country.

For decades, the Berlin Wall was a potent symbol of the containment of people. Although the emigration policy of East Germany was clearly embodied in stone, other states with restive populations and pent-up demand for outmigration had policies that were equally effective (albeit less newsworthy). The Soviet Union, the East European countries of the Soviet bloc, and China all had precisely enunciated rules and regulations that dictated who could leave the country and under what conditions. Such interference by the authorities is deemed necessary because the demand for exit visas would overwhelm the labor market, triggering a shortage of workers and an upward pressure on wages. Moreover, when educated people emigrate, the harm to the economy is even greater due to the loss of human capital (as discussed in Chapter 4). When fertile young people emigrate, there is a potential demographic cost, as the country is robbed of their offspring (in other words, future workers). When workers emigrate, the government suffers the loss of their tax revenues; when healthy individuals emigrate, the investments of the health system have been lost, and so forth.

As a result of these economic considerations, some countries control emigration through a complex system of exit permits. The difficulty of obtaining these is inversely related to the outflow of migrants. Governments shroud the emigration process in secrecy, they establish elaborate bureaucratic requirements, and they purposefully increase the complexity and the time requirements of the process, all in order to discourage the potential migrant. Exit permits are so difficult to obtain that success comes only after pressure is exerted from the international community. For instance, in the United States the Jackson-Vanik Amendment, passed during the Nixon administration, linked the USSR's most-favored-nation status to the opening up of its emigration policies.[74] Sometimes, emigration is effectively discouraged by the prohibitively high cost of exit permits. This has a dual effect: containing the population and raising government revenue. It has also been found that some countries have selective emigration policies, depending on the ethnicity of the migrant (such a policy reflects the goal of cleansing a society of undesirable populations, as occurred in Romania with the sale of exit permits to Jews).

The evidence with respect to trends in emigration policies is somewhat mixed. On the one hand, countries with previously tightly controlled borders have witnessed significant liberalization. The most poignant example pertains to the former Soviet bloc: indeed, when the Berlin Wall was dismantled on November 9, 1989, it was actually the controlled exit policies that came crumbling down, precipitating enormous migration flows.[75] On the other hand, some countries continue to closely monitor their borders. In the early 2000s, Cuba still restricts the free outflow of people, albeit inconsistently. Even though numerous citizens are desperate enough to attempt the crossing of the Florida Straits, large-scale exoduses such as the 1980 Mariel Boatlift underscore the fickleness of Cuban emigration policy.

Contrary to countries that restrict the outflow of their populations, there are others where it is encouraged (such as Bangladesh, Pakistan, the Philippines, Mexico, and Sri Lanka).[76] They actively pursue policies of labor emigration for several reasons. First, they want to relieve the domestic employment pressures by decreasing demand for labor. Second, they want their workers to gain work experience in order to bring the acquired skills back home and aid in the development of their countries. Third, they want the migrant workers to send home remittances, preferably in foreign currencies. These positive effects are viewed as offsetting the negative effects of brain drain and loss in labor.

Refugees and Involuntarily Displaced Peoples

In 1995, the annual report of the UNHCR stated that "the end of the Cold War generated a strong sense of optimism about the international refugee situation. With the rivalry of the superpowers over, it was thought many conflicts would be resolved, large numbers of refugees would be able to go back to their homes and resources being used for relief could be moved to rehabilitation and development."[77] It then went on to state that "precisely the opposite has happened." In fact, at the turn of the new millennium, there were some thirty-five million people across the globe living in refugee and involuntarily displaced people's encampments. Many of them linger there for years and even decades, as their status remains unresolved and no host country agrees to receive them. In South Africa, between 1960 and 1980, more than 3.5 million people were dispersed and then assigned to encampments, where most have stayed; Eritreans fled to Sudan more than thirty years ago, and some 300,000 still live in camps there; Vietnamese boat people left their country in 1975, and 40,000 are still encamped across Southeast Asia; hundreds of thousands of Tutsi refugees went to Burundi in 1962, only to be joined in the same encampments by their nationals in the 1990s; and native peoples of North America were resettled in the past century on reservations, and more than one million are still there. Clearly, the number of people who live in encampments is not negligible.[78] Also not negligible is the number of countries that host encampments: at this time, over ninety countries have camps with more than 1,000 inhabitants. In Africa by 1992, only four states had neither gained nor lost more than 1,000 refugees.[79] If we add to the above countries that are home to encampment residents, namely the ones that have produced the involuntary displacement, then the total number of countries associated with permanent encampments rises to well over 100.

Involuntary displacement by definition implies the absence of choice. That condition is further aggravated by the constraints placed by home and host countries on displaced people's ability to return home or to make a new life in the host country. Although migrants do not have choices, their hosts do. When faced with hordes of refugees at their borders, host governments have to make choices about accepting them or turning them away. If the governments permit entry, they must then decide whether refugees will be dispersed or concentrated within compact geographical areas. They also decide whether refugees will be integrated or quarantined. The choices made by the host authorities reflect their country's immigration, manpower, and social policies (which in turn are based on the projected economic, political, and social impact of the incoming populations). The choices also follow from the host country's international commitments and obligations (which are based on its adherence to international guidelines pertaining to treatment of refugees). Finally, the choices also reflect the host country's position within the community of nations. This includes its geopolitical relations with its refugees' home countries and/or its religious ties to the refugees.

In a previous study, I identified the following four sentiments underlying refugee policy: intolerance, reluctant hospitality, laissez-faire hospitality, and unconditional welcome.[80] These sentiments may be viewed as markers along a spectrum in which active intolerance and unconditional welcome represent the least common extremes. An example of the former is when Vietnamese boat people arrived in Singapore and were not allowed to disembark. With respect to the latter, some authorities actively provide economic and political opportunities, as the Indians did for the Tibetans. Most refugees are met with reluctant or laissez-faire hospitality. Reluctant hospitality occurs when host countries accept refugees with less than enthusiasm. They provide them with basic infrastructure and condone minor economic activity but then create such unpalatable conditions that refugees initiate their exodus (as illustrated by the Vietnamese refugees in Hong Kong). With laissez-faire hospitality, authorities condone the presence of refugees, recognizing the positive contributions of their encampments to their own economies (in terms of labor and skills, demand, trickle down from international aid). They do nothing, however, to encourage long-term integration.

Clearly, there are constraints on movements of involuntarily displaced peoples when host countries base policy on intolerance or reluctant hospitality. Even in cases when encampment residents are allowed to linger, however, host governments may impose restrictions on their activities that limits their ability to return home or integrate in their new locations. These restrictions, which sometimes also apply to migrants and immigrants, impose limitations on the individuals' right of movement, right of employment, right to own property, and right to citizenship. Also relevant is institutionalized discrimination and the extent to which ethnic groups are treated differently under law. Rights and discrimination, as supported by host institutions and policies, indicate whether displaced persons are politically acknowledged and legally protected within host states. Clearly, if camp residents have the right to move within the host state, they will have greater employment options because they can search across a broader territory. To the extent that they have the right to work outside the camp, residents' choices are increased, and their legal status provides some protection from exploitation. Displaced persons who can apply for citizenship are more likely to feel permanently ensconced in a host state and therefore more likely to take steps toward economic integration (such as investment and risk taking). Finally, camp residents who do not suffer from legalized discrimination against their particular ethnic group are more likely to feel welcome and therefore to seek integration.

Impediments to the Circular
Flow of Populations: Conclusions

The discussion of the impediments to the circular flow of population movements suggests that, despite globalization, there is not freedom of movement. It also suggests that constraints on movements do not have equal impact on all types of travelers. Choice and duration of stay once again emerge as crucial variables distinguishing travelers, insofar as institutional restrictions imposed on tourists (voluntary, temporary travelers) are less prohibitive than those imposed on migrants. They are the greatest in the case of involuntary migrants. As the duration of a migrant's stay increases, so does the institutional restriction associated with his or her stay. Also, as population movements become more involuntary, institutional restrictions increase. Indeed, LDC governments often impose stringent policies that dictate immigration and emigration. In a world characterized by globalization and unprecedented population movements, third world countries are increasingly taking control of their borders and making policy decisions pertaining to which movements to encourage and which to prohibit.

Notes

1. Frances Brown, *Tourism Assessed: Blight or Blessing?* (Oxford: Butterworth-Heinemann, 1998); Donald Reid, *Tourism, Globalization and Development* (London: Pluto Press, 2003), p. 3.

2. Cynthia Enloe, *Bananas, Beaches and Bases: Making Feminist Sense of International Politics* (London: Pandora, 1990), p. 31.

3. John Lea, *Tourism and Development in the Third World* (London: Routledge, 2001), p. 2.

4. Melanie Smith, *Issues in Cultural Tourism Studies* (London: Routledge, 2003), p. 10.

5. Reid, *Tourism, Globalization and Development,* p. 1.

6. Reiner Jaakson, "Globalization and Neocolonialist Tourism," in *Tourism and Postcolonialism*, ed. C. Michael Hall and Hazel Tucker (London: Routledge, 2004), p. 176.

7. Peter Burns, "Social Identities, Globalization and the Cultural Politics of Tourism," in *Global Tourism*, 3rd ed., ed. William Theobald (Amsterdam: Elsevier, 2005), p. 391.

8. J. Beynon and D. Dunkerley, eds., *Globalization, the Reader* (London: Athlone Press, 2000), p. 26.

9. World Tourism Organization, *Enhancing the Economic Benefits of Tourism for Local Communities and Poverty Alleviation* (Madrid: 2002), p. 23.

10. *American Way*, November 1, 2004, p. 78.

11. Allan M. Williams and C. Michael Hall, "Tourism, Migration, Circulation and Mobility: The Contingence of Time and Place," in *Tourism and Migration: New Relationships Between Production and Consumption*, ed. C. Michael Hall and Allan M. Williams (Dordrecht, The Netherlands: Kluwer Academic Publishers, 2002), p. 2.

12. Jagdish Bhagwati, *In Defense of Globalization* (Oxford: Oxford University Press, 2004); Martin Wolf, *Why Globalization Works* (New Haven, CT: Yale University Press, 2004).

13. Yossi Shain, *Marketing the American Creed Abroad* (Cambridge: Cambridge University Press, 1999), chaps. 3, 5, esp. pp. 170–171.

14. C. M. Rogerson and Em. M. Letsoalo, "Resettlement and Under-Development in the Black 'Homelands' of South Africa," in *Population and Development Projects in Africa*, ed. John I. Clarke, Mustafa Khogali, and Leszek A. Kosinski (Cambridge: Cambridge University Press, 1985), p. 189.

15. Raoul Bianchi, "Tourism and the Politics of Mobility: Freedom, Risk and Security in a Mobile World" (paper presented to the International Studies Association Annual Convention, Honolulu, Hawaii, March 1–5, 2005).

16. Valene Smith, *Hosts and Guests: The Anthropology of Tourism*, 2nd ed. (Philadelphia: University of Pennsylvania Press, 1989), p. 9.

17. Thomas Friedman, *The World Is Flat* (New York: Farrar, Strauss, and Giroux, 2005).

18. It is also possible that the presence of tourists may cause frustration and despair, leading to hostility. This has led some to replace the term *demonstration effect* with *confrontation effect*. Brian Archer, Chris Cooper, and Lisa Ruhanen, "The Positive and Negative Impacts of Tourism," in *Global Tourism*, 3rd ed., ed. William Theobald (Amsterdam: Elsevier, 2005), p. 89.

19. These universal values are far from being universally upheld, however. Adamanta Pollis and Peter Schwab questioned whether human rights were relevant to non-Western societies or socialist ideologies by arguing that economic, cultural, and collective rights had as much validity and legitimacy as individual civil and political rights. Adamanta Pollis and Peter Schwab, "Human Rights: A Western Construct with Limited Applicability," in *Human Rights: Cultural and Ideological Perspectives*, ed. Adamanta Pollis and Peter Schwab (New York: Praeger Publishers, 1979).

20. *Economist*, September 25, 2004, p. 50.

21. Jaakson, "Globalization and Neocolonialist Tourism," p. 180.

22. Jozsef Borocz, *Leisure Migration: A Sociological Study in Tourism* (Tarrytown, NY: Elsevier, 1996), p. 3.

23. Alan A. Lew and Alan Wong, "Tourism and the Chinese Diaspora," in *Tourism and Migration*, ed. C. Michael Hall and Allan M. Williams (Dordrecht, The Netherlands: Kluwer Academic Publishers, 2002), p. 2005; T. E. Coles and D. J. Timothy, eds., *Tourism, Diasporas and Space* (London: Routledge, 2004).

24. The term *diaspora* comes from the Greek for dispersal and connotes just that, people dispersed outside their national borders. For a comparison of diasporas through the ages, see Michael Mandelbaum, "Introduction" in *The New European Diasporas, National Minorities and Conflict in Eastern Europe*, ed. Michael Mandelbaum (New York: Council on Foreign Relations Press, 2000), p. 2.

25. For this reason, some governments are threatened by the diaspora and prohibit contact with the population. For a discussion of such a policy in Uganda and Rwanda, see Philip Gourevitch, *We Wish to Inform You that Tomorrow We Will Be Killed with Our Families* (New York: Picador USA, 1999), p. 73.

26. Shain, *Marketing the American Creed.*

27. Ibid., p. x. Although Nathan Glazer and Daniel Patrick Moynihan stated that ethnic influences have become very important determinants of policy in the United States, that view was countered by Alexander De Conde, who argued that immigrant groups have little real power, despite the fact that it looks as if they do (Nathan Glazer and Daniel Patrick Moynihan, eds., *Ethnicity: Theory and Experience* [Cambridge: Harvard University Press, 1975], pp. 23–24; Alexander DeConde, *Ethnicity, Race and American Foreign Policy: A History* [Boston: Northeastern University Press, 1992], p. 200).

28. *Economist*, August 19, 2000, p. 11.

29. Dawid de Villiers, "Foreword," in *The Political Economy of Tourism Development in Africa*, ed. Peter U.C. Dieke (New York, Cognizant Communications Corporation, 2000), p. xi.

30. Louis D'Amore, "Tourism—A Vital Force for Peace," *Annals of Tourism Research* 15, no. 2 (1988), pp. 269–271.

31. James Mak, *Tourism and the Economy* (Honolulu: University of Hawaii Press, 2004), p. ix.

32. Waleed Hazbun, "Mapping the Landscape of the 'New Middle East': The Politics of Tourism Development and the Peace Process in Jordan," in *Jordan in Transition, 1990–2000*, ed. George Joffe (New York: Palgrave, 2002), p. 332. See also Shimon Peres, *The New Middle East* (New York: Henry Holt, 1993).

33. Dallen Timothy, Bruce Prideaux, and Samuel SeongSeop Kim, "Tourism at Borders of Conflict and (De)militarized Zones," in *New Horizons in Tourism*, ed. Tej Vir Singh (Cambridge, MA: CABI Publishing, 2004); Y. Kim and J. L. Crompton, "Role of Tourism in Unifying the Two Koreas," *Annals of Tourism Research* 17, no. 3 (1990).

34. www.travelwirenews.com/eTN/23MAR2005.htm (accessed March 23, 2005).

35. *Miami Herald*, June 21, 2005.

36. David Weaver, "Tourism and Political Geography in Southern Africa," in *The Political Economy of Tourism Development in Africa*, ed. Peter U.C. Dieke (New York: Cognizant Communications Corporation, 2000), p. 56.

37. *Economist*, May 8, 2004, p. 41. Tour operators argue that insecurity is exaggerated and that land mines are the main security problem. The minister of tourism in Mirwais Sadiq claimed that the country was perfectly safe (just before he was assassinated in 2004).

38. Smith, *Issues in Cultural Tourism Studies*, p. 3.

39. Archer, Cooper, and Ruhanen, "The Positive and Negative Impacts," p. 86.

40. Amy Chua, *World on Fire: How Exporting Free Market Democracy Breeds Ethnic Hatred and Global Instability* (New York: Anchor Books, 2004).

41. Archer, Cooper, and Ruhanen, "The Positive and Negative Impacts," p. 86.

42. Although this ban had been lifted by the successor to King Hassan, in an effort to develop sympathy among the Sahawaris, the fear of their association with the Polisario liberation movement continues to be strong. *Economist*, January 22, 2000, p. 48.

43. *Miami Herald*, September 12, 2004. For this reason, the Chinese tourist has been called the holy grail of Asia. Estimates indicate that the average Chinese tourist spends $1,500 on shopping in Guam, triple what the Japanese tourist spends. *New York Times*, May 13, 2004.

44. Philippe Legrain, *Open World: The Truth About Globalization* (London: Abacus, 2002), p. 8.

45. Z. Sardar and M. Wynn Davis, *Why Do People Hate America?* (London: Icon Books, 2002), quoted in Smith, *Issues in Cultural Tourism*, pp. 3–4.

46. Sardar and Davis, *Why Do People Hate America?*

47. David Fisher, "A Colonial Town for Neocolonial Tourism," in *Tourism and Postcolonialism*, ed. C. Michael Hall and Hazel Tucker (London: Routledge, 2004), p. 127.

48. *Economist*, July 31, 2004, p. 33.

49. Ibid.

50. S. Britton, "The Political Economy of Tourism in the Third World," *Annals of Tourism Research* 9, no. 3 (1982); C. Michael Hall and Hazel Tucker, eds., *Tourism and Postcolonialism* (London: Routledge, 2004).

51. Smith, *Issues in Cultural Tourism*, p. 4.

52. A. Mathieson and G. Wall, *Tourism: Economic, Physical and Social Impacts* (Harlow, UK: Longman, 1992).

53. Enloe, *Bananas, Beaches and Bases,* p. 31.

54. There is evidence that foreign investment in LDCs from other LDCs seems to have advantages over Western multinationals. According to the World Bank, the reach of some developing countries such as India, South Africa, Brazil, Malaysia, and China is spreading. It is still not large enough, however,

to be considered a viable replacement for Western investment. Global Development Finance, *Annual Report* (Washington, DC), April 6, 2005.

55. Mathieson and Wall, *Tourism: Economic, Physical and Social Impacts.*

56. Lea, *Tourism and Development,* p. 25.

57. David Harrison, "Tourism in Africa: The Social and Cultural Framework," in *The Political Economy of Tourism Development in Africa,* ed. Peter U.C. Dieke (New York: Cognizant Communication Corporation, 2000), p. 37.

58. Robert A. Poirier, "Tourism in the African Economic Milieu: A Future of Mixed Blessings," in *The Political Economy of Tourism Development in Africa,* ed. Peter U.C. Dieke (New York: Cognizant Communication Corporation, 2000), p. 30.

59. Harrison, "Tourism in Africa," p. 37.

60. Mowforth and Munt, *Tourism and Sustainability.*

61. Mathieson and Wall, *Tourism: Economic, Physical and Social Impacts.*

62. Lea, *Tourism and Development,* p. 66.

63. Davydd Greenwood, "Culture by the Pound: An Anthropological Perspective on Tourism as Cultural Commoditization," in Smith, *Hosts and Guests,* p. 173.

64. Jean Holder, "The Caribbean: Far Greater Dependency on Tourism Likely," *Courier* 122 (July/August 1990), p. 76, cited in Martin Mowforth and Ian Munt, *Tourism and Sustainability: New Tourism in the Third World,* 2nd ed. (London: Routledge, 2003), p. 64.

65. Martin Mowforth and Ian Munt, *Tourism and Sustainability: New Tourism in the Third World,* 2nd ed. (London: Routledge, 2003), p. 63.

66. H. G. Matthews, cited in C. Michael Hall and Hazel Tucker, "Tourism and Postcolonialism: An Introduction," in Hall and Tucker, *Tourism and Postcolonialism,* p. 5.

67. Fisher, "A Colonial Town for Neocolonial Tourism," p. 127.

68. These forces have been discussed in Milica Z. Bookman, *Ethnic Groups in Motion: Economic Competition and Migration in Multiethnic States* (London: Frank Cass, 2002), chap. 4.

69. Michael Fix and Jeffrey S. Passel, *Immigration and Immigrants: Setting the Record Straight* (Washington, DC: Urban Institute Press, 1994), p. 13.

70. Doris Meissner, Robert D. Hormats, Antonia Garrigues Walker, and Shijuro Ogata, *International Migration Challenges in a New Era* (New York: Trilateral Commission, 1993), p. 13.

71. Peter Stalker, *Workers Without Frontiers: The Impact of Globalization on International Migration* (Boulder: Lynne Rienner Publishers, 2000), p. 108.

72. Myron Weiner, "Security, Stability and International Migration," in *International Migration and Security,* ed. Myron Weiner (Boulder, CO: Westview Press, 1993), p. 10.

73. Bookman, *Ethnic Groups in Motion,* chap. 7.

74. This action underscored the power of the Jewish diaspora in the United States that spearheaded this effort in order to increase the number of Soviet Jews who could emigrate to Israel.

75. Myron Weiner, *The Global Migration Crisis* (New York: Harper-Collins, 1995).

76. In Mexico, immigrants were granted the right to a form of dual citizenship so that they could maintain ties to their homeland, retain their property rights, and possibly return, even if they had accepted foreign citizenship. The effect was that more Mexicans were willing to leave and take multiple citizenships. Christopher Rudolph, "Migration and the Evolving Security Agenda of Advanced Industrial Democracies: Toward an IR Theory of Migration Policy" (paper presented to the International Studies Association Annual Convention, Los Angeles, March 2000), p. 3.

77. UN High Commissioner for Refugees, *The State of the World's Refugees* (Geneva, Switzerland: United Nations, 1995), pp. 34–35.

78. Milica Z. Bookman, *Ethnic Groups in Motion,* pp. 141–142.

79. *La Republica*, August 20, 1992.

80. Milica Z. Bookman, *After Involuntary Migration: The Political Economy of Refugee Encampments* (Lanham, MD: Lexington Books, 2002).

Selected Bibliography

Aitken, C., and C. M. Hall. "Migrant and Foreign Skills and Their Relevance to the Tourism Industry." *Tourism Geographies: An International Journal of Place, Space and the Environment* 2, no. 3 (2000): 66–86.

Alam, A. "The New Trade Theory and Its Relevance to the Trade Policies of Developing Countries." *The World Economy* 23, no. 8 (1995): 367–385.

Appleyard, R. "International Migration and Development—An Unresolved Relationship." *International Migration* 30, no. 3-4 (1992).

Archer, B. H., and J. Fletcher. "The Economic Impact of Tourism in the Seychelles." *Annals of Tourism Research* 23, no. 1 (1996): 32–47.

Arzt, Donna E. *Refugees into Citizens.* New York: Council on Foreign Relations, 1997.

Bales, Kevin. *Disposable People: New Slavery in the Global Economy.* Berkeley: University of California Press, 2004.

Bell, M., and G. Ward. "Comparing Temporary Mobility with Permanent Migration." *Tourism Geographies: International Journal of Place, Space and the Environment* 2, no. 3 (2000).

Bell-Fialkoff, Andrew. *Ethnic Cleansing.* New York: St. Martin's Griffin, 1999.

Beynon, J., and D. Dunkerley, eds. *Globalization, the Reader.* London: Athlone Press, 2000.

Bhagwati, Jagdish. *In Defense of Globalization.* Oxford: Oxford University Press, 2004.

Bianchi, R. V. "Migrant Tourist-Workers: Exploring the Contact Zones of Post-Industrial Tourism." *Current Issues in Tourism* 3, no. 2 (2000).

Bird, R. M. "Taxing Tourism in Developing Countries." *World Development* 20 (1992): 1145–1158.

Black, Richard, and Vaughan Robinson, eds. *Geography and Refugees.* London: Belhaven Press, 1993.

Boniface, Priscilla. *Tasting Tourism: Travelling for Food and Drink.* Aldershot, Hampshire, UK: Ashgate, 2003.

Bookman, Milica Z. *After Involuntary Migration: The Political Economy of Refugee Encampments.* Lanham, MD: Lexington Books, 2002.

———. *The Demographic Struggle for Power: The Political Economy of Demographic Engineering in the Modern World.* London: Frank Cass, 1997.

———. *Ethnic Groups in Motion: Economic Competition and Migration in Multiethnic States.* London: Frank Cass, 2002.

Borocz, Jozsef. *Leisure Migration: A Sociological Study in Tourism.* Tarrytown, NY: Elsevier, 1996.

Brand, Laurie. "Development in Wadi Rum? State Bureaucracy, External Funders, and Civil Society." *International Journal of Middle East Studies* 33 (2001).

Briassoulis, Helen, ed. *Tourism and the Environment.* 2nd ed. Boston: Kluwer Academic Publishers, 2000.

Britton, S. G. "The Political Economy of Tourism in the Third World." *Annals of Tourism Research* 9, no. 3 (1982): 331–358.

Brown, Frances. *Tourism Reassessed: Blight or Blessing?* Oxford: Butterworth-Heinemann, 1998.

Bruner, E. "The Maasai and the Lion King: Authenticity, Nationalism and Globalization in African Tourism." *American Ethnologist* 28, no. 4 (2001): 881–908.

Buckley, Ralf. "Public and Private Partnerships Between Tourism and Protected Areas: The Australian Situation." *Journal of Tourism Studies* 13, no. 1 (2002).

Butcher, J. *The Moralisation of Tourism: Sun, Sand . . . and Saving the World?* London: Routledge, 2003.

Castles, Stephen, and Mark J. Miller. *The Age of Migration.* New York: Guildford Press, 1993.

Cater, E. "Ecotourism in the Third World: Problems for Sustainable Tourism Development." *Tourism Management* 14, no. 2: 85–90.

Chambers, E., ed. *Tourism and Culture: An Applied Perspective.* New York: State University of New York Press, 1997.

Chatty, D. "Enclosures and Exclusions: Wildlife Conservation Schemes and Pastoral Tribes in the Middle East." *Forced Migration Review* 2 (1998).

Cheng, Lucie, and Edna Bonacich, eds. *Labor Immigration Under Capitalism: Asian Workers in the United States Before World War II.* Berkeley: University of California Press, 1984.

Choucri, Nazli. "Cross-border Movements of Population in a 'Fair Globalization.'" *Development* 48, no. 1 (2005).

Chua, Amy. *World on Fire: How Exporting Free Market Democracy Breeds Ethnic Hatred and Global Instability.* New York: Anchor Books, 2004.

Cohen, E. "Contemporary Tourism and the Host Community in Less Developed Areas." *Tourism Recreation Research* 28, no. 1 (2003).

————. "Nomads from Affluence: Notes on the Phenomenon of Drifter-Tourism." *International Journal of Comparative Sociology* 14, no. 1–2 (1973).

————. "The Sociology of Tourism: Approaches, Issues and Findings." *Annual Review of Sociology* 10 (1984).

Cohen, Erik H. "Tourism and Religion." *Journal of Travel Research* 24, no. 4 (2003).

Cohen, Roberta, and Francis M. Deng. *Masses in Flight.* Washington, DC: Brookings Institution Press, 1998.

————, eds. *The Forsaken People, Case Studies of the Internally Displaced.* Washington, DC: Brookings Institution Press, 1998.

Copeland, B. R. "Tourism, Welfare and De-industrialization in a Small Open Economy." *Economica* 58, no. 4 (1991): 515–529.

Coshall, John T. "The Threat of Terrorism as an Intervention of International Travel Flows." *Journal of Travel Research* 41, no. 1 (2003).

Crouch, David, and Luke Desforges. "The Sensuous in the Tourist Encounter: Introduction to the Power of the Body in Tourist Studies." *Tourist Studies* 3, no.1 (2003).

Crouch, Geoffrey. "Demand Elasticities for Short-Haul Versus Long-Haul Tourism." *Journal of Travel Research* 33, no. 2 (1994).

Crush, J. S., and P. A. Wellings. "The Southern African Pleasure Periphery 1966–83." *Journal of Modern African Studies* 21, no. 4 (1983): 673–698.

D'Amore, Louis. "Tourism—A Vital Force for Peace." *Annals of Tourism Research* 15, no. 2 (1988): 269–271.

Deihl, C. "Wildlife and the Maasai." *Cultural Survival Quarterly* 9, no. 1 (1985).

De Kadt, E., ed. *Tourism: Passport to Development?* New York: Oxford University Press, 1979.

Diamond, J. "Tourism's Role in Economic Development: The Case Reexamined." *Economic Development and Cultural Change* 25, no. 3 (April 1977).

Diaz Benavides, David, and Ellen Perez-Ducy, eds. "Background Note by the OMT/WTO Secretariat." *Tourism in the Least Developed Countries.* Madrid: World Tourism Organization, 2001.

Dieke, Peter U.C., ed. *The Political Economy of Tourism Development in Africa.* New York: Cognizant Communications, 2000.

Dixon, John, et al. *Tourism and the Environment in the Caribbean.* Environment Department Papers 80. Washington, DC: World Bank, 2001.

Doswell, Roger. *Tourism: How Effective Management Makes the Difference.* London: Butterworth-Heinemann, 1997.

Dwyer, Larry, Peter Forsyth, and Prasada Rao. "Destination Price Competitiveness: Exchange Rate Changes Versus Domestic Inflation." *Journal of Travel Research* 40, no. 3 (2002).

Ehrenreich, Barbara, and Arlie Russel Hochschild, eds. *Global Women: Nannies, Maids and Sex Workers in the New Economy.* New York: Metropolitan Books, 2003.

Eltis, D. "Free and Coerced Transatlantic Migrations: Some Comparisons." *American Historical Review* 88 (1983).

Enloe, Cynthia. *Bananas, Beaches and Bases: Making Feminist Sense of International Politics.* London: Pandora, 1990.

Falvey, Rodney, and Norman Gemmell. "Are Services Income Elastic? Some New Evidence." *Review of Income and Wealth* 42 (1996).

Featherstone, M., ed. *Global Culture: Nationalism, Globalization and Modernity.* London: Sage, 1990.

Fennel, David. *Ecotourism: An Introduction.* London: Routledge, 1999.

Fix, Michael, and Jeffrey S. Passel. *Immigration and Immigrants: Setting the Record Straight.* Washington, DC: Urban Institute Press, 1994.

Frelick, Bill. *The Wall of Denial: Internal Displacement in Turkey.* Washington, DC: US Committee for Refugees, 1999.

Good, Kenneth. *Bushmen and Diamonds.* Discussion Paper no. 23. Uppsala, Sweden: Nordic Africa Institute, 2003.

Gordenker, Leon. *Refugees in International Politics.* New York: Columbia University Press, 1987.

Gosh, R. N., M.A.B. Siddique, and R. Gabbay, eds. *Tourism and Economic Development: Case Studies from the Indian Ocean Region.* Aldershot, Hampshire, UK: Ashgate, 2003.

Gunn, C. A. *Tourism Planning; Basics, Concepts, Cases.* London: Taylor and Francis, 1994.

Gurr, Ted Robert. *Minorities at Risk.* Washington, DC: United States Institute of Peace, 1983.

Hall, C. Michael, and Hazel Tucker, eds. *Tourism and Postcolonialism.* London: Routledge, 2004.

Hall, C. Michael, and Allan M. Williams, eds. *Tourism and Migration: New Relationships Between Producers and Consumers.* Dordrecht, The Netherlands: Kluwer Academic Publishers, 2002.

Hammar, Tomas, Grete Brochmann, Dristof Tamas, and Thomas Faist, eds. *International Migration, Immobility and Development.* New York: Berg, 1997.

Hampton, M. "Backpacker Tourism and Economic Development." *Annals of Tourism Research* 25, no. 3 (1998).

Harrison, David, ed. *Tourism and the Less Developed Countries.* London: Belhaven Press, 1992.

Hatton, Timothy J., and Jeffrey G. Williamson. *The Age of Mass Migration.* New York: Oxford University Press, 1998.

Hitchcock, M. "Ethnicity and Tourism Entrepreneurship in Java and Bali." *Current Issues in Tourism* 3, no. 3 (2000).

Honey, Martha. *Ecotourism and Sustainable Development: Who Owns Paradise?* Washington, DC: Island Press, 1998.

Hutnyk, J. *The Rumor of Calcutta: Tourism, Charity and the Poverty of Representation.* London: Zed Books, 1996.

Ionnides, Dimitri. *The Economic Geography of the Tourist Industry.* London: Routledge, 1998.

Isaacson, Rupert. *The Healing Land: The Bushmen and the Kalahari Desert.* New York: Grove Press, 2001.

Isbister, John. *The Immigration Debate.* West Hartford, CT: Kumarian Press, 1996.

Jackson, E. L., and T. L. Burton, eds. *Leisure Studies: Prospects for Twenty-First Century.* State College, PA: Venture Publishing, 1999.

Jafari, Jafar. "Tourism and Peace." *Annals of Tourism Research* 16 (1989).

————, ed. *Encyclopedia of Tourism.* London: Routledge, 2000.

Jenkins, C. L., and B. N. Henry. "Government Involvement in Tourism in Developing Countries." *Annals of Tourism Research* 9, no. 3 (1982).

Johnson, Peter, and Barry Thomas. *Choice and Demand in Tourism.* London: Mansell, 1992.

————, eds. *Perspectives on Tourism Policy.* London: Cassell Academic, 1993.

Kim, Y., and J. L. Crompton. "Role of Tourism in Unifying the Two Koreas." *Annals of Tourism Research* 17, no. 3 (1990).

Kirschenblatt-Gimblet, B. *Destination Culture: Tourism, Museums and Heritage.* Berkeley: University of California Press, 1998.

Kotler, P., J. Bowen, and J. Makens. *Marketing for Hospitality and Tourism.* Upper Saddle River, NJ: Prentice Hall, 1996.

Kuznets, Simon. Population Redistribution and Economic Growth, United States: 1870–1950. Philadelphia: American Philosophical Society, 1960.

Lansing, John, and Eva Mueller. *The Geographic Mobility of Labor.* Ann Arbor, MI: Institute for Social Research, 1967.

Lea, John. *Tourism and Development in the Third World.* London: Routledge, 2001.

Lee, Luke T. "Internally Displaced Persons and Refugees: Toward a Legal Synthesis?" *Journal of Refugee Studies* 9, no.1 (1996).

Legrain, Philippe. *Open World: The Truth About Globalization.* London: Abacus, 2002.

Lickorish, L. J., and C. L. Jenkins. *An Introduction to Tourism.* Oxford: Butterworth-Heineman, 1997.

Light, D. "Gazing on Communism: Heritage Tourism and Post-communist Identities in Germany, Hungary and Romania." *Tourism Geographies* 2, no. 2 (2000).

Lucas, Rosemary. *Employment Relations in the Hospitality Industry.* London: Routledge, 2004.

Lundberg, Donald, Mink Stavenga, and M. Krishnamoorthy. *Tourism Economics.* New York: Wiley, 1995.

MacCannell, Dean. *The Tourist: A New Theory of the Leisure Class.* 3rd ed. Berkeley: University of California Press, 1999.

Mak, James. *Tourism and the Economy.* Honolulu: University of Hawaii Press, 2004.

Mandelbaum, Michael, ed. *The New European Diasporas, National Minorities and Conflict in Eastern Europe.* New York: Council on Foreign Relations Press, 2000.

McLaren, Deborah. *Rethinking Tourism and Ecotravel.* 2nd ed. Bloomfield, CT: Kumarian Press, 2003.

Mathieson, A., and G. Wall. *Tourism: Economic, Physical and Social Impacts.* Harlow, Essex: Longman, 1982.

Meethan, K. *Tourism in Global Society: Place, Culture, Consumption.* New York: Palgrave, 2001.

Meissner, Doris, Robert D. Hormats, Antonia Garrigues Walker, and Shijuro Ogata. *International Migration Challenges in a New Era.* New York: Trilateral Commission, 1993.

Morais, Duarte B., Michael J. Dorsch, and Sheila J. Backman. "Can Tourism Providers Buy Their Customers' Loyalty?" *Journal of Travel Research* 42, no. 3 (2004).

Mowforth, Martin, and Ian Munt. *Tourism and Sustainability: New Tourism in the Third World.* London: Routledge, 2003.

Page, S. J. *Transport for Tourism.* London: Routledge, 1994.

Parnwell, Mike. *Population Movements and the Third World.* London: Routledge, 1993.

Pearce, D. *Tourism Development.* Harlow, Essex, UK: Longman, 1989.

Philipp, Steven. "Race and the Pursuit of Happiness." *Journal of Leisure Research* 32, no. 1 (2000): 121–124.

Pizam, Abraham, and Aliza Fleischer. "Severity Versus Frequency of Acts of Terrorism: Which Has a Larger Impact on Tourism Demand?" *Journal of Travel Research* 40, no. 3 (2002).

Pollis, Adamanta, and Peter Schwab, eds. *Human Rights: Cultural and Ideological Perspectives.* New York: Praeger Publishers, 1979.

Prebensen, Nina, Svein Larsen, and Birgit Abelsen. "I'm Not a Typical Tourist." *Journal of Travel Research* 41, no. 4 (2003).

Reid, Donald. *Tourism, Globalization and Development.* London: Pluto Press, 2003.

Richter, Linda. *Land Reform and Tourism Development in the Philippines.* Cambridge, MA: Schenkman Publishing, 1982.

———. "Not a Minor Problem: Developing International Travel Policy for the Welfare of Children." *Tourism Analysis* 10, no. 1 (2005).

———. *The Politics of Tourism in Asia.* Honolulu: University of Hawaii Press, 1989.

Rogerson, C. M., and Em. M. Letsoalo. "Resettlement and Under-Development in the Black 'Homelands' of South Africa." In *Population and Development Projects in Africa,* edited by John I. Clarke, Mustafa Khogali, and Leszek A. Kosinski. Cambridge: Cambridge University Press, 1985.

Rogge, John R. *Too Many, Too Long: Sudan's Twenty-Year Refugee Dilemma.* Totowa, NJ: Rowman and Allanheld, 1985.

Rogge, John R., ed. *Refugees: A Third World Dilemma.* Totowa, NJ: Rowman and Littlefield, 1987.

Rojek, C., and J. Urry, eds. *Touring Cultures: Transformations of Travel and Theory.* London: Routledge, 1997.

Saugestad, Sidsel. *The Inconvenient Indigenous*. Herndon, VA: Stylus Publishing, 2001.

Shain, Yossi. *Marketing the American Creed Abroad*. Cambridge: Cambridge University Press, 1999.

Sinclair, M. Thea, and Mike Stabler. *The Economics of Tourism*. London: Routledge, 1977.

Sindiga, I. *Tourism and African Development: Change and Challenge of Tourism in Kenya*. Aldershot, Hampshire, UK: Ashgate, 1999.

Sindiga, Isaac, and Mary Kanunah. "Unplanned Tourism Development in Sub-Saharan Africa with Special Reference to Kenya." *Journal of Tourism Studies* 10, no.1 (1999).

Singh, Tej Vir, ed. *New Horizons in Tourism*. Cambridge, MA: CABI Publishing, 2004.

Smith, Melanie. *Issues in Cultural Tourism*. London: Routledge, 2003.

Smith, Valene, ed. *Hosts and Guests: The Anthropology of Tourism Studies*. 2nd ed. Philadelphia: University of Pennsylvania Press, 1989.

Stalker, Peter. *Workers Without Frontiers: The Impact of Globalization on International Migration*. Boulder: Lynne Rienner, 2000.

Sung, Heidi H. "Classification of Adventure Travelers." *Journal of Travel Research* 42, no. 4 (April 2004).

Swanson, Kristen K., and Patricia E. Horridge. "A Structural Model for Souvenir Consumption, Travel Activities, and Tourist Demographics." *Journal of Travel Research* 42, no. 4 (May 2004).

Tarlow, Peter E., and Gui Santana. "Providing Safety for Tourists: A Study of a Selected Sample of Tourist Destinations in the United States and Brazil." *Journal of Travel Research* 40, no. 4 (2002).

Theobold, William, ed. *Global Tourism*. 3rd ed. Amsterdam: Elsevier, 2005.

Timothy, Dallen, Bruce Prideaux, and Samuel SeongSeop Kim. "Tourism at Borders of Conflict and (De)militarized Zones." In *New Horizons in Tourism,* edited by Tej Vir Singh. Cambridge, MA.: CABI Publishing, 2004.

Travel Industry World. *2001 Yearbook—The Big Picture*. Spencertown, NY: Travel Industry Publishing, 2002.

Turner, L. "The International Division of Leisure: Tourism in the Third World." *World Development* 4, no. 3 (1976): 253–260.

Urry, John. *The Tourist Gaze: Leisure and Travel in Contemporary Societies*. Newbury Park, CA: Sage Publications, 1990.

US Committee for Refugees. *World Refugee Survey 2000*. Washington, DC: 2000.

Van Der Post, Laurens. *The Lost World of the Kalahari*. New York: Morrow, 1958.

Verbeke, Jansen. *Marketing for Tourism*. London: Pitman, 1988.

Wahab, Salah, and Christopher Cooper, eds. *Tourism and the Globalization Age*. London: Routledge, 2001.

Weiner, Myron. "Security, Stability and International Migration." In *International Migration and Security,* edited by Myron Weiner. Boulder, CO: Westview Press, 1993.

Williams, Allan M, and C. Michael Hall, "Tourism and Migration: New Relationships Between Production and Consumption." *Tourism Geographies: International Journal of Place, Space and the Environment* 2, no. 3 (2000).

Williams, A. N., and G. Shaw, "Tourism: Candyfloss Industry or Job-Generator?" *Town Planning Review* 59 (1998).

Wolf, Martin. *Why Globalization Works.* New Haven, CT: Yale University Press, 2004.

Wolfe, R. J. "Recreational Travel, the New Migration." *Geographical Bulletin* 9 (1967).

Wood, Robert E. "Touristic Ethnicity: A Brief Itinerary." www.camden.rutgers .edu/~wood/Papers/touristic-ethnicity.pdf (accessed January 14, 2006).

World Bank. "Project: Transfrontier Conservation Areas and Tourism Development Project." Integrated Safeguards Data Sheet no. 25633, July 1, 2003.

———. "Sustainable Coastal Tourism Development." Project Appraisal Document, Report no. 20412-MOR, June 16, 2000.

———. "Tourism in Africa." Findings Report no.22617. *Environmental, Rural and Social Development Newsletter,* July 2001.

World Tourism Organization. *Compendium of Tourism Statistics.* Madrid: Annual volumes.

———. "Contribution of the World Tourism Organization to the SG Report on Tourism and Sustainable Development for the CSD 7 Meeting," "Addendum A: Tourism and Economic Development," April 1999.

———. *Enhancing the Economic Benefits of Tourism for Local Communities and Poverty Alleviation.* Madrid: 2002.

———. *Indicators of Sustainable Development for Tourism Destinations.* Madrid: 2004.

———. *Tourism and Poverty Alleviation.* Madrid: 2002.

———. *Tourism in the Least Developed Countries.* Madrid: 2001.

———. *Tourism, Peace and Sustainable Development for Africa.* Madrid: 2003. .

———. *Yearbook of Tourism Statistics.* Madrid: annual volumes.

World Tourism Organization, Tourism Policy Forum. "Tourism's Potential as a Sustainable Development Strategy." October 19–20, 2004, George Washington University, Washington, DC.

World Travel and Tourism Council. *Travel and Tourism—Forging Ahead.* The 2004 Travel and Tourism Economic Research Country League Tables. Madrid: 2004.

Index

Diaspora groups, 160, 163–166,
180(n24), 182(n74)
Direct demand for labor, 91–92
Direct population expulsion, 123–124,
126–130
Disappeared migrant workers, 104,
115(n52)
Disasters leading to migration:
expectations of tourist travel, 54;
international funds repairing damage
from, 73–74; involuntary migration
and environmental refugeeism, 30;
tsunamis, 54–55, 123, 156–157
Displacement: circular flow of
population movements, 7;
demonstration effect of tourism, 167;
governments preserving traditional
industries from, 111–112; involuntary
outmigration of tourism workers,
106–109; of local industry by tourism,
116(n65); multidirectional population
movements in the Caprivi Strip, 1. *See
also* Indigenous population
displacement
Djibouti: travel and tourism as related to
GDP, 13
Domestic migration: inmigration of
domestic workers, 104–106;
involuntary outmigration of tourism
workers, 106–109; large population
from, 17(n4); Williams and Hall's
four-phase model of tourism
migration, 27–28
Domestic tourism: demand determinants
for, 51; economic value of, 41(n27);
indigenous investors, 141;
international tourism and, 13, 20(n49);
spreading peace through, 166
Domestic workers, migration of,
104–106
Dominica: growth of GDP and growth of
travel and tourism, 76(table);
international tourist expenditure as a
percentage of GDP, 14(table); tourist/
resident ratio, 96(table); travel and
tourism industry employment,
92(table)
Dominican Republic: growth of GDP and
growth of travel and tourism,
76(table); international tourist
expenditure as a percentage of GDP,

14(table); tourist/resident ratio,
96(table); travel and tourism as a
percentage of GDP, 11(table), 12;
travel and tourism industry
employment, 92(table)
Dual citizenship, 183(n76)
Dual labor market, 97
Dual obstacles of gender and migrant
status, 105
Duration of movement, 8; classifying
tourists by incentive and capacity,
46–48; population movements
classified by duration and choice, 32
(table)
Duration of stay, 28–29

East Germany, 174
Eastern European Holidays, 165
Economic aid, 43(n45)
Economic expectations leading to
migration, 37
Economic growth and development:
changes to occupational structure of
the labor force, 40(n13); circular flow
of population movements, 7; cultural
tourism, 143; development assistance
programs, 70; development studies,
6–7; economic changes characterizing,
21; globalization and the spread of
market economics, 159–161; impact
of tourism on wildlife, 146–147;
impact on service sector, 39(n6);
interethnic competition and economic
growth, 38–39; as justification for
population displacement, 131; linking
development studies and tourism
studies, 6–7; long-term modern
economic growth, 39(n4); population
movements as labor adjustments to,
23–25; role of foreign capital, 33–36;
tourism as engine of growth, 75–81;
tourism's potential for, 35; tourist-
friendly LDCs, 10–16; tourist-led
development, 155–156;
underdevelopment and tourist
demand, 145–146
Economic issues: costs and benefits of
labor migration in tourism, 109–112;
dependency culture of tourism,
168–171; determining tourism
patterns, 51–53; economic benefits of

11(table); travel and tourism industry employment, 93(table)

Less developed countries (LDCs), 18(n21); increasing tourist flow, 3; nomenclature for, 18(n21); ramifications of economic development, 39(n5); structural transformation, 40(n8); tourism as engine of growth, 75–81; Williams and Hall's four-phase model of tourism migration, 27–28. *See also specific countries*

Liberia: travel and tourism as related to GDP, 13

Libya: exotic tourism, 49; growth of GDP and growth of travel and tourism, 77(table); tourist/resident ratio, 96(table); travel and tourism as a percentage of GDP, 11(table); travel and tourism industry employment, 92(table)

Loans and grants, 71–72

Local communities: artificiality of cultural tourism, 143–145; competition for resources between tourists and, 106–109; impact of tourism on, 55; involvement in population displacement, 133; job competition with foreign migrant workers, 104

Lomé Accord, 56

Lonely Planet guidebook, 166

Long-term modern economic growth, 39(n4)

Luxury tourism, 58–60

Maasai people, 125, 132

Macao: growth of GDP and growth of travel and tourism, 76(table); tourist/resident ratio, 96(table); travel and tourism as a percentage of GDP, 11(table); travel and tourism industry employment, 92(table)

Machu Picchu, Peru, 71

Madagascar: growth of GDP and growth of travel and tourism, 77(table); international tourist expenditure as a percentage of GDP, 14(table); tourist/resident ratio, 97(table); travel and tourism as a percentage of GDP,

11(table); travel and tourism industry employment, 93(table)

Madura Oya National Park, Sri Lanka, 124

Malawi: communal land ownership, 125; growth of GDP and growth of travel and tourism, 77(table); international tourist expenditure as a percentage of GDP, 14(table); political reasons for migration, 42(n36); tourist/resident ratio, 97(table); travel and tourism as a percentage of GDP, 11(table); travel and tourism industry employment, 93(table)

Malaysia: disappeared migrant workers, 104; education and training of tourist workers, 98; government propensity for tourism, 16; growth of GDP and growth of travel and tourism, 76(table); indigenous displacement to aid tourism, 120; international tourist expenditure as a percentage of GDP, 14(table); limiting cultural transfer, 159; tourist/resident ratio, 96(table); travel and tourism as a percentage of GDP, 11(table); travel and tourism industry employment, 92(table); waste management, 63

Maldives: growth of GDP and growth of travel and tourism, 76(table); international tourist expenditure as a percentage of GDP, 14(table); tourism as engine of growth, 75; tourist/resident ratio, 96(table); travel and tourism as a percentage of GDP, 11(table); travel and tourism industry employment, 92(table); wages of tourism workers, 99–100

Mali: growth of GDP and growth of travel and tourism, 77(table); international tourist expenditure as a percentage of GDP, 14(table); tourist/resident ratio, 97(table); travel and tourism as a percentage of GDP, 11(table); travel and tourism industry employment, 93(table)

Man-made disasters, 30

Mann, Thomas, 55

Manufacturing: characterization of economic development, 21–22; economic change and supply side of

About the Book

As travelers increasingly seek out the exotic wildlife and idyllic sunsets of the developing world, a complex relationship involving tourism, the migration of workers, and the involuntary displacement of peoples has emerged. Milica Bookman explores that relationship and the connection between population movements and economic development in third world countries.

Bookman's multicountry analysis demonstrates forcefully that tourism both induces migration and displacement and is enabled by them, in a self-reinforcing circular flow. These population movements, she argues, likewise are both a cause and effect of economic growth. They are not, however, a panacea for developing countries. Throughout her study, Bookman underscores the human costs of tourism-led development, emphasizing the need for greater attention to the social dislocations that it brings about.

Milica Z. Bookman is professor of economics at St. Joseph's University. She is author of eight books, including *Ethnic Groups in Motion* and *The Demographic Struggle for Power,* and is the recipient of the Tengelman Award for Excellence in Teaching and Research.